# BIRNBAUM'S FLORIDA FOR FREE

**STEPHEN BIRNBAUM**
EDITOR

**WENDY SPRITZER**
EXECUTIVE EDITOR

**Margaret Akra
Alison Frankel
Shawn H. Hancock
Lawrence T. Mahoney, Jr.
Andrew Rich
Marie B. Speed
David Wilkening**
CONTRIBUTING EDITORS

**Gail Silver**
ART DIRECTOR

**Steve Henry**
ILLUSTRATIONS

HEARST PROFESSIONAL MAGAZINES, INC.

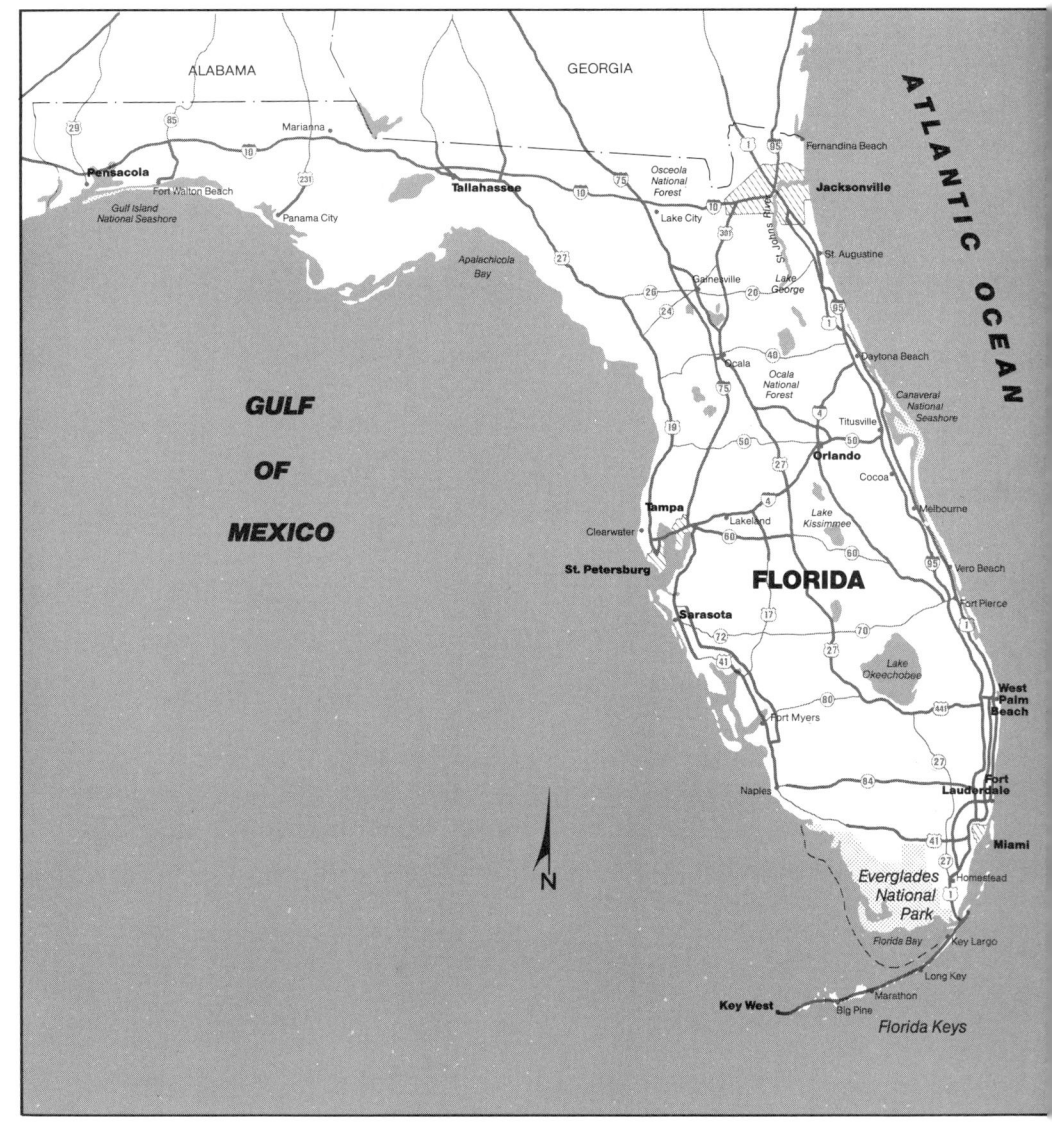

# TABLE OF CONTENTS

## POOLS AND BEACHES     7
Without a doubt the best for least, from north to south and west to east.

## HISTORIC SITES, GREAT GARDENS     23
Tours for history buffs and nature lovers.

## MUSEUMS AND GALLERIES     33
What's hanging around Florida, from world-renowned exhibits to private collections.

## WINDOW SHOPPING     45
Flea markets, malls, famous shopping streets—you don't have to buy to enjoy.

## WILD AND WONDERFUL     57
Animal and bird sanctuaries, preserves, forests, swamps. The natural denizens don't pay to enter, and neither do visitors.

## SITES AND SIGHTS     67
You can't join the shuttle crew, but you can watch them lift off, and that's only the most explosive example of wonderful and daffy places to go and things to do.

## SPORTS     77
Watch baseball's biggest stars shape up, join in the catch of the day, or simply cycle through the cypress.

## INDUSTRIAL TOURS     87
Get a behind-the-scenes look at how it's made—from orange juice to Tupperware.

## LIBRARIES, COLLEGES, AND UNIVERSITIES     93
Free films, beautiful grounds and gardens, interesting museums, and specialized collections.

## MILITARY AND GOVERNMENT SITES     103
Florida's major military bases all welcome visitors and offer organized tours.

## GREAT DRIVES     111
Take the back roads and discover the Florida of days gone by.

## ALMOST FOR FREE     119
Where to spend a little money for a lot of experience.

## DISCOUNT SHOPPING     127
Florida has almost as many factory outlets as alligators. Why resist fantastic savings on first-class goods?

## INFORMATION SOURCES     147
Where to get more information both before you go and while you're on the road.

## INDEX     153

Copyright © 1985 by Stephen Birnbaum

All rights reserved. No part of this work may be reproduced or transmitted in any form by any means, electronic or mechanical, including photocopying and recording, or by any information storage or retrieval system, without permission in writing from the copyright holders.

ISBN: 0-395-39410-4

*Other 1986 Birnbaum Travel Guides*

Canada
Caribbean, Bahamas, and Bermuda
Disneyland
Europe
Europe for Business Travelers
France
Great Britain and Ireland
Hawaii
Mexico
South America
United States
USA for Business Travelers
Walt Disney World

# A WORD FROM THE EDITOR

It has often been said—mostly by me, I think—that the next best thing to being born rich is traveling as though you were. And at a time when value for money is more important to travelers than ever before, this aphorism seems especially apt.

Carried to its logical extension, the very best way to travel must be at no charge at all, and even in an age when cynical souls contend that nothing-is-for-nothing, it may surprise you to learn that quite a bit is actually out there in the world to enjoy without cost. I say surprise because we, too, didn't start out with the idea that there are enough worthwhile, no-cost attractions and amusements to fill an entire book. But once we got into the subject in depth, we discovered that the myth of you-get-what-you-pay-for was just that—a myth.

This is the first of our ". . . For Free" guides, and we've focused on the state of Florida because it represents one of America's most fertile vacationlands. Once thought of as no more than a strip of pleasant beach in the southeasternmost corner of the country, the fact is that Florida is a wonderfully diverse place to explore, full of very special distractions and diversions.

We think that we've managed to collect all of the best costless holiday ideas that exist in the Sunshine State. To make this guide really complete, we've even added bits and pieces that we think cost-conscious travelers should know because their price is so low. This indispensable combination makes up a guide for savvy, frugal folk that proves once and for all that the quality of a travel experience need not depend solely on an extravagant price tag.

Obviously, any new guidebook must keep pace with and answer the real needs of today's travelers. That's why we've also tried to create a guide that's specifically organized, written, and edited for a modern traveling audience, for whom precise information is infinitely more desirable than mere quantities of unappraised data. We think that this book—and the other guides in our series—represent a new generation of travel guides; one that is especially responsive to contemporary needs and interests.

For years, dating as far back as Herr Baedeker, travel guides have tended to be encyclopedic, seemingly much more concerned with demonstrating expertise in geography and history than in any analysis of the sorts of things that most often concern today's typical tourist. But nowadays, when it is hardly necessary to tell a traveler where Miami is located, it's hard to justify devoting endless pages to historical perspectives. Rather, it becomes the responsibility of the editor to provide new perceptions and suggest new directions to make his guide genuinely valuable.

That's exactly what we've tried to do in every volume in our series. I think you'll notice a different, more contemporary tone to our text, as well as an organization and focus that are distinctive and functional. And even a random examination of what follows will demonstrate a substantial departure from the standard guidebook orientation, for we've attempted not only to provide information of a different sort, but we've also tried to present it in a context that makes it particularly accessible.

Needless to say, it's difficult to decide precisely what to include in any guidebook—and what to omit. Large numbers of specific questions have provided the real editorial skeleton for this book. The volume of mail I regularly receive seems to emphasize that modern travelers want very precise information, so we've tried to address that need and have organized our material in the most responsive way possible. Readers who want to know the best free beach near Sarasota or the best places to watch the major-league baseball teams prepare for their seasons will have no trouble finding that data in this guide.

Travel guides are, of course, reflections of personal taste, and putting one's name on a title page obviously puts one's opinions on the line. But I think I ought to amplify just what "personal" means. I do not believe in the sort of personal guidebook that's a palpable misrepresentation from the start. It is, for example, hardly possible for any single travel writer to visit thousands of sites and sights in any given year and provide accurate appraisals of each one.

I also happen to think that such an individual orientation is of substantially less value to readers. Visiting a single historic enclave for just 10 minutes or spending scant seconds surveying a scenic vista hardly equips anyone to provide advice that is of more than passing interest. No amount of doggedly alliterative or oppressively onomatopoeic text can camouflage a technique that is specious on its face. We have, therefore, chosen what I like to describe as the "thee and me" approach to editorial evaluations. What this really reflects is some personal sampling tempered by intelligent counsel from informed local sources, and these additional friends of the editor are almost always residents of the city and/or area about which they have been consulted.

I also should point out something about the person to whom this guidebook is directed. Above all, he or she is a "visitor." This means that selections have been specifically picked to provide a transient traveler with a representative, enlightening, stimulating, and, above all, pleasant experience.

Finally, I should point out that every good travel guide is a living enterprise; that is, no part of this text is cast in bronze. In our regular revisions, we refine, expand, and further hone all our material to serve your travel needs even better. To this end, no contribution is of greater value to us than your personal reaction to what we have written, as well as information reflecting your own experiences while using this book. We earnestly and enthusiastically solicit your comments on this book *and* your opinions and perceptions about places you have recently visited. In this way we will be able to provide the most current information—including the actual experiences of the travel public—and to make those experiences more readily available to others. Please write to us at 60 East 42nd St. New York, NY 10165.

We sincerely hope to hear from you.

—STEPHEN BIRNBAUM

# POOLS AND BEACHES

If every cove, bay, point, island, and headland of the coast of Florida were snapped taut as a piece of string, they would form a cord of seashore and sand 8,500 miles long. Small wonder, then, that water and beach and seabirds and driftwood and stinging, salty air are the Sunshine State's main attractions—unless, that is, one counts the sunshine itself.

What many people don't know is that Florida also has more lakes than any other state in the country, many of which are old-fashioned swimming holes that offer picnic areas and other recreational amenities. In fact, no point in Florida is more than 60 miles from some body of water.

On the Gulf Coast, beaches stretch around the Gulf of Mexico from Pensacola all the way south to the Ten Thousand Islands. The northern Gulf beaches are the whitest in the world—a dazzling spectacle of miles of snow-white particles. On the Atlantic side, beaches stretch from Fernandina in the north all the way to Key West, Florida's southernmost extremity. Parallel to this shoreline is old Highway A1A, hugging virtually the whole length of Florida's Atlantic coast and offering a generous number of parking spots and access roads to most of the best beaches.

Perhaps best of all, many of these beaches and lakes are open to the public at absolutely no charge. What follows is a select listing of the finest of Florida's free waters, north to south.

# NORTHERN FLORIDA

## THE GULF COAST

The beaches of Florida's northwestern coast extend from Pensacola Beach and around the Panhandle to Panama City, Fort Walton Beach, and Destin. This stretch of the state is promoted as the Emerald Coast, and U.S. Highway 98 runs along the length of it, providing access to all the beaches listed below.

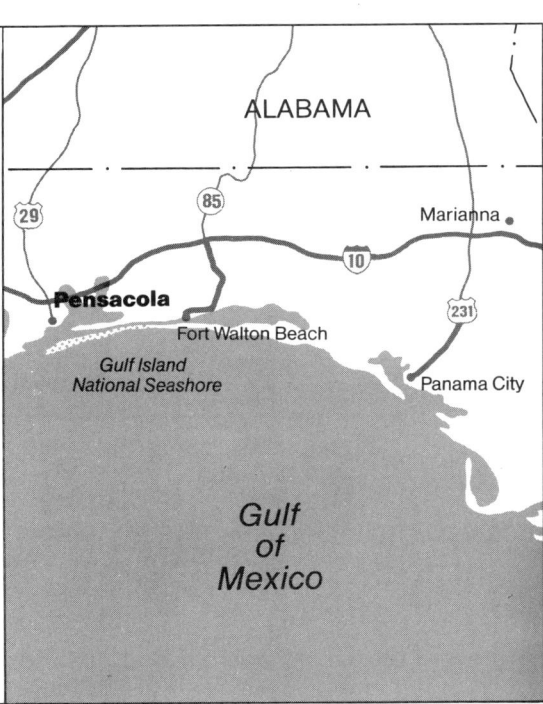

**PENSACOLA BEACH**—These fine, white, unspoiled sands stretch for miles along the Panhandle's Gulf Coast, anchored in the north by the city of Pensacola, an easy access point. Gulf waters are temperate and clear, and an added element of excitement will be provided by the near-inevitable flyover of the world-famous Blue Angels, the Navy's crack precision flying team, stationed at nearby Pensacola Naval Air Station. They're as good an excuse as any to remain flat on your back in that wonderful white sand, reading a novel or newspaper till you hear 'em roar by. Information: 800-874-1234; 800-343-4321 in Florida.

**FORT WALTON BEACH/DESTIN**—The Panhandle's spun-sugar beachfront property continues east from Pensacola to this pretty stretch of sand, midway between "Pensie" and raucous Panama City Beach (see below). If the pleasure of sand-strolling begins to pall, there's a public fishing and observation pier here that extends some 1,200 feet into the Gulf for a close look at the Gulf and its inhabitants. Information: 904-244-8191.

POOLS AND BEACHES/Northern Florida 9

**PANAMA CITY BEACH**—Adjacent to Pensacola and Fort Walton beaches, this 27-mile stretch of sand is famous for its "miracle strip"—resorts and amusement attractions mostly. It's not all honky-tonk, however; areas along the snow-white beach are secluded and quiet, offering havens from the hullabaloo for contemplating the deep, wide sea. There are also beach patrols to ensure safety. Information: 904-234-3193.

## THE EAST COAST

The shores of northern Florida's Atlantic coast don't have the Panhandle's exotic white sands, but they are shadowed by a series of spectacular barrier islands, and buttressed by dramatic dune formations. From Fernandina Beach in the north to Daytona farther south, eastern Florida's stretches of easy access sand vary from quiet, uncrowded havens to places overflowing with college students. Florida's legendary Highway A1A runs all along this coast and is the best route by which to get to the beaches.

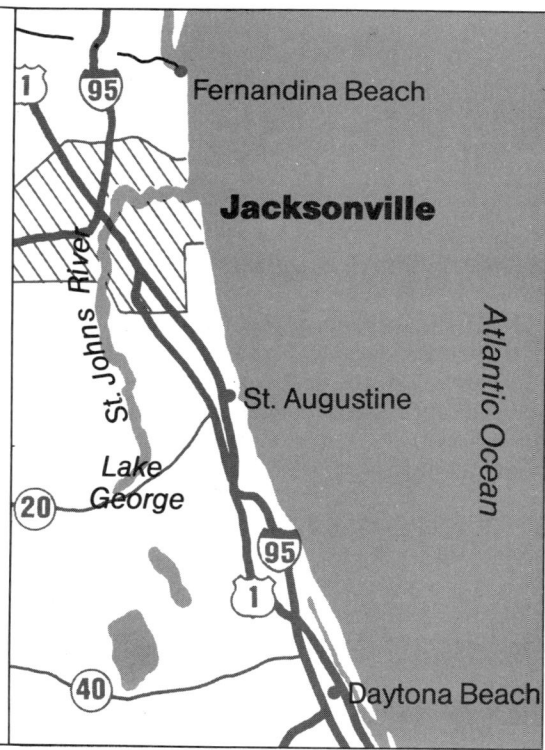

**FERNANDINA/AMELIA BEACH**—In this topmost corner of eastern Florida, almost like an arm flung out against the Atlantic, sits this 13-mile stretch of beach-cum-barrier island. It extends south from Cumberland Sound including Amelia Island, and all along its length there is swimming, sunning, surf-fishing, and shell collecting. Be warned, however, that this is the Atlantic coast: the sand is coarser than along the Gulf Panhandle, the waves are higher, and the water is colder. But oh, the sand dunes! Where the Gulf Coast is as flat as the bottom of a skillet, the coast here offers ups and downs in abundance. As of this writing, automobiles are not permitted on the beach without evidence of a paid permit. Information: 904-261-3248.

**LITTLE TALBOT ISLAND STATE PARK**—Directly south of the Fernandina/Amelia Beach on A1A and 17 miles east of Jacksonville is this state-owned camping and recreation area. There are picnicking facilities plus a lovely beach. Information: 904-251-3231.

**JACKSONVILLE AREA BEACHES**—Approximately 18 miles east of downtown are the Jacksonville Three: Atlantic Beach to the north, Neptune Beach in the center, and Jacksonville Beach to the south. These are hardly pristine strands of oceanfront, but rather busy community beaches with lifeguards on duty from 10 A.M. to 5 P.M. every day. Automobiles and alcoholic beverages are prohibited on all of these beaches. Jacksonville Beach has a fishing and observation pier for a small charge. Information: 904-249-3868.

**KATHRYN ABBY HANNA PARK**—There's a nominal charge for access to this recreation area located at the northernmost tip of Jacksonville Beach (approximately 18 miles east of Jacksonville). Facilities include pavilions, rest rooms, and outdoor cooking stations. Information: 904-249-4700.

**PONTE VEDRA and SOUTH PONTE VEDRA BEACHES**—This fine stretch of beachfront, some 20 miles southeast of Jacksonville, includes two exclusive resorts, Sawgrass and the Ponte Vedra Inn, but is otherwise open to the public. Limited-access roads lead to high, wooded dunes—some of the most beautiful on the coast—and a pure stretch of toe-tingling, coarse, crushed-shell sand beaches. Information: 904-354-5272.

**ST. JOHN'S COUNTY/ST. AUGUSTINE AREA BEACHES**—From the South Ponte Vedra area along Anastasia Island (roughly 5 miles due east of St. Augustine on Highway A1A), south past Crescent Beach to the Marineland attraction, stretch the high dunes and oak hammocks of these hard-packed sand beaches. Some allow automobile traffic, and there is, as of this writing, a car toll in effect in some areas. One great attraction of these beaches is their proximity to historic St. Augustine. Information: 904-824-8131.

**FLAGLER BEACH**—Public parking and camping areas are abundant on this strand between St. Augustine to the north and Ormond Beach/Daytona Beach to the south. Picnic facilities, saltwater fishing, and nature trails are among the recreational amenities. Information: 904-439-2943.

**DAYTONA BEACH**—Billed as the "World's Most Famous Beach," this resort area comprises 23 miles of fine-grained, smooth, packed sand and a noted boardwalk area. High-rise hotels and condominiums line the oceanfront, automobiles are permitted on the beach, and the area is within 90 minutes' drive of St. Augustine, Orlando (Walt Disney World), and the Kennedy Space Center. The beach is also famous for the college students that migrate here during the spring vacation break. Information: 904-255-0981.

## MAJOR SPRINGS

North-central Florida has an abundance of natural springs and lakes. Here are a couple of "swimming holes" that offer ice-cold, inland fun.

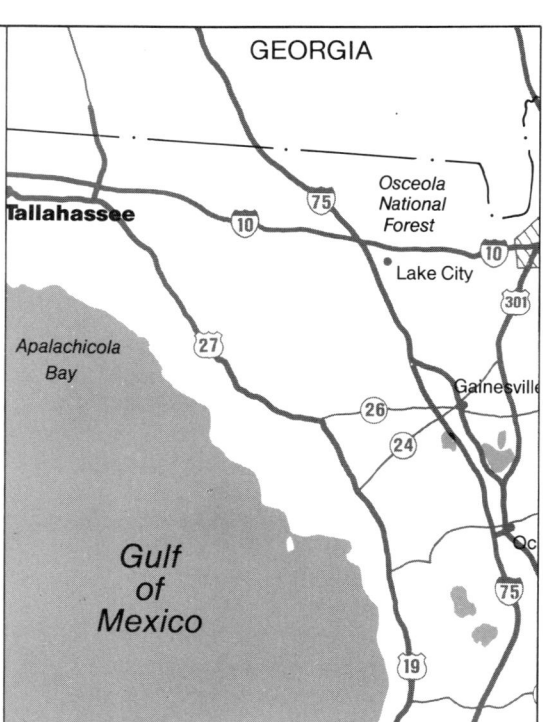

**MANATEE SPRINGS STATE PARK**, Chiefland—There's a nominal charge to enter this 1,900-acre park, where a crystal-clear spring remains at a constant 72 degrees year-round. Other amenities include nature trails, camping facilities, picnic tables and cooking areas, a boardwalk, and freshwater fishing. Information: Route 2; Box 617; Chiefland 32626 (904-493-4288).

**ICHETUCKNEE SPRINGS STATE PARK**—Northwest of Fort White, this state park can be reached via State Road 27 off Route 238. Within the park is a series of springs fed by the clear, ice-cold Ichetucknee River. Park facilities include swimming, regulated tubing, and snorkeling, and the river winds through hammock and swamp, providing opportunities to view many forms of wildlife. Open daily 8 A.M. to sunset. Information: RR 2; Box 108; Fort White 32038 (904-497-2511).

**OLUSTEE BEACH OCEAN POND RECREATION AREA**—Ocean Pond is a natural, 1,760-acre lake with day-use activities such as picnicking, swimming, and boating. The pond is located in Osceola National Forest; take U.S. 90 West to Highway 231, east of Lake City. Information: Osceola Ranger District; U.S. Forest Service; Route 7; Box 95; U.S. 90 West; Lake City 32055 (904-752-2577).

# CENTRAL FLORIDA

## THE GULF COAST

Around the Gulf Coast cities of Clearwater, St. Petersburg, and Tampa, the options from which to choose how and where to get your toes wet are wide and especially appealing. There is a constellation of beaches in the area as good as any in the state, several freshwater lakes, and even some free public pools. Go on, put your suit on.

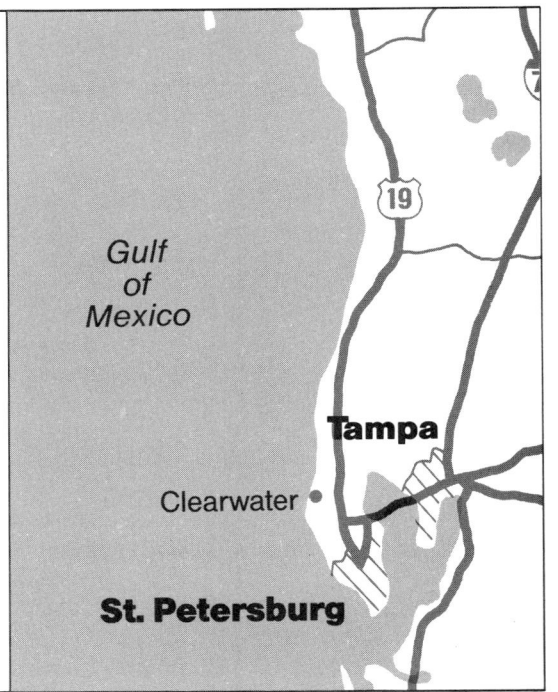

**BAHIA BEACH**—This 125-acre waterfront park, located on Tampa Bay in Ruskin, just north of St. Petersburg, has boat ramps and a docking facility. Information: 813-645-3291.

**E. G. SIMMONS PARK**—More than 1,000 feet of sandy beach are part of Ruskin's 500-acre recreational area, where fishing and canoeing, as well as simple swimming, are available. Facilities include a campground. Open daily 7 A.M. to sunset. Information: 813-645-3836.

**BELLEAIR BEACH**—Located between St. Petersburg and Clearwater beaches, this stretch of sand is so white that it looks as though it's been bleached. Information: 813-595-4575.

**FORT DE SOTO COUNTY PARK**—At this 900-acre St. Petersburg park visitors can swim in 5 small lakes. There are also protected plants on display and a wildlife sanctuary. Open sunrise to sunset. Information: 813-866-2484.

# POOLS AND BEACHES/Central Florida

**MADEIRA and REDINGTON BEACHES**—Here's where you find the fine stuff: more than 6 miles of spun-sugar sand beaches stretch north from Johns Pass, along the Gulf shore near St. Petersburg. Information: 813-393-1847.

**NORTH SHORE PARK**—St. Petersburg's 2,500-acre public park includes a bathing beach, tennis courts, and baseball diamonds. Open daily. Information: 813-893-7335.

**TREASURE ISLAND BEACH**—Like all good buried treasure, what's precious here is what isn't seen: garbage and dirt. Out-of-towners may be drawn to this 4-mile stretch of sand near St. Petersburg for its name, but city residents come because it's kept so clean. Information: 813-367-4529.

**CLEARWATER BEACH**—More than 3.3 miles of lusciously soft, white sand that can be blinding in the sunlight. Information: 813-446-2424.

**BROOKER CREEK PARK**—There's swimming in the park's Lake Tarpon, where lifeguards are on duty daily during summer months and on weekends during the rest of the year. It's north of Clearwater, in Palm Harbor. Open 7 A.M. to sunset. Information: 813-784-4686.

**TAMPA MUNICIPAL SWIMMING POOLS**—The Tampa Recreation Department operates 11 public pools. Three of them—Bob Hicks, Forest Hills, and Sulphur Springs—are open year-round. The others are usually open from June 10 through Labor Day. Addresses: **Bob Hicks Memorial**, 4120 West Mango (813-839-4246); **Angus R. Goss Memorial**, Central and Cayuga Avenues (813-239-3676); **Baldomero Lopez**, 3200 Spruce Street (813-876-5775); **Cuscaden Swimming Pool**, 2800 15th Street (813-248-9611); **Cyrus Green Swimming Pool**, Buffalo Avenue and 22nd Street (813-248-8501); **Forest Hills Swimming Pool**, 10208 North Boulevard (813-932-1320); **Interbay Swimming Pool**, 4321 Estrela (813-876-1245); **Riverfront Handicap Pool**, 1000 North Boulevard (813-253-6038); **Roy Jenkins Swimming Pool**, 154 Columbia Drive (813-251-0142); **Sulphur Springs Swimming Pool**, 8108 North Nebraska Avenue (813-932-8156); **Martin Luther King, Jr. Pool**, 2200 North Oregon Avenue (813-253-5700).

## Travel Tip: HURRICANE WATCH

Florida is hit by more hurricanes than any other state, though no major storms have struck heavily populated areas in the past 20 years. Hurricanes are most likely to hit Florida in September, but the official storm season extends from June through November.

# 14 POOLS AND BEACHES/Central Florida

## INLAND

While in Florida, one is never more than an hour or so from the coast (west or east), but the state's midriff has enough watery attractions to make a long trip to a coastal beach unnecessary. There's an ample supply of cool, lovely parks with lakes and pools.

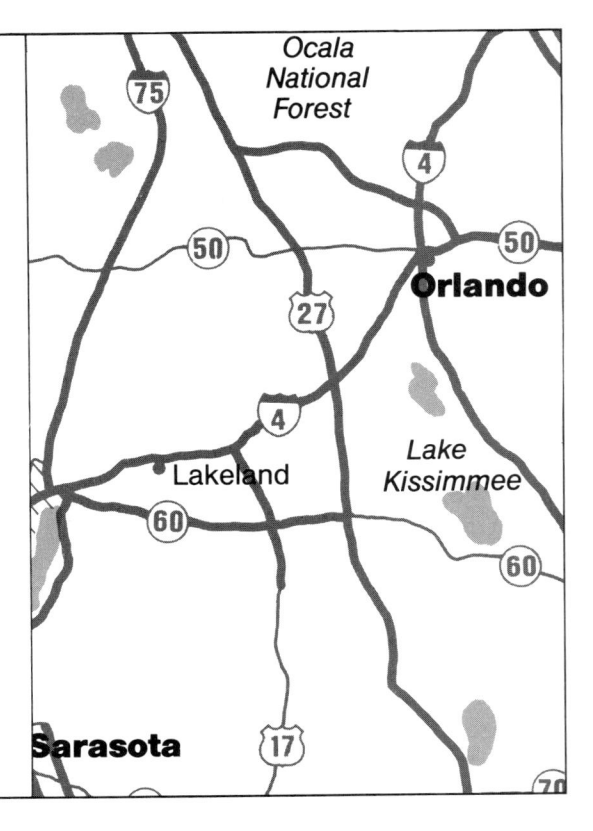

**KELLY PARK**—At this Apopka park, just northwest of Orlando, 26,000 gallons of clear, 62-degree water flow each minute from Rock Springs. Kelly is cherished for its beauty and renowned for its superb swimming facilities, and is so very popular that it's wise to arrive early on summer weekends. Picnic tables are plentiful, camping is available, and there are nature trails and a boardwalk bordering Rock Springs. The park is located about 5½ miles north of Apopka, just off Rock Springs Road (State Road 435). Information: 305-889-4179.

**LAKE FAIRVIEW RECREATION COMPLEX**—This is one of Orlando's most popular parks, with 23 acres that include a swimming beach, picnic facilities, boat ramp and dock, and an open play area for children. The park is on the southeast corner of Lee Road and U.S. 441. Information: 305-849-2288.

**LAKE LOUISA STATE PARK**—A few miles southwest of Clermont, off Lake Nellie Road, this 1,790-acre park is great for swimming and other water activities. There's also a nature study center. Open 8 A.M. to sunset, year-round. Information: 904-394-2880.

**JAYCEE BEACH**—Also in Clermont is this freshwater beach on Lake Minneola. It's a family-oriented spot, with white sand, boat docks, and kids—particularly in summer when it's especially busy. It remains open year-round. Information: 904-394-4191.

**MOSS PARK**—Tall, moss-draped trees shadow swimmers and boaters at this massive recreational retreat in the heart of Orlando. There are more than 1,550 acres located between Lakes Hart and Mary Jane. Open daily. Information: 305-273-2327.

**ORLO VISTA PARK AND COMMUNITY CENTER**—Another Orlando park, endowed with a beach as well as ball fields, tennis courts, exercise and jogging trails, and picnic grounds. Open daily 9 A.M. to 7 P.M. (to 5 P.M. in winter). Information: 305-299-6124.

**DINKY DOCK**—A small beach on Lake Virginia, on the campus of Rollins College, located north of Orlando in the tony town of Winter Park. Canoes can be rented. Open 8 A.M. to 8 P.M. during the summer; 7 A.M. to 6 P.M. in winter. Located on the corner of Ollie Avenue and Lake Virginia. Information: 305-644-9860.

## Travel Tip: BEFORE YOU GO...

- Cancel all regular home deliveries.
- Arrange for the lawn to be mowed regularly.
- Have mail forwarded, held by the post office, or picked up at your house, along with any leaflets, notices, or notes that might have been left in the door.
- Put your social security number on all appliances that are likely to be stolen in the event of a robbery.
- Leave a house key with a friend, in case an emergency entry is necessary, as well as your itinerary (with telephone numbers where you can be reached along the way).
- Empty the refrigerator, turn down the thermostat.
- Lock all doors and windows.
- Leave various lights on inside the house, preferably on timers, to discourage burglars.
- If you have an answering machine, do not leave a message saying how long you will be gone or specifying the exact date of your return. Keep it vague, and call in often for messages.

## 16 POOLS AND BEACHES/Central Florida

## THE EAST COAST

The best beaches on the east coast of central Florida are found at Canaveral National Seashore and Cocoa Beach, where sun, sand, and ocean await. An added bonus here is the opportunity to be where the action is when the space shuttle (or some other space-bound vehicle) blasts off at Cape Canaveral.

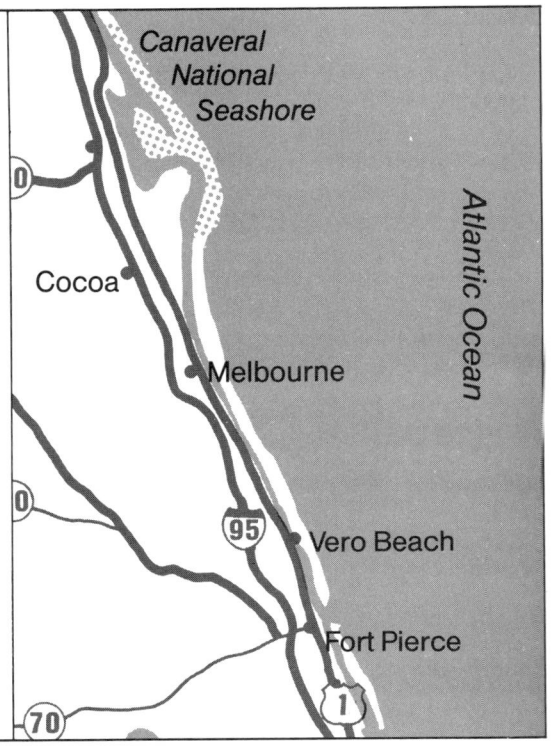

**NEW SMYRNA BEACH**—This is one of the quietest and most conservative of all central Florida beaches, on the east coast between Daytona Beach and Titusville. Information: 904-428-2449.

**PLAYALINDA**—The name means "pretty beach," and this 5-mile stretch of sand—part of the Canaveral National Seashore—lives up to its billing. Apparently nature agrees; it has a wide variety of wildlife and vegetation, and conservationists regard Playalinda as one of the state's last unspoiled beaches. Information: 305-867-4675.

**CAPE CANAVERAL**—Popular for surfing, swimming, and, if your timing is right, watching a space shuttle launch. Lifeguards are on duty during weekends only from March 30 through June 10; then daily from June 11 through September 2. Beach access is at Polk, Madison, and Jackson Avenues, and ample parking is available. Information: 305-783-1100.

**JETTY PARK CAMPGROUND**—Near the major port of Canaveral, this is the only beachfront campground in the area and its protected beach is perfect for

## POOLS AND BEACHES/Central Florida

swimming and sunning. There's also fishing off the rock jetty and from the seawall. Port Canaveral and Jetty Park are just a few miles beyond the end of the Beeline Expressway. Information: 305-783-7222.

**COCOA BEACH**—Another spot from which to view space launches. It's also a very popular place for surfers. Information: 305-632-6095.

**LORI WILSON PARK**—Also in Cocoa, this park has 7 acres of tropical hammock and is one of the few reminders of Florida's original natural coastline. There's also a picnic shelter with grills, a playground, and a boardwalk leading to the beach. Information: 305-453-1090.

**MELBOURNE**—This east coast city (south of Cocoa) has several lovely parks: **Long Point Park**, located 2 miles north of Sebastian Inlet and 1 mile west of Highway A1A, with a swimming lake with bathhouses, plus playgrounds, camping facilities, boat launching places, and a country store; **Wickham Park**, 1 mile west of U.S. 1 on Parkway Drive with 2 swimming lakes and picnic facilities, as well as an archery and shooting range; **Paradise Beach Park**, on A1A, with a 10-acre beach, a boardwalk, and picnic facilities; **Spessard Holland Park and Golf Course**, also on A1A, covers 160 acres with a 1,200-foot-long boardwalk and 3,600 feet of beachfront (golf information: 305-723-1590); and **Rhodes Park** on Babcock Street, which has a large swimming lake with picnic tables and grills. Information: 305-724-5400.

**SEBASTIAN INLET STATE RECREATION AREA**—Situated between Melbourne and Vero Beach, this area has facilities for surfing, fishing, sunbathing, swimming, and other water sports. Information: 305-727-1752 or 305-589-3754.

*Travel Tip:* **REMINDER FOR SWIMMERS**

Never swim immediately after eating, and never swim alone. Remember: a green beach flag indicates safe waters; yellow, swim with caution; red, danger and do not swim. Some beaches are afflicted with tar deposits from ship spills; they can be removed from the soles of the feet with a little kerosene, which most hotels keep on hand. Just ask.

SAVVY TRAVELER

# SOUTHERN FLORIDA

## THE GULF COAST

Before southern Florida's west coast unravels into the maze of mangrove mysteries in the Everglades, there are some of the best surf 'n' sun 'n' shell-collecting beaches in the world, stretching from Longboat Key down to Marco Island. U.S. Highway 41 hugs the coast all along its length here, and offers easy access to its beaches.

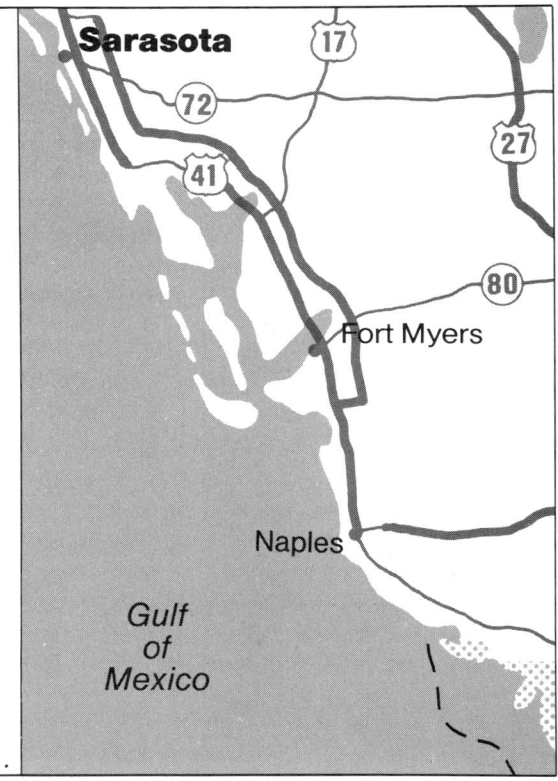

**LONGBOAT KEY**—This posh resort area has lovely white-sand beaches on the Gulf of Mexico. One of the best, **Whitney Beach**, is dominated by cabbage palms and Spanish bayonets. Information: 813-383-1212.

**SIESTA BEACH**—This sugar-white, firm, sandy beach, just 5 miles west of Sarasota, also has a pool, kiddie rides, good shelling, and dolphins frolicking in the gentle Gulf. Information: 813-955-8187.

**POINT O'ROCKS**—This isolated beach, near Siesta Key, is famous for the colorful rocks of all sizes found along its sands. Information: 813-955-8187.

**VENICE BEACH**—Famous for sharks' teeth that wash up on shore. The winged-roof pavilion is a pleasant place for a picnic. Information: 813-488-2236.

**ENGLEWOOD**—This may be the prettiest beach on Florida's southern Gulf Coast. There is considerable surf plus gorgeous cabbage palms. Situated 10 miles south of Venice. Information: 813-474-5511.

**GASPARILLA SOUND**—There's a great deal of mystery surrounding this area. Pirate gold is allegedly buried here and the place is supposedly haunted by the ghost of Gasparilla. There are also Calusa Indian mounds to observe, but touching is illegal. Information: 813-627-2222.

**PINE ISLAND**—One of Florida's largest but least-known coastal islands is located west of Fort Myers on Pine Island Road (Route 78). There are patches of sandy beach sprinkled between the dominant growth of mangroves, some of which are rookeries for pelicans. Information: 813-283-0888.

**FORT MYERS BEACH**—Key West boasts that it has America's best sunsets, but the twilight view of the horizon here—across the open Gulf of Mexico—is also a stunner. The beach is slow-paced and frequented mainly by families. And there's that sun that sets every evening. Information: 813-463-6451.

**SANIBEL and CAPTIVA ISLANDS**—Word is that these are the best beaches for shell collecting in the Western Hemisphere. The only way to be sure is to put them to the test firsthand. Find out why shellers are said to be afflicted by the "Sanibel stoop." (There's a $3 toll to cross the causeway; beaches are free.) Information: 813-472-1080.

**NAPLES BEACH**—Another of the best places in the state to watch the sun set. (Have we said this before?) The best view is from the Naples Pier, which juts out into the Gulf. Information: 813-262-6141.

**MARCO ISLAND**—The best swimming and sunning are on the western side of the island, where it's less crowded and the water is not quite as salty. Information: 813-394-7549.

---

## Travel Tip: FLIGHT KIT TIP

Savvy travelers like to have at hand a small bag with the basics for an overnight stay, particularly if they are traveling by plane. Always keep necessary medicine, valuable jewelry, travel documents, or business documents in your handbag, briefcase, or hand luggage. Never check these things with your luggage.

# THE EAST COAST

Southern Florida's east coast beaches include some of the most famous stretches of sand in the world. This is the area of the earth where legions of college students play beach blanket bingo every spring vacation and summer, and generations of northeasterners and midwesterners have come in midwinter to escape snowy cabin fever.

**HUTCHINSON ISLAND**—From Fort Pierce south to Stuart, there are 20 miles of superb oceanfront along Highway A1A. The western side of this barrier island faces the Indian River, one of Florida's most famous citrus-growing areas. Information: 305-287-1088.

**JUPITER ISLAND/JUPITER INLET**—This magnificent stretch of sand includes Blowing Rocks Preserve, where waves crash against limestone-coral formations and the 150-year-old Jupiter Lighthouse. Information: 305-746-7111.

**THE PALM BEACHES**—This stretch includes Juno Beach, North Palm Beach, Lake Park, Riviera Beach, and Palm Beach. Portions of these beaches are quite narrow, especially when the tide comes in. All can be reached from Highway A1A. Information: 305-655-3282.

**DELRAY BEACH**—This stretch has been cultivated by the many "snowbirds" who winter in this area. The beach was recently widened and has become more conducive to sunbathing. Information: 305-278-0424.

**POMPANO BEACH**—This public beach is particularly wide and has picnic facilities, a fishing pier, and a playground. Information: 305-941-2940.

**FORT LAUDERDALE**—Some of the finest Atlantic Ocean beachfront south of Daytona. It can get a bit crowded and overflow with college students during the weeks of spring break. But even that has its own peculiar, mad charm. Information: 305-462-6000.

**DANIA**—Just south of the Fort Lauderdale strip, this small, pretty beach is a favorite of local residents. Information: 305-927-3378.

**HOLLYWOOD**—This 6-mile stretch of sand has a 4-mile-long boardwalk with shops and restaurants. There's also the Beach Theatre Under the Stars, a 1,000-seat arena where free theatrical performances are held year-round. The backdrop is a series of high rises that stretch from Hollywood to Hallendale. Information: 305-920-3330.

**MIAMI BEACH**—The ultimate American seashore resort. Off Collins Avenue are 10 miles of urban beaches that have lately been undergoing a bit of a renaissance. The single best sunning spot here is at South Beach's Lummus Park. Information: 305-672-1270.

**SURFSIDE**—A favorite of wintering Canadians, this built-up neighbor of Miami Beach is a mixture of often bizarre motels and condos. Information: 305-866-6020.

**HAULOVER BEACH**—Just north of the towers of Miami Beach, this is a wonderful oceanfront park created by Dade County. There are dunes and access to Miami's longest fishing pier. Information: 305-375-4694.

## Travel Tip: SUN SENSE

Don't underestimate the Florida sun, even when you're not on the beach. Slather on sunscreen for extra protection when you're out sightseeing, on foot or in a car. Hats come in handy, as do lightweight, long-sleeved shirts. Believe it or not, light rays reflected from the pavement can actually cause legs to become sunburned. A good once-over with moisturizing lotion at the end of the day will help to keep skin soft and resilient.

## THE KEYS

The Florida Keys are not especially prime beach country; the shore is composed mostly of rock flats—great for fishing, but a topography that makes beaches a scarce commodity. In fact, the only sand beaches are man-made, and there is virtually no surf since the coral reef extends almost 4 miles into the ocean, breaking any waves that might try to roll in.

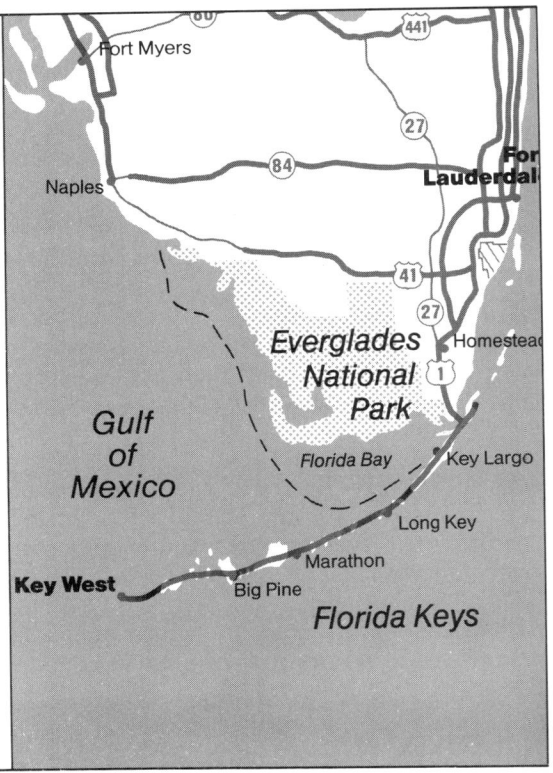

**Key Largo**, the largest of the Keys, has a series of small, covelike beaches on the Florida Bay side. **Tavernier** and **Plantation**, just to the south, have a handful of pretty Atlantic Ocean stretches. **Islamorada** is a major resort area and offers fine beaches on all sides. **Lower Matecumbe Beach** has a good Atlantic stretch of white sand and some Jamaican coconut palms. **Marathon** has a few Atlantic beaches that are not fenced off or posted by motels and homes. **Big Pine Key**, the second-largest of the islands, has some white sand coves amid the mangrove on its Gulf side. Miniature Key deer, a protected species, can sometimes be seen on this wilderness coast. **Key West**, the most famous of the islands, has several public strands: **Smathers Beach**, just west of the airport on South Roosevelt Boulevard, is the longest beach on the island, with family groups predominating on the quiet eastern end and with some shaded picnic tables; **Memorial Beach**, on Atlantic Boulevard near the south end of White Street, has a 7-foot-wide, 100-yard-long wooden pier that angles into the water; **South Beach**, where Duval Street meets the ocean, is more peaceful than the others and has a 50-yard-long concrete pier that is good for sunbathing.

# HISTORIC SITES, GREAT GARDENS

In 1513 Spanish explorer Ponce de Leon arrived on the east coast of Florida looking for the Fountain of Youth. His search may have been a dismal failure, but his landing at what is now St. Augustine did lend a certain immortality to that site. America got its first permanent European settlement, founded in 1565, 42 years before the settlement of Jamestown and 55 years before the Pilgrims landed at Plymouth Rock. And although those latter two settlements are memorialized today as historic sites, St. Augustine remains a living city—one that has gone to enormous effort to preserve and protect its precious heritage.

But Florida's rich multinational history is not limited to just one city. The state first belonged to Spain, was traded briefly to England, and was finally sold to the United States in 1821. Thanks in part to state and federal laws, much remains of this tumultuous past.

But it is not only man who has thrived in Florida. The earliest Spanish settlers brought seeds from around the world, and many of these foreign exotics flourished alongside native flora. The result is a variety and diversity of plants found almost nowhere else in the world in such ready proximity, and a number of magnificent gardens have sprung up to enhance and enrich this wealth. These, too, are a large part of the Florida culture that is free for the visiting.

# NORTHERN FLORIDA

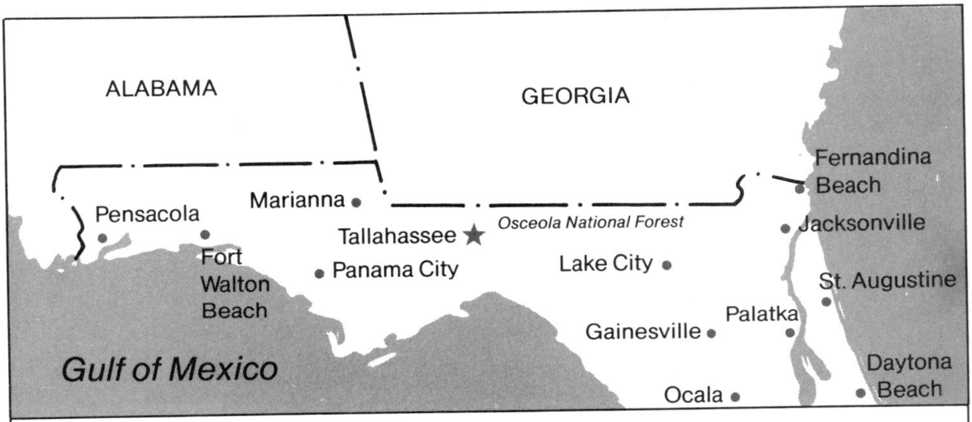

From the 16th-century conflicts between Spain and France to the Civil War, battles raged all across northern Florida. Many significant battle sites, national monuments, and historic homes have been preserved and are open to the public free of charge. And, of course, the historic city of St. Augustine—where buildings have been restored and original forts reinforced—is located on the east coast.

## HISTORIC SITES

**NATURAL BRIDGE HISTORIC SITE**, Woodville—Located near Tallahassee, this was the site of the 1865 Battle of Natural Bridge during which Confederate troops held back Union forces trying to capture Florida's capital. There are picnic grounds, fishing, and 6 acres of trails. Information: 904-925-6216.

**BROKAW-MCDOUGALL HOUSE**, Tallahassee—This mid-19th-century classical revival residence is distinguished by its fine craftsmanship and the beauty of its restored garden. Open Mondays through Fridays 8 A.M. to 5 P.M. 329 North Meridian; Tallahassee 32301 (904-488-3901).

**CENTRE STREET HISTORIC DISTRICT**, Fernandina Beach—The downtown area of this northern beach town is known as the "birthplace of America's shrimping industry." There are a number of interesting Victorian-style buildings to explore. Open all year. Maps and additional information are available at the Fernandina Beach Chamber of Commerce; 102 Centre Street; Fernandina Beach 32034 (904-261-3248).

**KINGSLEY PLANTATION**, Fort George Island—This graceful plantation on the east coast, just off Highway A1A, includes two of the state's oldest houses—the Kingsley house (1817) and Don Juan McQueen's house (1792). Open daily 8 A.M. to 5 P.M.; tours are offered at 9:30 A.M., 11 A.M., 1:30 P.M., and 3 P.M. Box 321; Fort George Island 32226 (904-251-3122).

**FORT CAROLINE NATIONAL MEMORIAL**, Jacksonville—A 138-acre park on the St. John's River commemorates the 16th-century attempts by the French to found a permanent settlement in Florida. Open daily 9 A.M. to 5 P.M. 12713 Fort Caroline Road; Jacksonville 32225 (904-641-7155).

**FORT MATANZAS NATIONAL MONUMENT**, St. Augustine—Located 16 miles south of the city, this classic coquina (soft, white limestone formed of broken shells and corals cemented together) Spanish fort served as a strategic-warning post during the 17th and 18th centuries. It also marks the site of a 1565 battle with French troops in which Spain reaffirmed her claim to Florida. Open daily 8:30 A.M. to 5:30 P.M. Highway A1A; St. Augustine 32086 (904-471-0116).

**CATHEDRAL OF SAINT AUGUSTINE**—This 18th-century structure was the home of the oldest Catholic parish in America. It was damaged by fire in 1887 and then restored. Open daily from sunrise to sunset. Cathedral and St. George Streets; St. Augustine 32084 (904-824-2806).

**MISSION OF NOMBRE DE DIOS**, St. Augustine—This was the nation's first mission (its first mass was celebrated in 1565). There's a 208-foot stainless steel cross that was erected in 1965 to commemorate the 400th anniversary of the landing of the Spaniards in St. Augustine. Open daily 8 A.M. to sunset. San Marcos Avenue at Old Mission Avenue; St. Augustine 32085 (904-824-2809).

**XIMENEZ FATIO HOUSE**, St. Augustine—This house was built in 1798 and restored as an inn in 1855 with period furnishings and a lovely garden. Guided tours are available. Open March 1 through August 31 on Mondays, Thursdays, Fridays, and Saturdays 11 A.M. to 4 P.M.; Sundays 1 P.M. to 4 P.M. 20 Aviles Street; St. Augustine 32084 (904-829-3575).

**BRONSON-MULHOLLAND HOUSE**, Palatka—This cypress home was built in 1854 in simplified Greek revival style and is an example of some of the unusual antebellum architecture found in this part of the state. Open Tuesdays, Thursdays, and Sundays 2 P.M. to 5 P.M. 501 North 2nd Street; Palatka 32077 (904-325-9347).

> ### *Travel Tip:* HIKING
>
> *Now shall I walk or shall I ride?*
> *"Ride," Pleasure said.*
> *"Walk," Joy replied.*
>
> Florida has trails galore, almost none of them uphill. They are one of the great pleasures of the state's many parks, nature preserves, and public gardens, treasures to be discovered simply by setting off.
>
> When you do, wear loose, comfortable clothing, sturdy shoes, and a hat to keep the sun at bay. Day packs and roomy pockets leave arms free to swing at your sides. Useful packables include binoculars and a bird-identification book, a Swiss army knife, a canteen of water, trail mix for a quick pick-me-up snack, a compass, and mosquito-repellent spray (better than the stick form of repellent because clothes as well as skin should be doused).
>
> For more information about Florida's hiking and canoe trails, as well as a copy of the booklet *Florida State Parks—The Real Florida* write the Department of Natural Resources; Bureau of Education and Information; Marjory Stoneman Douglas Building; 3900 Commonwealth Blvd.; Tallahassee, FL 32303 (904-488-7326).

## GREAT GARDENS

**EDEN STATE GARDENS**, Point Washington—Overlooking Choctawhatchee Bay in the Panhandle, these gardens flourish on the site (and around the remains) of a large 19th-century sawmill complex. Closed Tuesdays and Wednesdays. Tours are offered on the hour from 9 A.M. to 4 P.M. Grounds open at 8 A.M. Box 26; Point Washington 32454 (904-231-4214).

**RAVINE STATE GARDENS**, Palatka—About 20 miles southwest of St. Augustine are these gardens set in and around an 85-acre site. Among the plantings, the azaleas are particularly beautiful; they reach their peak in the period from mid-February through mid-March. The grounds include nature and jogging trails and picnic areas. Open daily 8 A.M. to sunset. Box 1096; Palatka 32078-1096 (904-328-4366).

**SUGAR MILL GARDENS**, Port Orange—Located 5 miles south of Daytona are these gardens centered around the ruins of an English sugar mill and the site of an original Spanish Franciscan mission founded in 1602. Open daily 11 A.M. to 4:15 P.M. 950 Old Sugar Mill Road; Port Orange 32019 (904-767-1735).

# CENTRAL FLORIDA

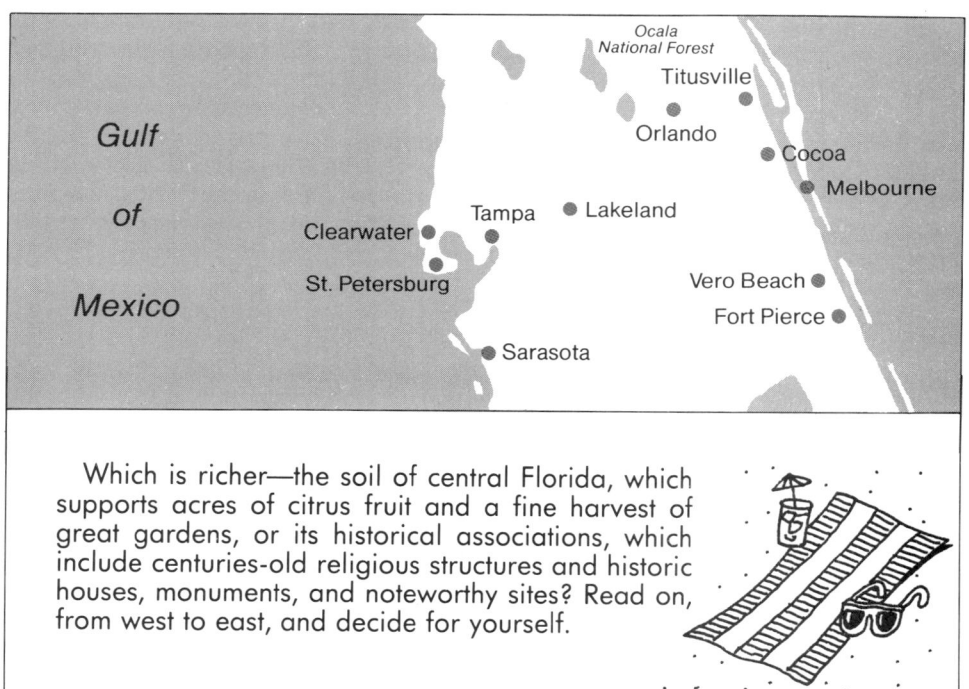

Which is richer—the soil of central Florida, which supports acres of citrus fruit and a fine harvest of great gardens, or its historical associations, which include centuries-old religious structures and historic houses, monuments, and noteworthy sites? Read on, from west to east, and decide for yourself.

## HISTORIC SITES

**PLANT HALL**, Tampa—The interest here is not botany, but the building itself, part of the University of Tampa. It's an 1891 Moorish-influenced structure, with 13 silver-domed minarets. It was originally built as the lavish Tampa Bay Hotel and is generally considered a unique example of American Moorish-style architecture. It became part of the university in 1933 and is one of the few genuine historic landmarks in the Tampa area. There are tours every Tuesday and Thursday at 1:30 P.M. from September 1 through the end of May. University of Tampa; Tampa 33606 (813-253-3333).

**YBOR SQUARE**, Tampa—This 1880s landmark area includes brick buildings that served as cigar factories and the headquarters of the Latin Quarter's political and social life. Most of the brick masonry, grillwork, and wooden interiors of the original structures have been preserved or restored. Open

Mondays through Saturdays 10 A.M. to 6 P.M.; Sundays noon to 6 P.M. Box 384; Tampa 33601 (813-247-4497).

**SAINT LEO ABBEY**, St. Leo—Nestled among beautiful rolling hills about 30 miles northwest of Lakeland is what is believed to be Florida's only functioning abbey, founded by the Order of St. Benedict in 1889. Visitors are always welcome. State Road 52; St. Leo 33574 (904-588-8290).

**HERITAGE PARK**, Largo—This historical park portrays the pioneer days of Pinellas County through a collection of buildings, including the oldest structure in the county—the McMullen-Coachman log house—built in the 1850s. Also on display is Seven Gables, a 13-room home built in the 1850s, and the Plant-Sumner House, built in 1896. Guided tours Tuesdays through Saturdays 10 A.M. to 4 P.M. 11909 125th Street North; Largo 33544 (813-462-3474).

**YULEE SUGAR MILL RUINS**, Homosassa—This 4-acre plantation, 50 miles north of Clearwater, functioned as a supplier of sugar products for southern troops during the Civil War. The native limestone mill, torched by a Union naval force during the war, has been partially restored. Open daily 8 A.M. to sunset. State Road 490; Homosassa 33605 (904-795-3817).

**HOLY TRINITY EPISCOPAL CHURCH**, Fruitland Park—This Gothic church, located about 40 miles northwest of Orlando, was built in 1888 and is well known for its stunning stained glass and its handmade mahogany altar. Visitors are welcome, but it's wise to call first to be sure the church is open. Tuesdays, Wednesdays, and Thursdays 9 A.M. to noon. 600 Spring Lake Road; Fruitland Park 32731 (904-787-1500).

**DEBARY HALL**—Located about 20 miles north of Orlando, this 114-year-old historic mansion, the plantation house of Baron Frederick DeBary, played host to Goulds, Astors, Vanderbilts, and the Prince of Wales. Winslow Homer often came here to paint. Especially interesting is a century-old mounted display of birds native to the region. Open Mondays through Fridays 9 A.M. to 3 P.M. 210 Sunrise Boulevard; DeBary 32713 (305-668-5286).

**NEW SMYRNA SUGAR MILL RUINS**—The remains of this 19th-century sugar mill have been declared a state historic site. A portion of the original sugar mill remains, and the laborious step-by-step process of making sugar and molasses is explained on informational signs around the ruins. Open daily 9 A.M. to 5 P.M. Off State Road 44 on Mission Drive. Box 861; New Smyrna Beach 32069 (904-428-2126).

**ST. GABRIEL'S EPISCOPAL CHURCH**, Titusville—The city's oldest church was built in 1887, and it contains a fine collection of Victorian stained glass. Open daily. 414 Pine Street; Titusville 32782 (305-267-2545).

# GREAT GARDENS

**KAPOK TREE INN**, Clearwater—Lavish formal gardens sprawl out from the famous Kapok Tree that blooms each February outside this lovely old restaurant. Open daily from noon to 10 P.M. 923 McMullen Booth Road; Clearwater 33517 (813-726-0504).

**SUNCOAST BOTANICAL GARDEN**, Largo—This herbarium has a collection of 600 specimens, a living plant collection, and one of the largest protected collections of wildflowers on Florida's west coast. There's also a nature conservation area. Open daily sunrise to sunset. 1040 125th Street North; Largo 33544 (813-321-1726).

**APOPKA**—Located 12 miles northwest of Orlando, the whole city of Apopka is known as the "indoor foliage capital of the world." The city is sprinkled with flower and plant shops, and an outdoor art and foliage festival is held every spring. Apopka Area Chamber of Commerce; 180 East Main Street; Apopka 32703 (305-886-1441).

**BIG TREE PARK**, Longwood—This heavily shaded park, about 12 miles north of Orlando, boasts rows of tall cypress trees that stand guard in a circle around the "Senator," one of the oldest and largest bald cypress trees in the country. The Senator is 125 feet tall, has a 47-foot circumference, and is estimated to be 3,500 years old. Open daily sunrise to sunset. U.S. Highway 17-92 on General Hutchinson Parkway; Longwood 32750 (305-323-2500).

**SLOCUM WATER GARDENS**, Winter Haven—One of the Southeast's most extensive displays of water plants. Open weekdays 8 A.M. to noon and 1 P.M. to 4 P.M.; Saturdays 8 A.M. to noon. 1101 Cypress Gardens Boulevard; Winter Haven 33880 (813-293-7151).

**CARL T. LANGFORD PARK**, Orlando—Visitors to this 19-acre park can stroll leisurely along boardwalks that are flanked by tropical foliage. The elevated nature trail is designed to protect plants (such as banana, citrus, and magnolia trees) and animals (opossums and raccoons, among others). There are signs posted to identify the various trees and plants. There are also picnic shelters, barbecue pits, a playground, and a tennis court. Open daily 5 A.M. to sunset. Central Boulevard near Fern Creek and Hampton Avenues. Orlando Parks and Recreation Bureau; 1103 South Westmoreland; Orlando 32805 (305-849-2283).

**LAKE EOLA PARK**, Orlando—Specialty gardens are regularly changed at this 11.2-acre park, located at the corner of Robinson and Rosalind in downtown Orlando. Open daily from sunrise to sunset. (305-849-2283).

**DICKSON AZALEA PARK**, Orlando—Another haven where a 3-mile trail is carved into a ravine. Informational signs describe plants and wildlife. Open 5 A.M. to sunset. Located on Rosearden Drive at the corner of Robinson Street. Orlando Parks and Recreation Bureau; 1103 South Westmoreland; Orlando 32805 (305-849-2283).

**MEAD GARDENS**, Winter Park—Several nature trails and ponds, with connecting streams, are found in this haven. Azaleas provide most of the spring color, and walking tours are also available. There's also a greenhouse. Open 8 A.M. to 6 P.M. daily. Denning Drive; Winter Park 32789 (305-644-9860).

**FLORIDA FEDERATION OF GARDEN CLUBS**, Winter Park—The building of this organization's headquarters, its gardens, and a lovely wildflower display are all open to the public, but by reservation only. Tours can be arranged Mondays through Fridays 9 A.M. to 5 P.M. 1400 South Denning Drive; Winter Park 32790 (305-647-7016).

**CHALET SUZANNE**, Lake Wales—This country inn's collection of winding brick walkways, pastel-shaded streets, and hand-painted tiles, located about 40 miles southwest of Orlando, reminds some visitors of a modern fantasy world. The restaurant here serves excellent meals, and rooms are available for overnight stays, but there's no charge just to take a look around. Closed Mondays June through September. On U.S. Highway 27. Box AC; Lake Wales 33853 (813-676-6011).

**ERNA NIXON PARK**, Melbourne—This 52-acre hammock of magnificent hardwood trees, palms, and ferns is preserved in its natural state. Some of the trees are several hundred years old. Open 10 A.M. to 6 P.M. Wednesdays through Sundays. The South Brevard Junior Service League, the Florida Native Plant Society, and the ranger on duty offer guided tours for children's groups. Brevard County Parks and Recreation; Wickham Park; 2500 Parkway; Melbourne 32935 (305-725-0511).

**FLORIDA INSTITUTE OF TECHNOLOGY BOTANICAL GARDENS**, Melbourne—This is a beautifully landscaped 125-acre campus, about a quarter of which is covered by a lush hammock of palms (hundreds of species), natural streams, water oaks, and tropical vegetation. Open during daylight hours. 150 West University Boulevard; Melbourne 32901 (305-768-8000).

---

*Travel Tip:* **REMEMBER . . .**
Pack half the clothes you think you'll need—and twice the money.

*SAVVY TRAVELER*

# SOUTHERN FLORIDA

Historically, southern Florida is the new guy on the block—most of the state's notable historic battles raged farther north, and so few war scars exist here. But when the world finally arrived here—in the 1920s, 1930s, and 1940s—it came on with a vengeance, leaving a distinctive architectural heritage (Miami's art deco district, for one) that provides a glimpse of Florida life during the early part of this century.

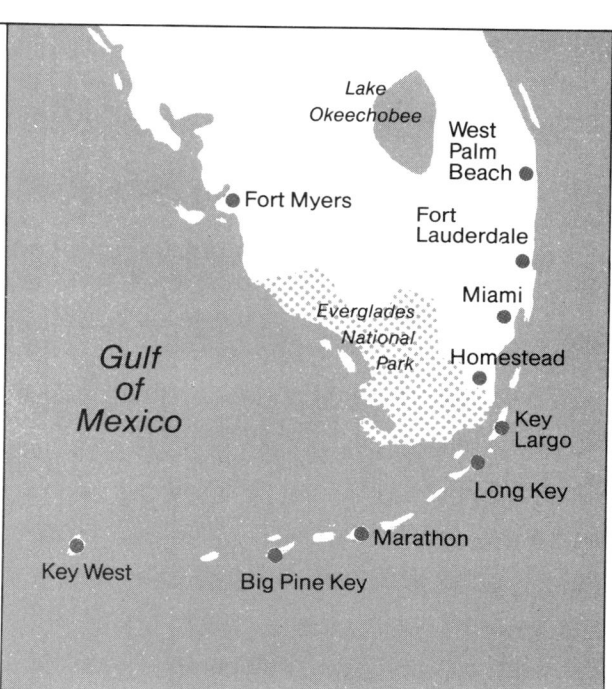

## HISTORIC SITES

**HIMMARSHEE VILLAGE**, Fort Lauderdale—There are four restored homes here, built in 1895 by Phelemon Bryan and Edwin Thomas King, who helped bring the iron horse to what was then swamp and piny woods. There are free tours of the King-Cromartie House, the onetime residence of the Kings. It's a two-story structure that houses what was Fort Lauderdale's first indoor toilet. It was also one of the first homes to have electricity and a telephone. 229 Southwest Second Avenue; Fort Lauderdale (305-462-8803).

**ART DECO DISTRICT**, Miami Beach—This area offers a rare combination: the movieland charm of the 1930s set in a lively neighborhood of the 1980s. This National Historic District is officially bounded by 6th Street on the south, 23rd Street on the north, Ocean Drive to the east, and Alton Road to the west. In it are about 800 buildings, including examples of streamline moderne and depression moderne as well as Mediterranean revival, Spanish colonial and beaux arts styles. Almost everywhere there are unique murals, decorative iron and etched-glass work, exquisite bias reliefs, colored neon, and other delights—so stand back, look up, and go into building lobbies. Buildings of particular interest include the Washington Storage Building and the Hotel Neron. Special events take place regularly, and many of them are free. Maps are available at the Miami Design Preservation League; 1236 Ocean Drive; Miami Beach 33139 (305-672-2014).

**PORTER HOUSE**, Key West—This 2½–story mansion is a fine example of Key West's indigenous conch houses. It has a rare mansard roof with gabled dormers. A marker in the corner of the yard, worth a look, relates Dr. Joseph Y. Porter's medical and pirate-chasing exploits. Dr. Porter did research on yellow fever and served as Florida's first public health officer. Corner of Caroline and Duval Streets; Key West 33040 (305-296-6206).

**THE BAHAMA HOUSE**, Key West—Built in the Bahamas and disassembled for shipment to Key West, this elegant dwelling, now a private residence, has a white picket fence, wide verandas, and a twin-gabled roof. 730 Eaton Street; Key West 33040 (305-296-6206).

# GREAT GARDENS

**MORIKAMI MUSEUM**, Delray Beach—This museum is the lasting testament of G. M. Morikami, last of the Japanese pineapple farmers who cultivated rich black Palm Beach County soil. Open Tuesdays through Sundays 10 A.M. to 5 P.M. 4000 Morikami Park Road; Delray Beach 33444 (305-499-0631).

**HIALEAH PARK RACE TRACK**—When the horses aren't running (that's all but 70 days of the year), the park and track—with their elegant royal palms, Australian pines, and large flock of pink flamingos—are open to the public, 9:30 A.M. to 5 P.M. daily. 79th Street and East 4th Avenue; Hialeah 33013 (305-885-8000).

**SIMPSON PARK**, Miami—A tiny patch of tropical hardwood forest, including Caribbean species, set in the shadow of the city's booming Brickell Avenue District. Open daily 7 A.M. to 7 P.M. 55 Southwest 17th Road; Miami 33129 (305-856-6801).

**FRUIT AND SPICE PARK**, Homestead—Located about 20 miles south of Miami, there are more than 500 varieties of exotic fruits such as the carambola and the cashew, with samples often available. Open daily 10 A.M. to 5 P.M. Southwest 248th Street and 187th Avenue; Homestead 33031 (305-247-5727).

# MUSEUMS AND GALLERIES

Sun and sea may seem to come first in Florida, but the fact is the state also offers a fairly broad cultural scene, including a wide and varied group of museums and galleries—from tiny one-room exhibitions tracing a single city's history to large, multibuilding institutions displaying works that represent centuries of civilization.

Whether one is interested in aviation, history, science, fine arts, or railroad memorabilia, there's a special museum or gallery in the Sunshine State devoted to it. The United States Naval Aviation Museum in Pensacola offers one of the nation's finest collections of old aircraft and World War I artifacts while Orlando's Loch Haven Art Center has a particularly notable collection of pre-Columbian art. In addition, many of the state's colleges and universities have fine art galleries and museums on their campuses. And entry is usually possible without charge. Even major museums, such as Miami Beach's Bass Museum, open their doors without charge once a week. So it's just a question of knowing when to be where.

To take the mystery out of museum going, here's a guide to the best free museums and galleries in the state, including those major institutions that offer specific free days. (Note: museum and gallery hours change frequently, so it's a good idea to call before visiting.)

# NORTHERN FLORIDA

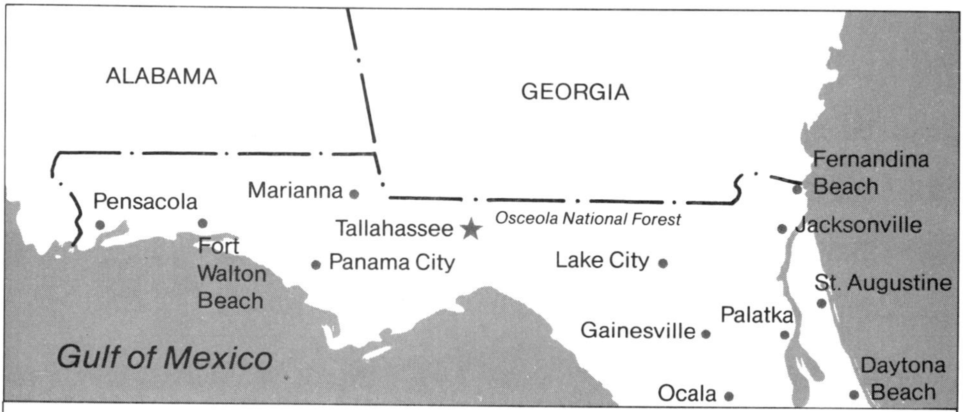

History and fine arts seem to be the main preoccupations of the area's free museums and galleries. Some display artifacts from the many wars and battles fought in the region; others are a showcase for the work of local and world-renowned artists.

**PENSACOLA HISTORICAL MUSEUM**—A 2,000-volume library, 18th- and 19th-century men's and women's accessories, Indian artifacts, and a large collection of the type of glass negatives used before celluloid was invented highlight this museum's holdings. Open Mondays through Saturdays 9 A.M. to 4:30 P.M. Closed holidays. 405 South Adams Street; Pensacola 32501 (904-433-1559).

**PENSACOLA MUSEUM OF ART**—The permanent collection of paintings, graphics, and watercolors is augmented by a 300-volume library of art reference materials. Open Tuesdays through Fridays 10 A.M. to 5 P.M.; Saturdays 10 A.M. to 4 P.M. Closed holidays. 407 South Jefferson Street; Pensacola 32501 (904-432-6247).

**UNITED STATES NAVAL AVIATION MUSEUM**, Pensacola—Here are 100 of the craft that first put aerial warfare into the skies, with 40 on display at any one time. Also part of the collection is the oldest Navy aircraft engine, and numerous World War I artifacts. Open daily 9 A.M. to 5 P.M., except Thanksgiving, Christmas, and New Year's Day. Naval Air Station; Navy Boulevard; Pensacola 32508 (904-452-3604).

**MUSEUM OF FLORIDA HISTORY**, Tallahassee—Befitting a museum in the state capital, the collections here are given over to displays on archaeological, historical, and contemporary Florida; one of the most interesting is the Spanish New World coin collection. Open Mondays through Fridays 9 A.M. to 4:30 P.M.; Saturdays 10 A.M. to 4:30 P.M.; Sundays and holidays noon to 4:30 P.M. Closed Christmas. R.A. Gray Building; Pensacola and Borrough Streets; Tallahassee 32301 (904-488-1484).

**TALLAHASSEE JUNIOR MUSEUM**—Fifty-five acres of nature trails wind through the grounds, and a 19th-century working farm depicts Florida's pioneer days. There's also a one-room schoolhouse and a grist mill. Open Tuesdays through Saturdays 9 A.M. to 5 P.M.; Sundays 12:30 P.M. to 5 P.M. 3945 Museum Drive; Tallahassee 32304 (904-576-1636).

**FLORIDA STATE FINE ARTS GALLERY**, Tallahassee—This campus-affiliated operation is known for its Peruvian, European, and contemporary art. Open Mondays through Fridays 10 A.M. to 4 P.M.; weekends 1 P.M. to 4 P.M. Fine Arts Building; Florida State University; Tallahassee 32306-2037 (904-644-6836).

**CUMMER GALLERY OF ART**, Jacksonville—As attractive as the 12 galleries of European painting, sculpture, prints, and tapestries are 2½ acres of formal gardens. And not to be missed is Cummer's 720-piece collection of early Meissen porcelain. Open Tuesdays through Fridays 10 A.M. to 4 P.M.; Saturdays noon to 5 P.M.; Sundays 2 P.M. to 5 P.M. 829 Riverside Avenue; Jacksonville 32204 (904-356-6857).

**JACKSONVILLE MUSEUM OF ARTS AND SCIENCES**—The "children's museum," as it is still called locally though its name was changed a few years ago, represents the physical, natural, and life sciences—a bonanza of answers to the questions how and where and why. Facilities include a planetarium and a replica of an 1879 Gothic church. Open Tuesdays through Fridays 9 A.M. to 5 P.M.; Saturdays 11 A.M. to 5 P.M.; Sundays 1 P.M. to 5 P.M. 1025 Gulf Life Drive; Jacksonville 32207 (904-396-7062).

**JACKSONVILLE ART MUSEUM**—The museum specializes in 20th-century graphics and paintings, but it is best-known for its collection of oriental ceramics. Open Tuesdays, Wednesdays, and Fridays 10 A.M. to 4 P.M.; Thursdays 10 A.M. to 10 P.M.; weekends 1 P.M. to 5 P.M. Closed during August. 4160 Boulevard Center Drive; Jacksonville 32207 (904-398-8336).

**MUSEUM OF ARTS AND SCIENCES**, Daytona Beach—The arts are represented by the largest collection of Cuban art in the free world plus works by contemporary Florida artists; the sciences find a home in the 140-seat planetarium. The museum is set on a 60-acre nature preserve and there are lovely trails that wind around the grounds. Open Tuesdays through Fridays 9 A.M. to 4 P.M.; Saturdays and Sundays noon to 5 P.M.; and Wednesdays 7:30 P.M. to 9 P.M. 1040 Museum Boulevard; Daytona Beach 32014 (904-255-0285).

**FLORIDA STATE MUSEUM**, Gainesville—You have to go to college—or at least to the campus of the University of Florida—to learn about the human history and natural ecology of the southeastern United States and Caribbean; but the museum's exhibits on the archaeology and herpetology of these areas tell the whole story. Open Mondays through Saturdays 9 A.M. to 5 P.M.; Sundays and holidays 1 P.M. to 5 P.M. Museum Road; University of Florida; Gainesville 32611 (904-392-1721).

**UNIVERSITY GALLERY**, Gainesville—Also on the campus are the Florida archives of photography, and permanent collections of Indian sculpture and pre-Columbian artifacts. Open Mondays through Fridays 9 A.M. to 5 P.M.; Sundays 1 P.M. to 5 P.M. Corner of Southwest 13th Street and Stadium Road; Gainesville 32611 (904-392-0201).

## Travel Tip: PERSONAL-EFFECTS INSURANCE

The airlines, Amtrak, and bus companies provide only limited protection against the loss or damage of baggage in their care. The limits of their liability are included as part of the fine print on every ticket, and are as follows: Airlines insure luggage and contents for a maximum of $1,250 on domestic flights, and $9.07 a pound on international flights; Amtrak takes responsibility for a maximum of $500 per passenger; and the buses assume responsibility for considerably less, about $250 maximum per passenger. These maximum payments are not automatic; payments will be based on the value of the baggage and its contents. If your luggage disappears en route, or is damaged, deal with the situation immediately, at the airport, train station, or bus station. If an airline loses your luggage, you will be asked to fill out a Property Irregularity Report before you leave the airport. If your property disappears elsewhere, make a report to the police at once.

# CENTRAL FLORIDA

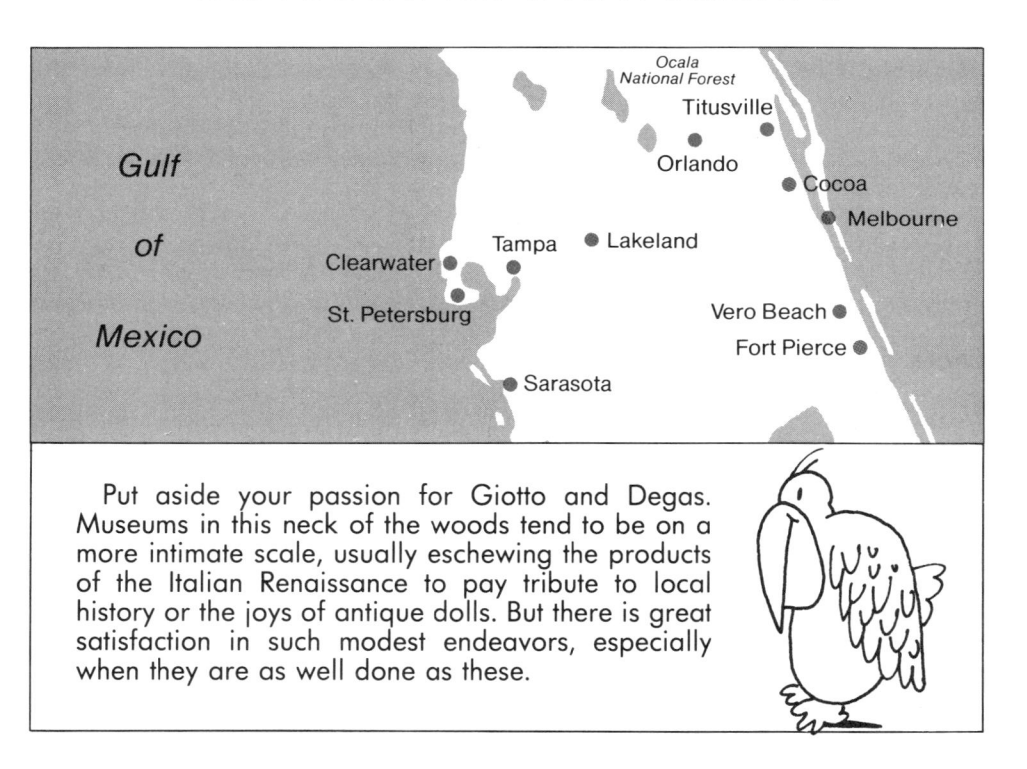

Put aside your passion for Giotto and Degas. Museums in this neck of the woods tend to be on a more intimate scale, usually eschewing the products of the Italian Renaissance to pay tribute to local history or the joys of antique dolls. But there is great satisfaction in such modest endeavors, especially when they are as well done as these.

**DUNEDIN HISTORICAL SOCIETY MUSEUM**—Located in the town's old railroad station, this is a must for aficionados of the choo-choo, with relics from the first railroad system on Florida's West Coast. Some items date from as early as 1889, the Middle Ages in Florida terms. Open Tuesdays and Saturdays 10 A.M. to noon; Thursdays 9:30 A.M. to 11:30 A.M. Closed June 1 through October 1. 341 Main Street; Dunedin 33528 (813-733-1291).

**FLORIDA GULF COAST ART CENTER**, Belleair—Primarily a teaching center, there are also changing exhibits of contemporary regional art. From September through May hours are 10 A.M. to 4 P.M. Tuesdays through Saturdays; 2 P.M. to 5 P.M. Sundays. Closed June, July, and August, and holidays. 222 Ponce de Leon Boulevard; Belleair 33516 (813-584-8634).

**PINELLAS COUNTY HISTORICAL MUSEUM**, Largo—A complex of historic homes and buildings, with guides in period costume and craftsmen working in traditional modes, which offers a glimpse into the early days in a Florida settlement. A collection of 5,000 photographs completes the picture. Open Tuesdays through Saturdays 10 A.M. to 4 P.M.; Sundays 1 P.M. to 4 P.M. 11909 125th Street North; Largo 33544 (813-462-3474).

**THE BEACH ART CENTER**, Indian Rocks Beach—A slightly different view of the area's history—as it was recorded on canvas, including a 6-foot by 40-foot mural depicting the history of the area. Open Mondays through Fridays 9 A.M. to 4 P.M.; Saturdays 9 A.M. to noon. 1515 Bay Palm Boulevard; Indian Rocks Beach 33535 (813-596-4331).

**HILLSBOROUGH COUNTY HISTORICAL MUSEUM AND LIBRARY**, Tampa—Displays include Civil War memorabilia and Spanish-American war items, as well as exhibits re-creating local history. Open Mondays through Fridays 10 A.M. to 4 P.M. Closed holidays. Hillsborough County Courthouse; 491 Pierce Street; Tampa 33602 (813-272-5919).

**MUSEUM OF NATURAL HISTORY**, Tampa—Natural history and lots of it at this city attraction. Open Tuesdays and Thursdays 10:30 A.M. to 4 P.M.; Saturdays 1 P.M. to 4 P.M. 1101 East River Cove Avenue; Tampa 33604 (813-272-5840).

**TAMPA MUSEUM**—A collection of 20th-century paintings and prints, and pre-Columbian and Native American artifacts. Open Tuesdays, Thursdays, and Fridays 10 A.M. to 6 P.M.; Wednesdays 10 A.M. to 9 P.M.; Saturdays 9 A.M. to 5 P.M.; Sundays 1 P.M. to 5 P.M. 601 Doyle Carlton Drive; Tampa 33602 (813-223-8128).

**ELLIOTT TEACHING GALLERY/ART CENTER OF ECKERD COLLEGE**, St. Petersburg—This permanent college collection of graphics includes works by Rivers, Motherwell, Roth, Gottlieb, and Nolan. Paintings, drawings, and prints by local artists are also on display. Open Mondays through Fridays 10:30 A.M. to 4:30 P.M. Closed June, July, and August. 4400 54th Avenue South; St. Petersburg 33733 (813-867-1166).

**SCIENCE CENTER OF PINELLAS COUNTY**, St. Petersburg—A changing roster of science exhibits is featured here. Open Mondays through Fridays 9 A.M. to 4 P.M. Closed holidays. 7701 22nd Avenue North; St. Petersburg 33710 (813-384-0027).

**THE MUSEUM OF FINE ARTS**, St. Petersburg—Traveling exhibitions, especially those devoted to the French impressionists, are a frequent part of the agenda here. There's also a fine collection of black-and-white photographs. Open Tuesdays through Saturdays 10 A.M. to 5 P.M. 255 Beach Drive Northeast; St. Petersburg 33706 (813-896-2667).

**ROYELLOU MUSEUM**, Mount Dora—The highlights of an eclectic display are the prison cells of an old jailhouse and antique firefighting equipment. This museum is about 25 miles northwest of Orlando. Open Wednesdays 2 P.M. to

4 P.M.; Saturdays 10 A.M. to 4 P.M. South of Donnelly Park in Mount Dora. Box 196; Mount Dora 32757 (904-383-2165).

**MAITLAND ART CENTER**—An unusual complex of Aztec-style buildings designed by artist and architect André Smith. A changing roster of exhibits feature local, regional, and national artists. An artist-in-residence demonstrates how to draw with grease pencils and ink directly onto century-old limestone. Gardens and courtyards surround the facilities. Open Tuesdays through Fridays 10 A.M. to 4 P.M.; weekends 1 P.M. to 4 P.M. 231 West Packwood Avenue; Maitland 32751 (305-645-2181).

**LOCH HAVEN ART CENTER**, Orlando—One of the finest collections of pre-Columbian art in the entire Southeast, as well as African and 20th-century American art. Major traveling exhibits often make stops here. Open Tuesdays through Fridays 10 A.M. to 5 P.M.; Saturdays noon to 5 P.M.; Sundays 2 P.M. to 5 P.M. 2416 North Mills Avenue; Orlando 32803-1483 (305-896-4231).

**ORANGE COUNTY HISTORICAL MUSEUM**, Orlando—At a complete hot-type newspaper composition room donated by the *Orlando Sentinel*, visitors can see what printing a newspaper was like before the computer age. There's also the new Firehouse Museum housing antique firefighting equipment, plus a blacksmith shop, a 1,000-year-old canoe, and a pioneer kitchen. Open Tuesdays through Fridays 10 A.M. to 4 P.M.; weekends 2 P.M. to 5 P.M. 812 Rollins Street; Orlando 32803 (305-898-8320).

**OSCEOLA CENTER FOR THE ARTS**, Kissimmee—The complex includes various art displays, a 249-seat auditorium, classrooms, and a gallery. Free Saturdays and Sundays 2 P.M. to 5 P.M. 2345 East Spacecoast Highway; Kissimmee 32742 (305-846-6257).

**POLK PUBLIC MUSEUM**, Lakeland—The permanent collection includes pre-Columbian art, 18th-century European ceramics, and contemporary art. Open Tuesdays through Fridays 9 A.M. to 5 P.M.; Saturdays 10 A.M. to 4 P.M.; Sundays 1 P.M. to 4 P.M. 800 East Palmetto Street; Lakeland 33801 (813-688-7743).

**THE DEPOT MUSEUM**, Lake Wales—A 1916 Pullman car and various other Seaboard Coastline railroad memorabilia are on display as well as clothing, tools, and other artifacts from the town's early days. Open Mondays through Fridays 9 A.M. to 5 P.M.; Saturdays 10 A.M. to 4 P.M. 325 South Scenic Highway; Lake Wales 33853 (813-676-5443).

**GENERAL SANFORD MEMORIAL LIBRARY MUSEUM**, Sanford—This town was incorporated in 1876, and much of its history resides right here, exhibit by exhibit. Open Wednesdays, Thursdays, Fridays, and Sundays 3 P.M. to 5 P.M. 520 East First Street; Sanford 32771 (305-322-2212).

**FORT CHRISTMAS MUSEUM**—This is a faithful and artful replica of the type of bulwark used for protection against the Indians during the Second Seminole War (1835–1842). Open Tuesdays through Saturdays 10 A.M. to 5 P.M.; Sundays 1 P.M. to 5 P.M. 1300 Fort Christmas Road; Christmas 32709 (305-568-4149).

# SOUTHERN FLORIDA

This is rich country for culture vultures. Museums host major international exhibitions regularly and carry well-endowed permanent collections. Galleries tend toward the trendy and quirky, which makes gallery-going a treat. And the colleges and universities of the Miami area are home to some excellent museums and galleries that display permanent collections, as well as shows featuring work by students and professors.

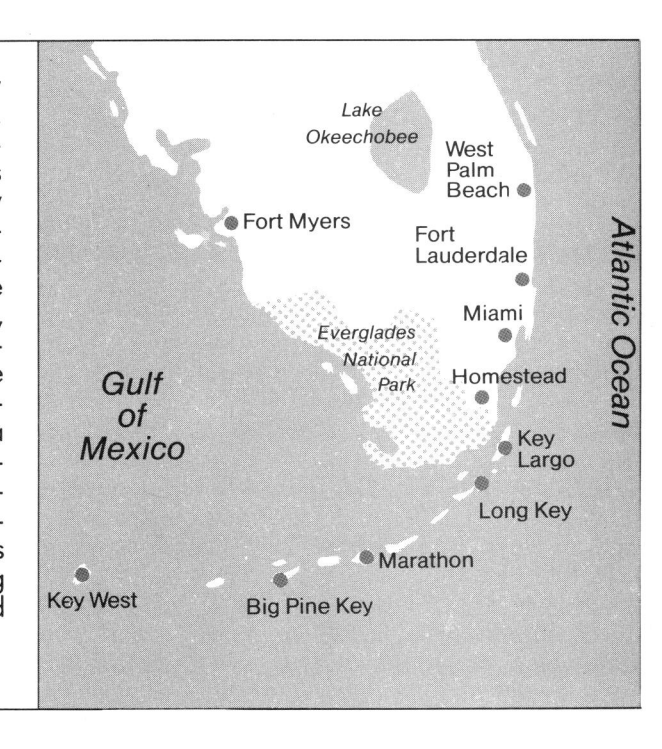

**ART LEAGUE OF MANATEE COUNTY**, Bradenton—Works by local artists including oils and sculptures. Open daily 10 A.M. to 6 P.M. (Closed during summer.) 209 9th Street West; Bradenton 33505 (813-746-2862).

**JOAN HODGELL GALLERY**, Sarasota—Considered Southern Florida's best source of works by young contemporary artists in various media. Open Mondays through Saturdays 10 A.M. to 6 P.M. or by appointment. 46 South Palm Avenue; Sarasota 33577 (813-366-1146).

**FOSTER HARMAN GALLERY OF AMERICAN ART**, Sarasota—Paintings and sculptures by nationally recognized artists, as well as local talents. Open Mondays through Saturdays 10 A.M. to 5 P.M. from mid-October through May. Closed Mondays during June, July, and August. 1415 Main Street; Sarasota 33577 (813-955-1002).

**I. IRVING FELDMAN GALLERIES**, Sarasota—Contemporary works and limited-editions are the special interest here. Open Tuesdays through Saturdays 10 A.M. to 4 P.M. from November 1 through April 30; or by appointment from May through October. 540 John Ringling Boulevard, Suite B; St. Armand's Circle; Sarasota 33577 (813-388-2805).

**OEHLSCHLAEGER GALLERIES**, Sarasota—One of the state's major showcases for contemporary American and European artists. Open Tuesdays through Sundays 10 A.M. to 6 P.M. 28 South Boulevard of the Presidents at St. Armand's Circle; Sarasota 33577 (813-388-3312).

**NATIONAL WILDLIFE GALLERY**, Fort Myers—Manatees, tarpon, sea gulls, and pelicans are the subjects of portraits hung at this gallery. But how did they arrange sittings? Open Mondays through Fridays 8:30 A.M. to 6:30 P.M.; Saturdays 8:30 A.M. to 4 P.M. 12995 Cleveland Avenue; Fort Myers 33907 (813-939-2425).

**TOWER GALLERY OF ART**, Fort Myers—Gulf sunsets, shrimp boats, and other southwest Florida themes depicted in various media. Open Mondays, Tuesdays, Wednesdays, and Saturdays 10 A.M. to 6 P.M.; Thursdays and Fridays 10 A.M. to 9 P.M.; Sundays noon to 5 P.M. 127 Bell Tower Shopping Center; Fort Myers 33907 (813-433-0070).

**THALHEIMER'S GALLERY**, Naples—Beautiful antique jewelry, and, for more modern tastes, 2 custom designers on staff. Also oriental rugs and limited-edition porcelains and bronzes. Open daily 9 A.M. to 1 P.M. from May through October. 2095 East Tamiami Trail; Naples 33962 (813-744-4666).

**FOUR WINDS GALLERY**, Olde Naples—Represents the work of our best Native American artists—stunning silver and gold jewelry, pottery, weavings, and sculpture. Open daily 10 A.M. to 5 P.M. Closed during August. 1167 Third Street; Olde Naples 33940 (813-263-7555).

**NAPLES ART GALLERY**—Of particular interest here are the hand-blown glass pieces and onyx sculptures. Open Mondays through Saturdays 9:30 A.M. to 5 P.M. 275 Broad Street South; Naples 33940 (813-262-4551).

**ST. LUCIE COUNTY HISTORICAL MUSEUM**, Fort Pierce—The focus is history, from prehistoric fossils to pioneer-era relics. Open Wednesdays through

Sundays 10 A.M. to 4 P.M. Closed July, August, and September. 414 Seaway Drive; Fort Pierce 33449 (305-464-6635).

**HIBEL MUSEUM OF ART**, Palm Beach—This beautifully laid-out facility is a tribute to American lithographer, sculptor, and painter Edna Hibel. Open Tuesdays through Saturdays 10 A.M. to 5 P.M.; Sundays 1 P.M. to 5 P.M. 150 Royal Poinciana Plaza; Palm Beach 33480 (305-833-6870).

**NORTON GALLERY AND SCHOOL OF ART**, West Palm Beach—Considered one of the foremost small museums in the United States, with exhibits often augmented by loans from private collections of knowledgeable Palm Beach residents. Open Tuesdays through Saturdays 10 A.M. to 5 P.M.; Sundays 1 P.M. to 5 P.M. 1451 South Olive Avenue; West Palm Beach 33401 (305-832-5194).

**BASS MUSEUM**, Miami Beach—The tapestries and oriental bronzes are first-rate, as are the 14th-century textiles and paintings. Free only on Tuesdays from 10 A.M. to 5 P.M. 212 Park Avenue; Miami Beach 33139 (305-673-7533).

**METROPOLITAN MUSEUM AND ART CENTER**, Coral Gables—The 6 galleries here feature a constant parade of traveling art exhibits. There's also an art school on the first floor. Free only on Wednesdays from 10 A.M. to 5 P.M. and 7 P.M. to 10 P.M. 1212 Anastasia Avenue; Coral Gables 33134 (305-442-1448).

**SOUTHERN CROSS OBSERVATORY**, Miami—Powerful telescopes atop the Museum of Science allow stargazing in a city known for its moon. Open Fridays and Saturdays 8 P.M. to 10 P.M.; Sundays 2 P.M. to 4:30 P.M. and 8 P.M. to 10 P.M. 3280 South Miami Avenue; Miami 33129 (305-854-4242).

**LOWE ART MUSEUM**, Coral Gables—The University of Miami's ranking art museum boasts a permanent collection of notable Renaissance paintings and modern art. Open Tuesdays through Fridays noon to 5 P.M.; Saturdays 10 A.M. to 5 P.M.; Sundays noon to 5 P.M. 1301 Stanford Drive; Coral Gables 33146 (305-284-3535).

**BAY VISTA PHOTO GALLERY**, North Miami Beach—On the campus of Florida International University this gallery features both local and national photographers. Hours vary seasonally, so call ahead. Bay Vista Campus; Room 105; Biscayne Boulevard and Northeast 151st Street; North Miami Beach 33181 (305-940-5700).

**THE ART MUSEUM**, Miami—Getting hung isn't such a bad thing if you're an undergraduate fine arts student at the Tamiami Campus of Florida International University. It simply means your work has been chosen to join that of your professors on the school museum walls. Tamiami Campus; Southwest Eighth Street and Southwest 107th Avenue; Miami 33199 (305-554-2890).

**THE CAREFULLY CHOSEN**, Miami—Showcasing works by Jewish artists. Open Mondays through Fridays 10 A.M. to 4 P.M.; or by appointment. 109 Northeast 39th Street; Miami 33137 (305-576-8808).

**CIRCLE GALLERY**, Miami—Located in the Hyatt Regency Hotel, this large showplace has a good selection of sculptures and lithographs. Open Mondays through Fridays 10 A.M. to 7 P.M.; Saturdays 10 A.M. to 5 P.M. 400 Southeast Second Ave.; Miami 33131 (305-371-2766).

**LA PETITE GALLERY**, Miami—Tucked away in Burdine's department store, there's a changing roster of fine-art exhibits. Open Mondays through Saturdays 10 A.M. to 6 P.M. 22 East Flagler Street; Miami 33131 (305-835-5151).

**WIRTZ GALLERY**, South Miami—Here is an opportunity to see work by local artists. Open Mondays through Fridays 9:30 A.M. to 4 P.M. In the First National Bank of South Miami; 5750 Sunset Drive; South Miami 33143 (305-667-5511).

**FRANCIS WOLFSON ART GALLERY**, Miami—A small but excellent gallery in the New World Center of Miami/Dade Community College, which regularly offers contemporary art exhibits. Open Mondays through Fridays 9 A.M. to 5:30 P.M. 300 Northeast Second Avenue; Miami 33132 (305-347-3278).

**BACARDI GALLERY**, Miami—In the former headquarters of Bacardi Imports, Inc., this fine gallery offers Miami's best shows of Latin American art. Open weekdays 9 A.M. to 5 P.M. 2100 Biscayne Boulevard; Miami 33137 (305-573-8511).

**THE ART RESOURCE**, Miami—Sculpture, weaving, and photography usually dominate the scene here. Open Mondays through Fridays 10 A.M. to 5 P.M. 3800 Northeast Second Avenue; Miami 33137 (305-573-6299).

**ART PLACE AT CAULEY SQUARE**, Miami—Located in a 50-year-old Dade County pine building in the South Dade area, with changing exhibits by Florida artists that often feature photography. Open Mondays through Saturdays 10 A.M. to 4:30 P.M.; or by appointment. 22400 Old Dixie Highway; Miami 33170 (305-258-4222).

**GLORIA LURIA GALLERY**, Bay Harbor Islands—This is one of the best known of the Greater Miami galleries. Open Tuesdays through Saturdays 10 A.M. to 5 P.M. 1033 Kane Concourse; Bay Harbor Islands 33154 (305-865-3060).

**GALERIA CAMHI**, Bay Harbor Islands—Recent major exhibitions have included works by Ben Shahn, Picasso, and other such luminaries. Open Mondays through Saturdays 9:30 A.M. to 5:30 P.M. 1027 Kane Concourse; Bay Harbor Islands 33154 (305-864-3560).

**GALLERY AT GROVE ISLE**, Coconut Grove—In a trendy Miami neighborhood, antique oriental art is displayed. Open Tuesdays through Saturdays 10 A.M. to 6 P.M.; by appointment on Sundays and Mondays. 4 Grove Isle Drive; Coconut Grove 33133 (305-858-1522).

**NETSKY GALLERY**, Coconut Grove—Contemporary works done in nontraditional materials make this gallery an especially lively showplace. Open Tuesdays through Saturdays 11 A.M. to 6 P.M.; Sundays noon to 5 P.M. 3107 Grand Avenue; Coconut Grove 33133 (305-448-6163).

**FORMA GALLERY**, Coral Gables—A good place to see Latin American fine art. Open Mondays through Fridays 10:30 A.M. to 5:30 P.M.; Saturdays noon to 4 P.M. 305 Alcazar Avenue; Coral Gables 33134 (305-442-9430).

**KEY LARGO ANTIQUES AND ART GALLERY**—Sculptor Thom Roberts produces work in black coral and ivory; there's also a permanent display of Japanese and Korean silks and chests. Hours vary so call ahead. Milemarker 98.6 Gulfside; Key Largo (305-852-5933).

**THE RAIN BARREL**, Islamorada—An artists' and craftsmen's colony with 6 different shops featuring leather work, stained glass, and batik. Open daily 9 A.M. to 5 P.M. 86700 Overseas Highway; Islamorada 33036 (305-852-3084).

**SEA CAPTAIN'S MEMOIRS GALLERY**, Islamorada—Nautical artwork, underwater photography, and handcrafted gifts such as wood sculpture. Open 10 A.M. to 4 P.M.; closed Wednesdays and Sundays. Milemarker 82 in the Islamorada Shopping Center; Box 895; Islamorada 33036 (305-664-8243).

**ISLAND GALLERY**, Marathon—Fine marine paintings are shown here, including works by official U.S. Coast Guard artist Eric S. Gebhardt. Open Tuesdays through Fridays 11 A.M. to 5 P.M. 10800 Overseas Highway; Marathon 33050 (305-743-0115).

**MARIAN STEVENS**, Key West—High-quality local and Caribbean paintings. Open daily 10 A.M. to 10 P.M. 221 Duval Street; Key West 33040 (305-296-5625).

**LUCKY STREET GALLERY**, Key West—Contemporary works, including ceramics, wood, and lithography are featured. Open daily 11 A.M. to 6 P.M. 322 Margaret Street; Key West 33040 (305-294-3973).

**GINGERBREAD SQUARE GALLERY**, Key West—A diverse group of local artists are represented in a gallery set in a tropical garden with tiled patios. Open daily 11 A.M. to 6 P.M. from October through May. Closed Tuesdays and Wednesdays during June, July, August, and September. 910 Duval Street; Key West 33040 (305-296-8900).

# WINDOW SHOPPING

To shop and not buy takes a bit of willpower, or more accurately, won't power. But given the right atmosphere and the right displays, window-shopping can prove to be a very fulfilling experience. Florida is chock-full of shopping malls where strolling the broad indoor lanes flanked with gardens can provide a pleasant (and cool) respite from the state's midafternoon heat. And when the impulse to buy becomes just too strong, there's usually a spot to give in without denting the family travel budget too deeply.

Flea markets are also a popular phenomenon in the Sunshine State. While most of these grand-scale events take place outside (so there aren't too many windows to scan), they do provide racks and tables full of everything from antiques and fine jewelry to knickknacks and junk. It's great fun to just paw through the piles.

There are also several cities and towns whose main streets reveal a bounty of beautiful windows. Winter Park's Park Avenue, for example, is a delightful place to spend the day just poking around the attractive boutiques and specialty stores. Worth Avenue in Palm Beach offers a stretch of some of the world's most expensive stores while the Coconut Grove section of Miami is packed with antique clothing stores, trendy shops and galleries, plus sidewalk vendors displaying jewelry, pottery, scarves, and other merchandise.

# NORTHERN FLORIDA

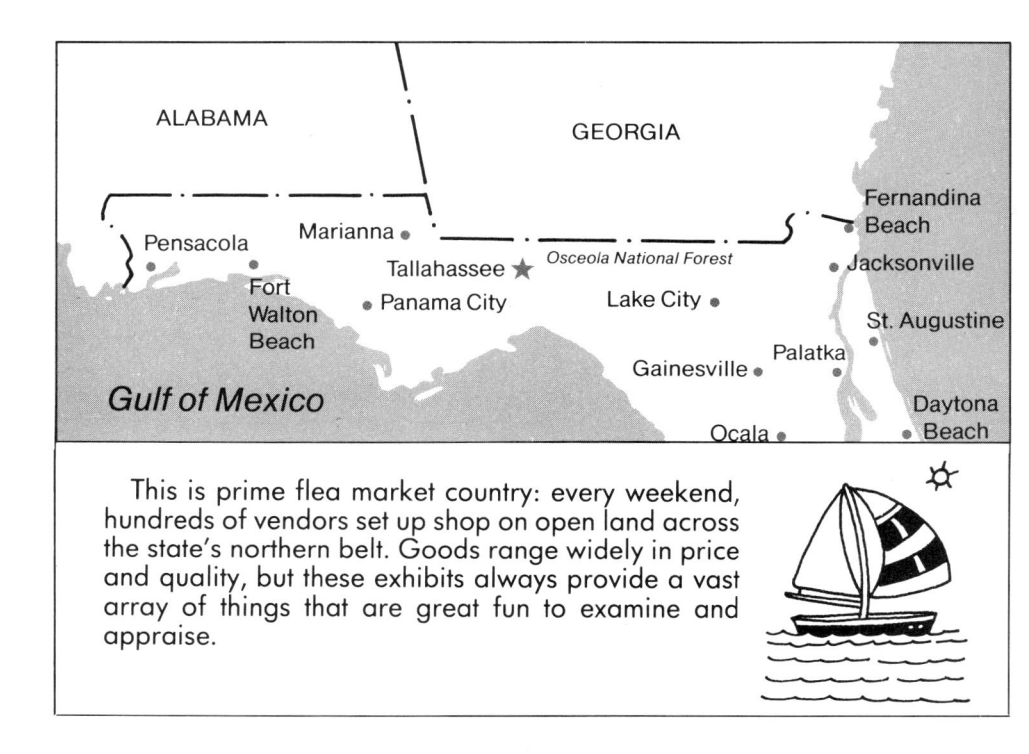

This is prime flea market country: every weekend, hundreds of vendors set up shop on open land across the state's northern belt. Goods range widely in price and quality, but these exhibits always provide a vast array of things that are great fun to examine and appraise.

**WALDO FLEA MARKET**—Located on Highway 301 north of Waldo between Starke and Gainesville, this large outdoor market is open on Saturdays and Sundays with vendors offering everything from farm tools to antiques. Open 7:30 A.M. to 5 P.M. Information: 904-468-2255.

**ORANGE PARK MALL**—A good place to stroll and window-shop. More than 140 stores, including *J. C. Penney* and *Sears*. Open Mondays through Saturdays 10 A.M. to 9 P.M.; Sundays 12:30 P.M. to 5:30 P.M. 1910 Wells Road; Orange Park 32073 (904-269-2422).

**THE MARKET PLACE**, Jacksonville—At the Lane Avenue exit of I-10, a large outdoor market is open weekends from 8 A.M. to 5 P.M. A leisurely stroll will reveal collectibles, produce, plants, tools, and lots more. 6839 Ramona Boulevard; Jacksonville 32205 (904-786-1153).

**REGENCY SQUARE MALL**, Jacksonville—There are 165 stores including *Sears*,

J. C. Penney, and Ivey's at this mall located about 4 miles east of downtown. Open Mondays through Saturdays 10 A.M. to 9 P.M.; Sundays 12:30 P.M. to 5:30 P.M. Arlington Expressway at Atlantic Boulevard; Jacksonville 32211 (904-725-3830).

**THE LIGHTNER MUSEUM**, St. Augustine—A small antiques mall is part of the museum complex, and it's an inviting place to poke around. The restaurant offers a nice spot of lunch. 75 King Street; St. Augustine (904-824-2874).

**ST. AUGUSTINE ANTIGUO**—A narrow 2-block section of the nation's oldest city, the main preservation area has been closed to all but pedestrian traffic. Visitors can stroll the streets where a bakery, various shops and restaurants, and an ice cream and candy store provide fine window-shopping (and a little snacking along the way). There are guides dressed in Spanish costumes to help direct traffic.

**DAYTONA FLEA MARKET**—A 10-acre, open-air spread off I-95 where fresh produce, collectibles, and jewelry are the mainstays. Open Saturdays and Sundays 7 A.M. to 4 P.M. Information: 904-252-1999.

## Travel Tip: HINTS FOR OLDER TRAVELERS

No longer limited by specific vacation schedules or the rigidity of the business week, older travelers can take advantage of off-season, off-peak travel times that are both less expensive and pleasanter than traveling during high season. Here are a few hints for making the most of a trip to the Sunshine State:
- Eat meals early (or late) to avoid restaurant crowds. If you have lunch at 11 A.M., a 4 P.M. dinner will be welcome.
- Don't try to save money by scrimping on food. Traveling takes energy and only a good meal can provide it.
- Protect yourself from the sun. Wear a hat and be sure not to stint on the sunscreen.
- Don't become overheated or dehydrated. Take rest stops in shady spots, and drink plenty of liquids.

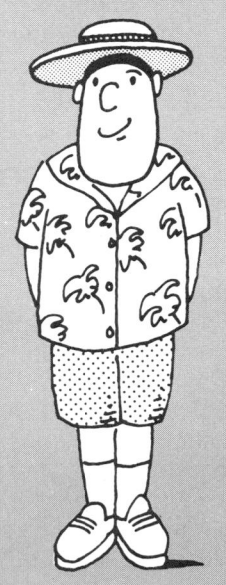

SAVVY TRAVELER

# CENTRAL FLORIDA

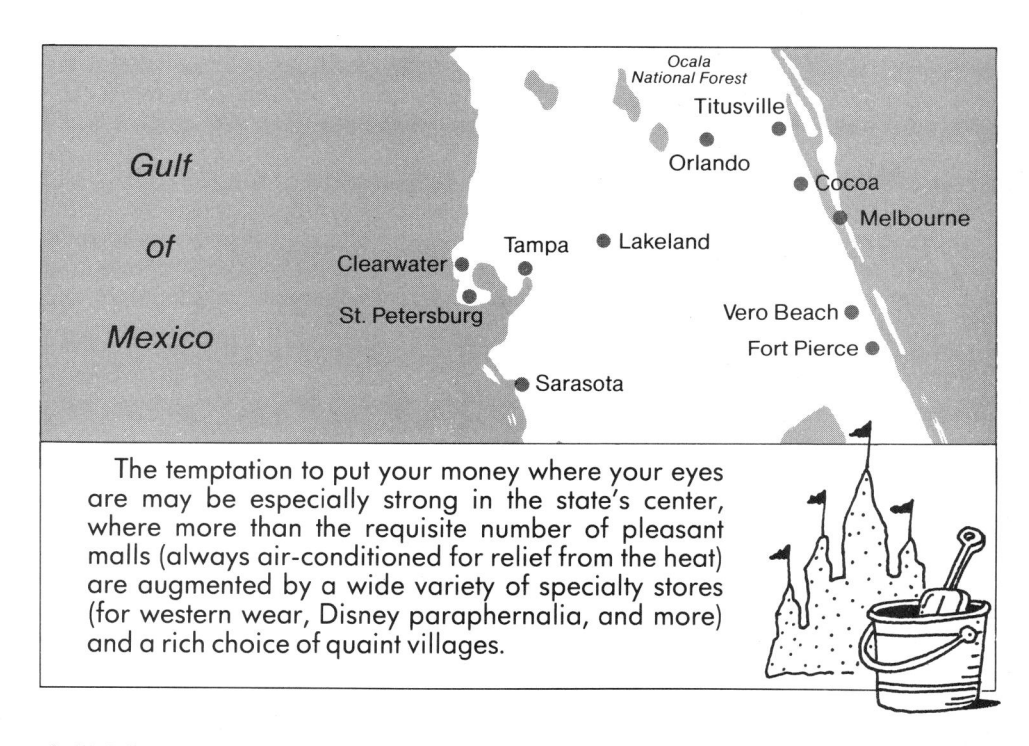

*Map showing Central Florida with locations: Ocala National Forest, Titusville, Orlando, Cocoa, Melbourne, Tampa, Lakeland, Clearwater, St. Petersburg, Vero Beach, Fort Pierce, Sarasota, and the Gulf of Mexico.*

The temptation to put your money where your eyes are may be especially strong in the state's center, where more than the requisite number of pleasant malls (always air-conditioned for relief from the heat) are augmented by a wide variety of specialty stores (for western wear, Disney paraphernalia, and more) and a rich choice of quaint villages.

**A PLACE FOR COOKS**, Clearwater—The heat is on in this 3,000-square-foot store jammed with every sort of cookware, bakeware, cutlery, and kitchen gadgets imported from more than 30 countries. There are also daily cooking demonstrations, and coffee and specialty food tastings. The store has more than 650 cookbook titles in stock and many unusual and hard-to-find kitchen tools. Open Mondays through Fridays 10 A.M. to 6 P.M.; Saturdays 10 A.M. to 5 P.M. 1447 South Fort Harrison Avenue; Clearwater 33516 (813-446-5506).

**BOATYARD VILLAGE**, Clearwater—A shopping-dining-entertainment complex, with 27 specialty shops overlooking a man-made lake. The Boatyard was constructed from antique wood and tin brought here from around the nation. This shopping center is well known for its frequent special events, including a chili cookoff and the annual Oktoberfest. Open Mondays through Thursdays 11 A.M. to 8 P.M.; Fridays and Saturdays 11 A.M. to 9 P.M.; Sundays noon to 6 P.M. 16100 Fairchild Drive; Clearwater 33520 (813-535-4678).

**COUNTRYSIDE MALL**, Clearwater—One of Florida's largest malls, it has more than 160 stores and shops. Open Mondays through Saturdays 10 A.M. to 9 P.M.; Sundays 12:30 P.M. to 5:30 P.M. 2601 Highway 19 North, Suite 842; Clearwater 33575 (813-796-1238).

**ROCKIN' RHYTHM QUALITY WESTERN WEAR**, Clearwater—Known as the South's only one-stop (or one-step) dance shop. Square dance, round dance, and clogging records and supplies are found here, plus a full line of clothing and shoes, boots, belts, buckles, and Stetson hats. Open Mondays through Saturdays 9 A.M. to 7 P.M.; Sundays noon to 5 P.M. 1894 Drew Street; Clearwater 33575 (813-461-1879).

**SUNSHINE MALL**, Clearwater—When the beach gets to be a bit much, this mall is just a few blocks away. There are 106 stores, including *J. C. Penney* and *J. Byrons*. Open Mondays through Saturdays 10 A.M. to 9 P.M.; Sundays noon to 5 P.M. Missouri Avenue at Druid Road; Clearwater 33516 (813-447-6073).

**GINJAN**, Indian Rocks Beach—A large selection of local and out-of-state newspapers, as well as magazines, hardcover books, greeting cards, and tobaccos. Open Mondays through Saturdays 8 A.M. to 5 P.M.; Sundays 8 A.M. to 1 P.M. 313 Gulf Boulevard; Indian Rocks Beach 33535 (813-596-7046).

**SEASIDE TREASURE INC.**, Indian Rocks Beach—All the necessities for the beach—towels, sportswear, suntan lotions—plus added surprises like 14-karat-gold jewelry, nautical-themed gifts, wind chimes, and beautiful shells and coral. Open daily 9 A.M. to 8 P.M. 1313 Gulf Boulevard; Indian Rocks Beach 33535 (813-595-3355).

**MANDALAY SURF AND SPORT**, Clearwater Beach—Surf's up at the area's largest full-service shop, where surfboards, swimwear, skateboards, and skim boards are on display—and hard to resist. Open daily 10 A.M. to 6 P.M. 522 Mandalay Avenue; Clearwater Beach 33515 (813-442-3227).

**PINELLAS COUNTY ANTIQUING**, St. Petersburg—More than 100 dealers are listed in this handy shopping guide to the area's better-known antique stores, which comes with a map. Contact Sue Tiffin; Posh Pineapple Antiques; 560 North Indian Rocks Road; Belleair Bluff 33540 (813-586-3006).

**TYRONE SQUARE MALL**, St. Petersburg—The more than 140 stores here include *Maas Brothers*, *Robinson's*, *J. C. Penney*, and *Sears*. Open Mondays through Saturdays 10 A.M. to 9 P.M.; Sundays 1:30 P.M. to 5:30 P.M. 6901 22nd Avenue North; St. Petersburg 32710 (813-345-0126).

**TIKI GARDENS**, Indian Shores—Ten gift shops are set in a re-created Polynesian village surrounded by exotic gardens. This unusual attraction has been called the most authentic replica of a Polynesian village anywhere on the

U.S. mainland. Open daily 9:30 A.M. to 10:30 P.M. 19601 Gulf Boulevard; Indian Shores 33535 (813-595-2567).

**WEBSTER FLEA MARKET**—Billed as the world's largest, with more than 1,500 vendors on 15 acres, hawking everything from junk to fine jewelry. The market is well known for antiques and fresh local vegetables. Open Mondays from 7 A.M. to 5 P.M. Webster is about 45 miles west of Orlando. Contact Sumter County Farmers Market, Inc.; Box 62; Webster 33597 (904-793-2021).

**T-SHIRT JUNCTION**, Lakeland—Central Florida's largest T-shirt store features more than 200 designs. Personalized lettering can be done while you wait. Custom screen printing is also available. Open Mondays through Saturdays 8 A.M. to 6 P.M. 1062 Highway 92 West; Lakeland 33823 (813-665-0385).

**ALTAMONTE MALL**, Altamonte Springs—With 165 stores, this is central Florida's largest mall. Retail operations here are typical of malls across the state, but there are also varied activities at the mall, including craft shows, karate demonstrations, and health programs. Open Mondays through Saturdays 10 A.M. to 9 P.M.; Sundays noon to 5:30 P.M. 451 Altamonte Avenue; Altamonte Springs 32701 (305-830-4400).

**FLEA WORLD**, Sanford—Billed as the largest *indoor* flea market in the country, and who's to argue with 1,200 booths, plus free entertainment on Fridays and Saturdays? The market is open Fridays, Saturdays, and Sundays 8 A.M. to 5 P.M. Highway 17–92; Sanford 32771 (305-321-1792).

**FLORIDA TWIN MARKETS**, Zellwood—More than 200 vendors from all over the country offer antiques and collectibles in enclosed buildings at this well-known flea market and antique center. The flea market is open weekends 8 A.M. to 5 P.M.; the antique center is open Saturdays 8 A.M. to 5 P.M. and Sundays 10 A.M. to 5 P.M. Highway 441; Box 939; Zellwood 32798 (305-886-TWIN).

**MOUNT DORA ANTIQUING**—Dozens of antique stores can be found in this lovely little New England–like city. Many of the stores are on Donnelly Street. A map is available from the Mount Dora Chamber of Commerce; Box 196; Mount Dora 32757 (904-383-2165).

**PARK AVENUE**, Winter Park—Upscale shops line the main street of Orlando's posh suburb. Park Avenue has long been famous for its expensive shops and elegant restaurants. Winter Park Chamber of Commerce; Box 280; Winter Park 32790 (305-644-8281).

**DOWNTOWN ORLANDO**—Stroll down lovely Orange Avenue, recently streetscaped and dotted with drake elms, through the newly renovated shopping area. Some of the most interesting shops include *Barnie's Coffee and*

*Tea Company, Florida Stamp and Sign and Pencrafters,* and *Gibbs-Louis,* one of Orlando's finer dress shops. Most stores are open weekdays 10 A.M. to 5:30 P.M. Greater Orlando Chamber of Commerce; Box 1234; Orlando 32802 (305-425-1234).

**THE MARKETPLACE**, Orlando—A New England–style shopping village, nestled around an unusual clock tower, where shops and eateries line old-fashioned cobblestone walkways. There are many fine specialty shops, boutiques, antique shops, and a natural food store here. Open Mondays through Thursdays and Saturdays 10 A.M. to 7 P.M.; Fridays 10 A.M. to 9 P.M.; Sundays noon to 5 P.M. 7600 Phillips Drive, Suite 73; Orlando 32819 (305-351-7000).

**WALT DISNEY WORLD VILLAGE**, Lake Buena Vista—The best way to take in this lovely shopping area is to wander at will. There are more than 20 stores, including clothing shops, a children's store, gift and toy emporiums, a Disney-character shop, a bookstore, and much more. There are also several places to snack or have a complete meal—and don't forget to have a look around on board the elegant *Empress Lilly* riverboat. Open daily 9:30 A.M. to 10 P.M. and there's often free entertainment in the evenings. Located on Buena Vista Drive, off Route 535. Box 40; Lake Buena Vista 32830 (305-828-3800).

**COCOA VILLAGE**, Merritt Island—This French Quarter–style section of downtown has recently been renovated, with antique shops and other stores clustered together off Harrison Street. There's also a variety of places to dine. A map is available from the Cocoa Beach Area Chamber of Commerce; 400 Fortenberry Road; Merritt Island 32952 (305-459-2200).

**FIFTH AVENUE**, Indialantic—A street lined with fine shops, including a dozen boutiques selling fashionable women's wear. There are also fine furniture stores and bookshops. Chamber of Commerce of South Brevard; 1005 East Strawbridge Avenue; Melbourne 32901 (305-724-5400).

**MELBOURNE SQUARE MALL**—The largest shopping complex in Brevard County has more than 150 stores, including such major chains as *Burdines, Jordan Marsh,* and *J. C. Penney.* Open Mondays through Saturdays 10 A.M. to 9 P.M.; Sundays noon to 5:30 P.M. 1700 West New Haven Avenue; Melbourne 32901 (305-727-2000).

**RON JON SURF SHOP**, Cocoa Beach—An enormous selection of boards, beach equipment, and related items. Bicycles, rafts, skim boards, and roller skates are available for rent. Open daily 8:30 A.M. to 11 P.M. 4151 North Atlantic Avenue; Cocoa Beach 32931 (305-784-1485).

**PEDDLER'S VILLAGE**, Rockledge—An old grove and packing house has been converted into a delightful shopping area with a dozen shops, including the charming *Peddler's Village General Store.* There's also Kris Kringle Square, where Christmas items are sold year-round. Open Mondays through Saturdays 10 A.M. to 5 P.M.; Sundays 11 A.M. to 5 P.M. 4657 South U.S. 1; Rockledge 32955 (305-632-1177).

# SOUTHERN FLORIDA

This is the land of ritzy window-shopping, from Las Olas Boulevard in Fort Lauderdale (where the windows are particularly well-dressed) and Worth Avenue in Palm Beach (where just about everything is too expensive to even consider buying) to Calle Ocho in Miami's Little Havana and the huge Omni International Mall. You might say browsing is the number one Miami vice.

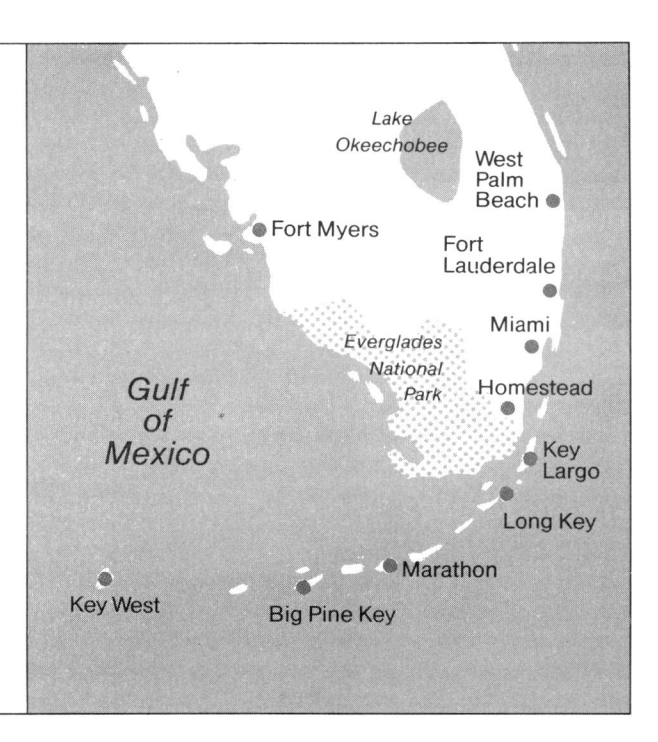

**ST. ARMAND'S CIRCLE**, Sarasota—A circle of lovely boutiques and restaurants ring a garden. High-fashion shops, some of the state's best art galleries, and some fine restaurants make this a destination for window-shoppers from as far away as St. Petersburg and Tampa. State Road 780; Sarasota (813-388-1554).

**SARASOTA SQUARE MALL**—Located about 8 miles south of the city, this center includes *Maas Brothers, Sears,* and *J. C. Penney.* Open Mondays through Saturdays 10 A.M. to 9 P.M.; Sundays 12:30 P.M. to 5:30 P.M. 8201 South Tamiami Trail; Sarasota 33583 (813-922-9609).

**FISHERMAN'S VILLAGE**, Punta Gorda—This complex includes a 1,000-foot-long pier, some 35 boutiques, and 6 restaurants, as well as a marina. 1200 West Retta Esplanade; Punta Gorda 33950 (813-639-8721).

**DOWNTOWN FORT MYERS**—Window-shopping in Fort Myers is a delightful and peaceful activity. The clothing stores, the smoke shop, and the magazine shop are particularly nice. The Caloosahatchee River marinas are across the way, where you can relax from all the walking. Fort Myers Chamber of Commerce; Box CC; Fort Myers 33902 (813-334-1133).

**EDISON MALL**, Fort Myers—Out of the downtown area, on the Tamiami Trail, this mall offers a *Maas Brothers*, *Burdine's*, *Sears*, and *J. C. Penney*. Open Mondays through Saturdays 10 A.M. to 9 P.M.; Sundays noon to 5 P.M. 4125 South Cleveland Avenue; Fort Myers 33901 (813-939-5464).

**ROYAL PALM SQUARE**, Fort Myers—Upscale shops include *Mole Hole* (for gifts) and *Yves St. Laurent*, making window-shopping a particular pleasure here. There are 36 stores and boutiques, plus a few restaurants. Open Mondays through Saturdays 10 A.M. to 6 P.M. 1400 Colonial Boulevard; Fort Myers 33907 (813-939-3900).

**NAPLES**—The most exclusive shops are in the area of Third Street and Fifth Avenue. Look in at *Cleopatra's Barge* for jewelry and *Mole Hole* for all kinds of gifts. Naples Chamber of Commerce; 1700 Tamiami Trail North; Naples 33940 (813-262-6141).

**PALM BEACH MALL**, West Palm Beach—An expansive spread of over a million square feet accommodates more than 100 stores, including *Burdine's*, *Lord & Taylor*, *J. C. Penney*, and *Jordan Marsh*. Open Mondays through Saturdays 10 A.M. to 9 P.M.; Sundays noon to 5:30 P.M. 1801 Palm Beach Lakes Boulevard; West Palm Beach 33401 (305-686-3513).

**WORTH AVENUE**, Palm Beach—One of the most elegant shopping streets in the world, of the kind that's often compared to Rome's Via Condotti and Paris's Rue Faubourg St-Honoré—a perfect atmosphere for window-shopping and people-watching.

**LAS OLAS BOULEVARD**, Fort Lauderdale—The windows of this neatly manicured retail district are small but interesting; if something catches your eye, go on in. The merchants along this stretch are among the nicest in Florida. There are also lots of benches along the route for relaxing or people-watching. Most of the stores are open Mondays through Saturdays 10 A.M. to 5 P.M. Information: 305-463-5750.

**GALLERIA**, Fort Lauderdale—*Neiman-Marcus*, *Saks Fifth Avenue*, *Lord & Taylor*, *Burdine's*, and *Jordan Marsh* are the anchors of this 140-shop mall.

There's enough to keep anyone busy for hours. Open Mondays through Saturdays 10 A.M. to 9 P.M.; Sundays noon to 5:30 P.M. 2414 East Sunrise Boulevard; Fort Lauderdale 33304 (305-564-1015).

**OMNI INTERNATIONAL MALL**, Miami—Located in the posh *Omni International Hotel*, this complex offers 165 shops, including *Jordan Marsh* and *J. C. Penney*, plus smaller shops and boutiques. Open Mondays through Saturdays 10 A.M. to 9 P.M.; Sundays noon to 5:30 P.M. 1601 Biscayne Boulevard; Miami 33132 (305-374-6664).

**THE FALLS**, Miami—A small but fancy shopping area set around man-made lakes. *Bloomingdale's* is the latest addition to more than 75 fine small shops. Open Mondays through Saturdays 10 A.M. to 9 P.M.; Sundays noon to 5 P.M. 8888 Howard Drive; Miami 33176 (305-255-4570).

**BAL HARBOUR SHOPS**—No doubt Miami's fanciest shopping area, with a *Neiman-Marcus* as its anchor. Open Mondays, Thursdays, and Fridays 10 A.M. to 9 P.M.; Tuesdays, Wednesdays, and Saturdays 10 A.M. to 6 P.M.; Sundays noon to 5 P.M. 9700 Collins Avenue; Bal Harbour 33154 (305-866-0311).

**DADELAND**, Miami—Hundreds of stores, including *Burdine's*, *J. C. Penney*, *Jordan Marsh*, and *Saks Fifth Avenue*, under the roof of one of the nation's largest malls. Open Mondays through Saturdays 10 A.M. to 9:30 P.M.; Sundays noon to 5:30 P.M. 7535 Dadeland Mall; Miami 33156 (305-665-6226).

---

*Travel Tip* · **PHOTO EQUIPMENT CHECKLIST**

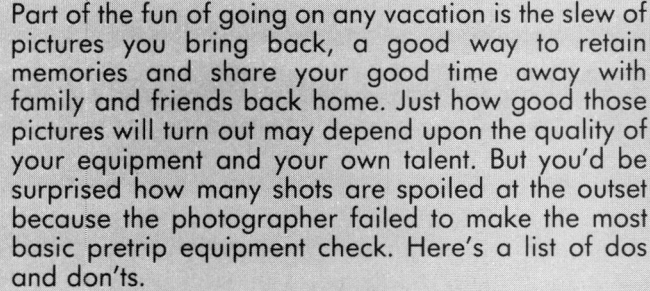

Part of the fun of going on any vacation is the slew of pictures you bring back, a good way to retain memories and share your good time away with family and friends back home. Just how good those pictures will turn out may depend upon the quality of your equipment and your own talent. But you'd be surprised how many shots are spoiled at the outset because the photographer failed to make the most basic pretrip equipment check. Here's a list of dos and don'ts.

• Check the camera's batteries regularly. Make a point of putting in new batteries before leaving home.

• Test a new camera with a roll of film *before* leaving. Give yourself time to see results before

**COCONUT GROVE**—The streets of this village in Miami (about 4 miles south of the downtown area) were made for walking. Galleries display watercolors by Miami artists and various forms of oriental pottery. Boutiques range from local designers' shops and antique clothing stores (*Nostalgia* is particularly interesting) to small new-wave outfits. There's also great shopping on the sidewalks, where vendors hawk silver jewelry, pottery, scarves, and T-shirts. Coconut Grove Chamber of Commerce; 3437 Main Highway; Coconut Grove 33133 (305-444-7270).

**MAYFAIR**, Coconut Grove—Three levels of lovely, and pricey, European and American shops, plus what locals claim is the best little branch of *Burdine's* in Florida. Much more suitable to window-shopping than a buying spree. Open Sundays through Wednesdays 11 A.M. to 7 P.M.; Thursdays and Fridays 11 A.M. to 9 P.M.; Saturdays 10 A.M. to 9 P.M. 2911 Grand Avenue; Coconut Grove 33133 (305-448-1700).

**CALLE OCHO**, Miami's Little Havana—The area's shopping center stretches for miles along Southwest 8th Street, where industrious merchants keep their storefronts spotlessly scrubbed and advertise lots of *"especials"* each day. There are colorful fruit stands, unique boutiques (some of the Cuban-design furniture is quite unusual), and some great spots for a cup of strong Cuban coffee. Shops are usually open Mondays through Saturdays 7:45 A.M. to 5 P.M., and sometimes later; closed Sundays. For information call the Latin Chamber of Commerce at 305-642-3870.

---

depending on new equipment in some distant place.
- Keep film in a plastic bag and avoid passing it through airport X-ray machines. Most security guards are happy to hand-check film and loaded cameras.
- Remember that Florida's hot sun can be as bad for film as it is for one's skin. So carry with you only the amount of film you need, and leave the rest in a cool hotel room. Never leave film in a hot, closed car.
- Never shoot into the sun. Maintain a distance of from 4 to 12 feet from subjects for best results. Except when actually shooting, keep your camera in a plastic bag while on the beach. Sand is destructive to virtually all photographic equipment.
- When buying film, always check the expiration date stamped on the box.

**MIRACLE MILE**, Coral Gables—Not quite a mile long and hardly a miracle, this strip along Coral Way is nonetheless quite attractive and its windows are particularly well dressed. There are more than 140 stores along the stretch from 37th Avenue to 42nd Avenue. Open Mondays through Saturdays 10 A.M. to 5 P.M. For information contact the Miracle Mile Merchants' Association at 305-445-0591.

**CUTLER RIDGE SHOPPING MALL**, Miami—The country's southernmost *Lord & Taylor* is here, as are 145 other shops. Open Mondays through Saturdays 10 A.M. to 9 P.M.; Sundays noon to 5:30 P.M. 20505 South Dixie Highway; Miami 33189 (305-235-8562).

**KEY WEST**—Duval and Front Streets are scattered with unconventional shops and interesting windows. *Fast Buck Freddie's* at 500 Duval Street has nice displays of fashionable clothes; *Carpets and Casuals* at 400 Duval Street features wicker and rattan furniture, rugs, and other home furnishings; *Key West Fragrances* at 540 Green Street offers unusual perfumes.

---

## *Travel Tip:* TRAVELING WITH KIDS

Traveling successfully with children is an art form in itself, and keeping kids occupied during a long trip (by car or plane) can help ward off the endless drone of, "Are-we-there-yet?" When traveling by car, it's wise to set up a series of intermediate goals to which children can look forward. Younger children can anticipate discovering the contents of a pint-sized suitcase packed with familiar games and toys—plus a few surprises. In addition, it's smart to take along snacks to keep things peaceful when stomachs start rumbling and food is miles away. Above all, take it easy and allow time for plenty of breaks en route. When traveling with children by plane, try to schedule flights for off-peak hours, when the chances are better that extra seats will be available. For takeoffs and landings, give babies a bottle, pacifier, or their own thumb to promote swallowing and avoid painful ear clogging. Airlines often offer special meals or snacks for kids; these can be ordered at no extra charge when reservations are made.

# WILD AND WONDERFUL

The wild side of Florida life extends far beyond those slithering toothy reptiles that make such good purses and belts. The state's forests, sanctuaries, refuges, preserves, and swamps harbor a variety of plants and animals that can be seen very few other places on earth, particularly in such close proximity. Some 300 varieties of birds, 600 species of fish, and countless mammals—marine and land-based—make their homes here.

It's a state where deer run free in parks and forests, manatees loll about in shallow waters, alligators skulk along canals, shorebirds come and go in dramatic formations at dawn and dusk, and turtles weighing up to 700 pounds amble out of the sea to lay eggs.

Florida also lays claim to the largest stand of royal palms in the world, in southern Florida, and Everglades National Park, a pristine wilderness full of flora and fauna so spectacular it invites a lifetime of contemplation to be truly appreciated.

There are nature centers that sponsor bird walks and turtle watches, but it's not necessary to join an organized group to see the untouched, natural side of the Sunshine State. The place is chock-full of opportunities to view nature unadorned, if you just know where to look.

So here is a guide to Florida's wild, wonderful—and free—side.

# NORTHERN FLORIDA

Northern Florida's topography supports two major national forests—Osceola and Ocala—both of which cover thousands of acres and offer fine opportunities to view plants, trees, and wildlife unique to the state. Florida also has become a major thoroughbred horse-breeding area, where hundreds of horse farms line the roads and allow a glimpse of future racing champs being put through their paces.

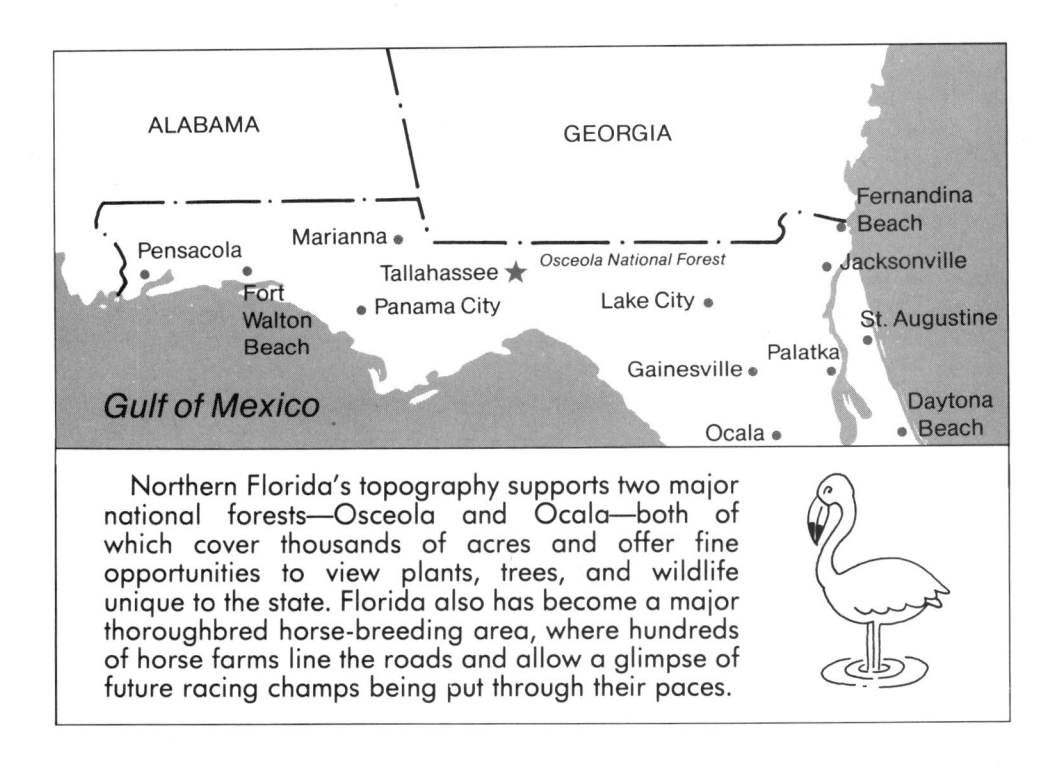

**ST. MARKS NATIONAL WILDLIFE REFUGE**—Located about 20 miles south of Tallahassee, these 65,000 acres of land and 31,500 acres of water are home to waterfowl, alligators, and birds of every sort—birders have reported sighting bald eagles, roseate spoonbills, and a variety of herons. This is where the St. Marks River empties into Apalachee Bay. There are several miles of driving trails, plus other scenic paths only accessible on foot. Historically, this has been one of the southernmost wintering areas for Canada geese. Open Mondays through Fridays 8 A.M. to 4:30 P.M.; Sundays 10 A.M. to 5 P.M. Box 68; St. Marks 32355 (904-925-6121).

**OSCEOLA NATIONAL FOREST**, Lake City—Perhaps best known as the site of the Battle of Olustee, the largest conflict of the Civil War fought in the state of Florida. The forest preserve encompasses 157,000 acres in all (including a 2,000-acre natural lake), and activities include fishing, camping, and some legal hunting. Open daily. Osceola Ranger District; U.S. Forest Service; Route 7; Box 423; Lake City 32055 (904-752-2577).

**PAYNES PRAIRIE STATE PRESERVE**, Micanopy—This marsh-and-wet-prairie refuge, located about 15 miles south of Gainesville, is home to waterfowl, wading birds, and alligators, among other animals. The preserve can be toured on foot or can be viewed from an observation tower. Open year-round 8 A.M. to sunset. Route 1; Box 41; Micanopy 32667 (904-466-3397).

**OCALA NATIONAL FOREST**—Known locally as "the big scrub," this forest has the largest concentration of sand pine in the world—as well as a great reputation among fishermen who treasure adjacent Lake George. It is also home to one of the largest deer herds in Florida. Special attractions include Juniper Springs and Alexander Springs, two natural recreation areas. Open daily 7 A.M. to sunset. Lake George Ranger District; Route 2; Box 701; Silver Springs 32670 (904-625-2520).

**OCALA STUD FARM**—One of many farms in this lush thoroughbred-breeding area. Foaling season runs from January to the end of May, and training season starts in September and lasts until it gets too hot to work the horses, usually about June. Training sessions are conducted from 7 A.M. to 10 A.M. and again from 1 P.M. to 3 P.M. At these interesting and often entertaining workouts, visitors can see horses swim in a pool designed especially for them. (According to trainers, swimming helps to strengthen horses' legs, while also keeping them cool.) Southwest 27th Avenue, 2 miles west of Ocala; 904-237-2171.

**BRIDLEWOOD FARM**, Ocala—The best time to visit this stable, just 5 miles west of I-75, is after January, when nature has done its work and many of the mares have foaled. Training sessions are held only in the mornings. Tours are self-guided, but trainers and staff members are more than happy to answer questions. 8318 Northwest 90th Terrace; Ocala 32675 (904-622-5319).

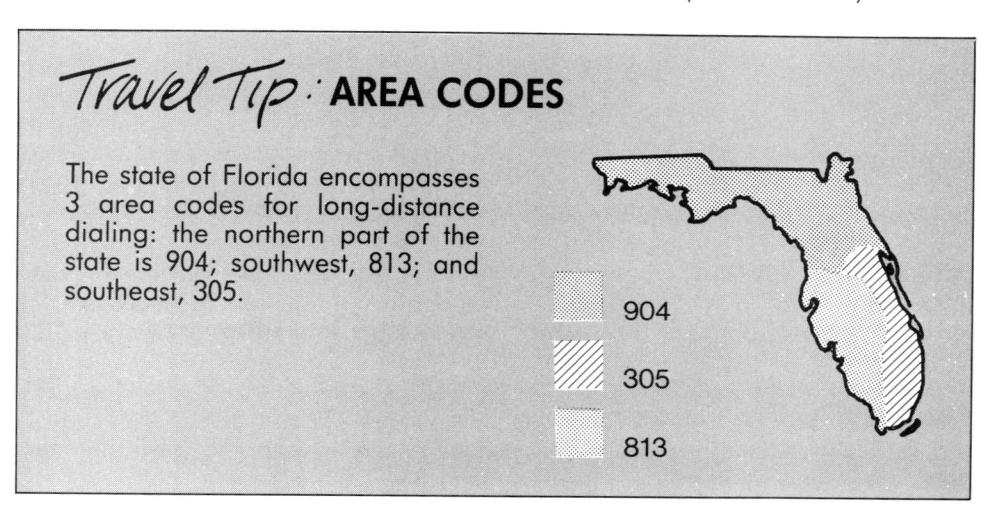

---

## *Travel Tip*: AREA CODES

The state of Florida encompasses 3 area codes for long-distance dialing: the northern part of the state is 904; southwest, 813; and southeast, 305.

- 904
- 305
- 813

# CENTRAL FLORIDA

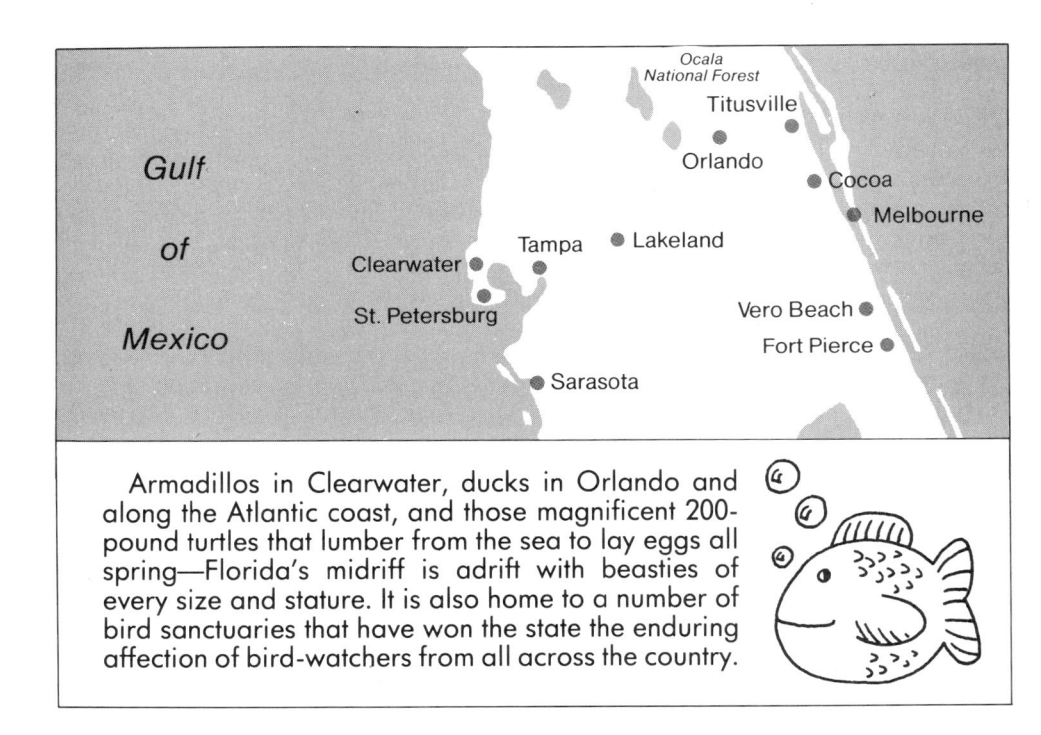

Armadillos in Clearwater, ducks in Orlando and along the Atlantic coast, and those magnificent 200-pound turtles that lumber from the sea to lay eggs all spring—Florida's midriff is adrift with beasties of every size and stature. It is also home to a number of bird sanctuaries that have won the state the enduring affection of bird-watchers from all across the country.

**FLORIDA TRAIL**, Clearwater—Armadillos, raccoons, and even deer and mountain cats can be found along this famous trail that stretches from the middle of Florida north to the foothills of Alabama. There's backpacking, day and night hikes, canoeing, tubing, and fossil hunting. One suggestion: You'll see more if you go on your own (or in a small group), since large tours tend to scare away the more timid of the animals. Information: Don Chambers; 2065 Highland Avenue North; Apartment D-105; Clearwater 33515 (813-447-8956).

**LAKE NATURE PARK**, Clearwater—Alligators, owls, and a reptile exhibit are features at this 50-acre facility, which also has a nature trail. Open Tuesdays through Sundays 10 A.M. to 5 P.M. 2750 Park Trail Lane; Clearwater 33519 (813-462-6024).

**SUNCOAST SEABIRD SANCTUARY**, Indian Shores—This is one of the largest bird sanctuaries in the entire Southeast; hundreds of crippled birds can be found recuperating here at any one time. Many of the herons, bald eagles, nighthawks, osprey, and pelicans, whose injuries won't allow them to fend for themselves, become permanent residents. Open daily 9 A.M. to sunset. 18328 Gulf Boulevard; Indian Shores 33535 (813-391-6211).

**ALDERMAN'S FORD**, Tampa—A self-guided nature tour along boardwalks and footbridges at this scenic 596-acre park takes in an enormous amount of the ecosystem's plant life. There's also a free canoe launch on the Alafia River, one of the most popular canoeing spots in the state. Open daily 8 A.M. to sunset. Highway 39 south of Highway 60. Hillsborough County Parks & Recreation Department; 1101 East River Cove Drive; Tampa (813-681-7990).

**EUREKA SPRINGS**, Tampa—Raccoons, rabbits, and opossum are just about as numerous as human visitors in this 38-acre park, which also offers rare plants, a greenhouse, interpretative trails, boardwalks, and a picnic area. Open daily 8 A.M. to 6 P.M. Northeast of the Florida State Fairgrounds between Highway 301 and Interstate 4. Route 9; Box 57E; Tampa 33610 (813-626-7994).

**LOWRY PARK**, Tampa—There's a small zoo here, with gibbons, lions, and other animals. Open weekdays 8 A.M. to 4 P.M.; Saturdays 11 A.M. to 3 P.M. 7525 North Boulevard; Tampa 33604 (813-933-3386).

**UPPER TAMPA BAY PARK**—Owls, hawks, and even a cougar have been sighted during the weekly nature study sessions held each Sunday at 2 P.M. A changing roster of programs focuses on Florida's snakes, endangered species, and other wildlife topics. 8001 Double Branch Road; Tampa 33615 (813-855-1765).

**E. G. SIMMONS PARK**, Ruskin—Bird-watching is a popular pastime among the shallow waters of the mangrove swamps surrounding this preserve. The 469-acre park also has picnic areas and a beautiful waterfront view. Open daily sunrise to sunset. 2401 19th Street Northwest; Ruskin 33570 (813-645-3836).

**FORT DE SOTO PARK**, St. Petersburg—At this 880-acre park, visitors can go eyeball-to-eyeball with raccoons, squirrels, and many different varieties of birds—some of which are found nowhere else in the country. Open daily sunrise to sunset. Tierra Verde; St. Petersburg 33715 (813-866-2484).

**SCIENCE CENTER OF PINELLAS COUNTY**, St. Petersburg—There are live animals, scientific exhibits, and a planetarium. Open Mondays through Fridays 9 A.M. to 4 P.M. 7701 22nd Avenue North; St. Petersburg 33715 (813-384-0027).

**FLORIDA AUDUBON SOCIETY**, Maitland—A center for birds of prey, with daily presentations of these denizens. Open Tuesdays through Saturdays 10 A.M. to 4 P.M.; raptor presentations are at 11 A.M. The aviary is closed Sundays and Mondays, but an art gallery and gift shop are open Mondays through Saturdays 10 A.M. to 4:30 P.M. 1101 Audubon Way; Maitland 32751 (305-647-2615).

**GENIUS DRIVE**, Winter Park—Several dozen kaleidoscopically colored peacocks strut their stuff around this 50-acre preserve, whose winding roads are ringed by mature orange trees and huge Spanish moss–draped oaks. Visitors can feed the handsome peacocks as they stroll the grounds. Call 305-644-9860 for hours. The circular Genius Drive can be found off Osceola Avenue through Henkel Circle or off Lakemont Avenue to Mizell Avenue in Winter Park. Winter Park Chamber of Commerce; Box 280; Winter Park 32790 (305-644-8281).

**LAKE DAVIS**, Orlando—Ducks and more ducks—diving and puddle ducks; redhead, canvasback, and ringneck ducks; lesser scaup, ruddy ducks, blue-winged teals, and northern shovelers—are among the birds found here. Open daily dawn to dusk. Orange County Parks Department; 118 West Kaley Street; Orlando 32806 (305-420-3640).

**WYNDHAM HOTEL**, Orlando—This may seem an unlikely spot for nature watching, but the hotel happens to have one of the largest collections of Japanese koi fish in the state, displayed in a lobby pool. Visitors can feed or even pet these extremely people-friendly fellows. Nearby, a 50-foot gilded bird cage houses a variety of tropical fowl and songbirds. Open anytime. 6677 Sea Harbor Drive; Orlando 32821 (305-351-5555).

**KISSIMMEE LIVESTOCK MARKET**—Various breeds of cattle are on display at the weekly livestock auctions held here Wednesdays at 1 P.M. Kissimmee Livestock Market; Box 2329; Kissimmee 32742–2329 (305-847-3521).

**PUSH, PULL, AND PADDLE**, Titusville—A ranger-guided tour explores the wildlife and seabirds of Canaveral National Seashore. Part of the trip is made in canoes (bring your own, or one can be provided), and it's a good idea to wear old clothes and sneakers. Reservations necessary. Tours are given Saturdays 10 A.M. to 2 P.M. State Road 402, 7 miles east of Titusville. Box 6447; Titusville 32782 (305-867-0634).

**SEA TURTLE LECTURES**, Titusville—Learn about the 200-pound giants who lumber out of the ocean from April to September to lay their eggs in the sand. Lecture schedules vary but classes usually are held on Sunday afternoons. Canaveral National Seashore Park Headquarters; State Road 402; Titusville 32782 (305-867-0634).

**MERRITT ISLAND NATIONAL WILDLIFE REFUGE**—This sanctuary for wintering waterfowl provides directions for self-guided walking and driving tours. Located 7 miles east of Titusville on State Road 402, near the Kennedy Space Center. Merritt Island National Wildlife Refuge; Box 6504; Titusville 32782 (305-867-0667).

**TURTLE WATCHES**, Canaveral National Seashore—They only come out at night—from May through August along this stretch of beach, loggerheads and giant green sea turtles, some of which weigh as much as 700 pounds, pay a visit to the beaches to deposit their eggs. Reservations for watches should be made during May; actual dates are set according to the tides. State Road 402; Titusville 32782 (305-867-0634).

# SOUTHERN FLORIDA

Even if southern Florida had only Everglades National Park in its wonderful wilderness inventory, it would still be one of the planet's richest areas for observing plants and wildlife. But this region of the state has much more. There are refuges and preserves where manatees, alligators, shorebirds, panthers, and otters find homes, not to mention Big Pine Key, site of the National Key Deer Refuge, where diminutive deer found nowhere else in the world roam.

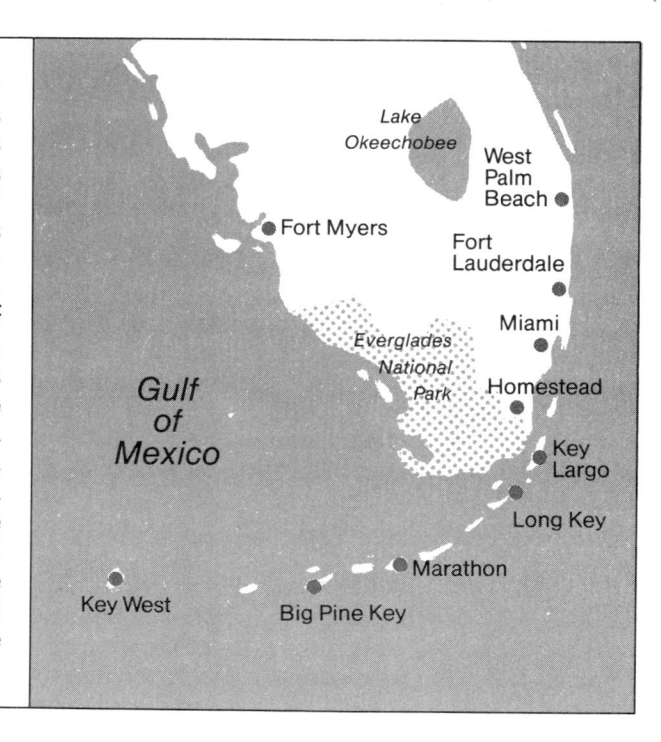

**JANES SCENIC DRIVE IN THE FAKAHATCHEE STRAND**, Copeland—The largest wild stand of royal palms anywhere grows in this southwestern corner of the state. During April and May, when millions of white spider lilies carpet the marshy prairie, this is also the spot to find the largest concentration (and widest variety) of native orchids in North America. Panthers and bobcats are also frequently sighted, and perfectly harmless for viewers who stay in their cars. Near the City of Everglades, north of the Tamiami Trail just west of State Road 29. Box 548; Copeland 33926 (813-695-4593).

**CONSERVANCY, INC.**, Naples—The Briggs Nature Center and the Rookery Bay National Estuarine Sanctuary fall under the auspices of Conservancy, Inc., and offer a wealth of opportunities to sight herons, egrets, sandpipers, bald eagles, ospreys, and hawks. There are also walking trails, an animal rehabilitation center, and an aviary. Open daily 9 A.M. to 5 P.M.; closed weekends from late May through late October. 1450 Merrihue Drive; Naples 33942 (813-262-0304).

**THE WEBB WILDLIFE PRESERVE**, Punta Gorda—This spectacular, 65,000-acre Gulf Coast preserve is particularly dramatic at sunset, when the waterbirds come home for the night. Park entrance is 5 miles south of Punta Gorda, east of U.S. 41 (813-639-1531).

**SHARK VALLEY**, Everglades National Park—Once 4,000, now 2,100, square miles of the world's finest saw-grass marsh, this pristine wilderness is given over to America's third-largest national park (and strangely enough, one of its least visited). The colorful and infinitely diverse species of wildlife in the Everglades combine to form what has been called nature's greatest nonstop variety show. Exotic and endangered water birds, alligators, colorful snakes, oversized turtles, bobcats, crocodiles, and even dolphins can all be seen in a single visit, not to mention mammoth butterflies and an insect and fish population that look as if they're dressed for Mardi Gras. There is a $2 fee to enter the park at the main gate, but at Shark Valley (off the Tamiami Trail near Miccosukee Indian Headquarters, midway between Miami and Naples), entry is free. Readily accessible from this entrance point are Otter Cave and the Bobcat Hammock. Open daily 8:30 A.M. to 6 P.M.; Shark Valley Visitor Center (305-221-8776).

**BISCAYNE NATIONAL PARK**, Homestead—Some 42 acres of islands and 92,000 acres of sea stretch from Biscayne Bay south to the Keys. Park entrance is free and there are numerous opportunities for free snorkeling trips and glass-bottom boat rides for close-up looks at coral reefs and the various colorful fish that call Biscayne home. The main park gate is at Southwest 238th Street and Canal Drive. Box 1369; Homestead; 33090-1369 (305-247-7275).

**J. N. "DING" DARLING NATIONAL WILDLIFE REFUGE**, Sanibel—Named for the cartoonist and devoted environmentalist. The best time to visit is around sunrise or sunset when grand formations of roseate spoonbills come and go. On the 5-mile drive through the refuge, herons, gulls, willets, and sandpipers are common sights. For walkers there are the interpretative walking trails. Open daily sunrise to sunset. One Wildlife Drive; Sanibel 33957 (813-472-1100).

**BARLEY BARBER SWAMP**, Southwestern Martin County—Florida Power & Light Company operates a 400-acre freshwater cypress swamp preserve where a wide variety of plants, trees, and wildlife can be viewed from a 5,800-foot-long boardwalk that forms a loop through the protected area. Points of interest are numbered along the trail, and on any given day one is apt to spot herons, egrets, bald eagles, woodpeckers, cardinals, sandpipers, alligators, snakes, frogs, turtles, otters, deer, opossum, raccoons, and armadillos. Five-hundred-year-old cypress trees are another highlight. Reservations are required for tours. Contact Florida Power & Light Company; Environmental Affairs; Box 14000; Juno Beach 33408 (305-863-3646).

**ARCH CREEK PARK AND MUSEUM**, North Miami—Eight lush acres of tropical and subtropical flora are tucked away near the bustling Miami metropolis. There's also a nature center, plus a museum featuring Indian artifacts, fossil exhibits, and other educational displays. An organized trail-walk is held every Saturday at 1 P.M. Open daily 9 A.M. to 5 P.M. 1855 Northeast 135th Street; North Miami 33181 (305-944-6111).

**GREYNOLDS PARK**, North Miami—Bird-watchers from both Miami and Fort Lauderdale head here, especially at sunrise and sunset, for a peek at the spectacular flights of ibis and spoonbills. The park has one of the largest rookeries in southern Florida and lays claim to the highest point in ultraflat Dade County—a 46-foot mound. Free bird walks are conducted Thursdays at 6 P.M. between May and September and at 5 P.M. from October through April. 17530 West Dixie Highway; North Miami 33154 (305-945-3425).

**PELICAN HARBOR SEABIRD STATION**, Miami—A chance to stroll about with dozens of pelicans and ask the question on everyone's mind: How do they stand for so long on just one leg? Open weekends 1 P.M. to 6 P.M. 1275 Northeast 79th Street Causeway, behind the State Marine Patrol Base (305-751-9840).

**LARRY AND PENNY THOMPSON PARK**, Miami—Early morning nature walks are a pleasure in this new park on the southwest fringe of the city. Open daily 10 A.M. to 5 P.M. 12451 Southwest 184th Street; Miami 33177 (305-257-1631).

**OLD CUTLER HAMMOCK NATURE CENTER**, Miami—A wide variety of nature programs are offered for a nominal fee on topics ranging from spiders and butterflies to owls and alligators. The center itself is open free of charge, as are its grounds, which include picnic facilities and fishing. Hours vary so call ahead for specifics. 17555 Southwest 79th Avenue; Miami 33157 (305-255-4767).

**CASTELLOW HAMMOCK**, South Dade County—A 50-acre tropical hammock, with nature trails, picnic shelters, and environmental displays. Interpretative field trips and programs are available upon request. The Nature Center is open daily 9 A.M. to 4 P.M. and the park is open dawn to dusk. 22301 Southwest 162nd Avenue; Goulds 33170 (305-245-4321).

**LAKE SURPRISE**, Key Largo—And you thought Florida only had alligators. The surprise here is the crocodile. Along U.S. 1 near this breeding ground, look for the sign that reads "Crocodile Crossing." They're a rare sight, but this is the best spot in the state for a lucky peek.

**NATIONAL KEY DEER REFUGE**, Big Pine Key—More than 250 diminutive deer, about the size of German shepherd dogs, are protected here. Bald eagles, egrets, and alligators can also be spotted. The refuge enforces strict regulations (never feed the deer), so be sure to check in at the Visitor Center for information about the rules. The refuge is open daily sunrise to sunset; the Visitor Center is open Mondays through Fridays 9 A.M. to 5 P.M. (When the center is closed, regulation brochures are available on a rack outside.) The Visitor Center is located 2 miles north of U.S. 1 on Country Road 940. Box 510; Big Pine Key 33043 (305-872-2239).

# A PRIMER ON FLORIDA'S OWN

**MANATEES:** These clumsy, fat, and rather lovable creatures are found along both coasts. Though huge, they are completely docile. Also known as sea cows, these odd mammals were allegedly mistaken for mermaids by sailors long ago. One of the best places to spot them is at the foot of Royal Palm Avenue in Coconut Grove, where they wallow and graze in shallow waters. Florida Power & Light publishes a free booklet about manatees that includes information about prime viewing spots. For a copy: Florida Power & Light; Box 029100; Miami 33102 (305-552-3891).

**FLORIDA RANGE CATTLE:** It's not the first thing that pops into most minds when Florida is mentioned, but the Sunshine State happens to be one of the nation's most active beef-producing areas. Range cattle seem a bit scrawny, but the resultant beef is quite good. The cattle are most commonly seen in Hendry County (west of Fort Myers), near State Road 80 west of Lake Okeechobee.

**SEA TURTLES:** From early June through mid-August female turtles—leatherbacks, greens, loggerheads, Kemp's ridleys, hawksbills, and olive ridleys—struggle ashore to lay their eggs along the Atlantic coast. The turtles range in weight from 150 to 700 pounds. Florida Power & Light sponsors turtle watches. To reserve a spot for a watch, contract Florida Power & Light; Box 029100; Miami 33102 (305-552-3891).

**BALD EAGLES:** With the single exception of Alaska, more bald eagles are found in Florida than in any other state in the Union. Some of the best places to see them are on the Gulf Coast, at Marco Island, and in the Ten Thousand Islands, south of Marco.

# SITES AND SIGHTS

Among Florida's most famous sights, you might not immediately remember to include the world's first house-eating sinkhole, a statue that cries, or the "haunted hill" of Lake Wales, but you really should. They're not only all free, but they are irrepressible fun. And there's lots more to see and enjoy in the Sunshine State, requiring not a single red penny. After all, that quintessential Florida sight, a rocket roaring up through the misty early-morning sunshine, is free to anyone willing to get up early enough to find a viewing spot on the sands across from Cape Canaveral on launch day. Those who have done it say it's well worth the effort. And there are other free opportunities for space enthusiasts at the Kennedy Space Center—it's just knowing where to find them.

And then there are the many festivals, planetarium shows, and, believe it or not, the state's renowned luxury resorts themselves. It's true that these glamorous retreats can prove a bit expensive for an overnight stay, but their grounds and lobbies are open to the public at no charge, and what better way to spend an afternoon than wandering through a well-kept garden or enjoying a romp through a resort's recreation areas?

Another Sunshine State sight worth investigating is that natural phenomenon known as the Gulf Stream, which flows so close to the Florida coast that it can be seen from the shores of Delray Beach.

Without further ado, here's the best of the Sunshine State, north to south, proving the old adage—some of the best things in life are free.

# NORTHERN FLORIDA

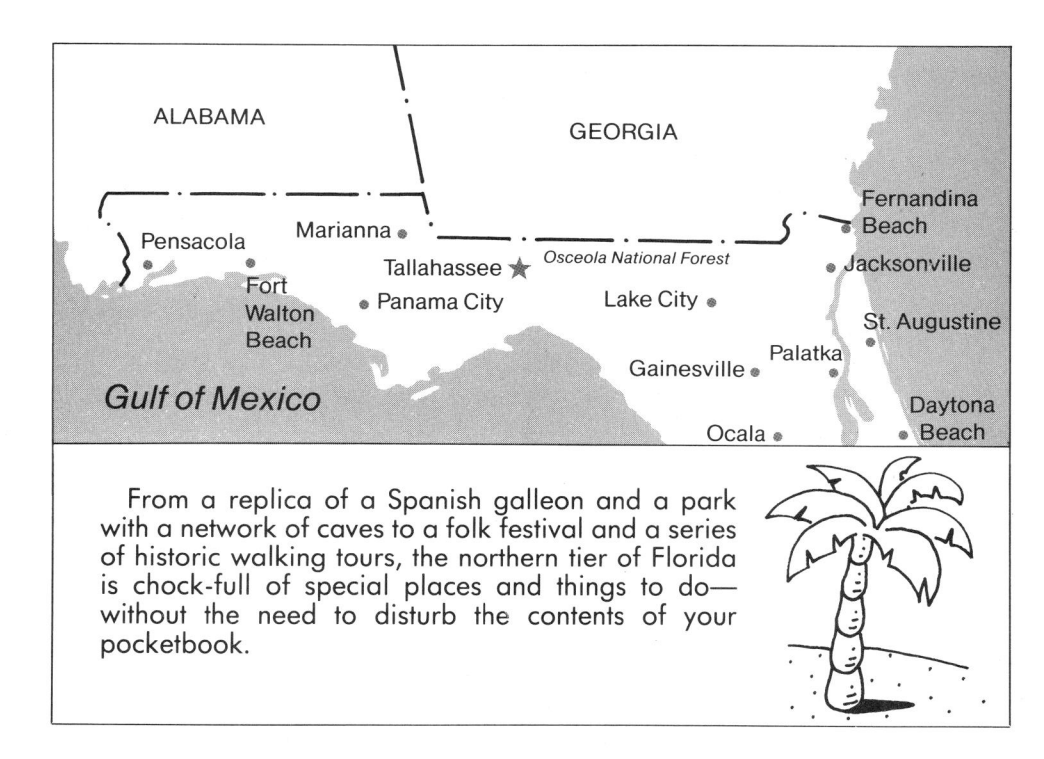

From a replica of a Spanish galleon and a park with a network of caves to a folk festival and a series of historic walking tours, the northern tier of Florida is chock-full of special places and things to do—without the need to disturb the contents of your pocketbook.

**ADVENTURES UNLIMITED**, Milton—This recreational area, about 20 miles north of Pensacola, offers canoeing and picnicking at Caldwater, Sweetwater-Juniper, and Blackwater creeks. Open daily; scheduled canoe trips run 8 A.M. to 3 P.M. Information: 904-623-6197.

**THE TREASURE SHIP**, Panama City Beach—Located on the eastern end of the beach, this larger-than-life replica of a 3-masted Spanish galleon houses restaurants, lounges, and gift shops. Open daily 4 P.M. to 10 P.M. 3605 Thomas Drive; Panama City Beach 32407 (904-234-8881).

**FALLING WATERS STATE RECREATION AREA**, Chipley—Nothing man-made here. The name of this 154-acre facility comes from a geological sink formation 100 feet deep and 15 feet in diameter—that's a big hole. Open year-round 8 A.M. to sunset. About 45 miles north of Panama City off Route 77 on Route 5; Box 660; Chipley 32428 (904-638-4030).

**FLORIDA CAVERNS STATE PARK**, Marianna—The limestone caverns of this famous network of caves, about 70 miles northeast of Panama City, were created centuries ago when what is now Florida was completely underwater. There's a charge for lighted tours of the caverns, but other park facilities include camping, fishing, and hiking. Information: 2701 Caverns Road; Marianna 32446 (904-482-3632).

**FLORIDA FOLK FESTIVAL**—Every year in May, the Stephen Foster Center in White Springs, about midway between Tallahassee and Jacksonville, becomes host to this collection of folk crafts, folk music, and native Florida "Cracker" foods (the likes of turtle, catfish, gator tail, and frog legs). Held Memorial Day weekend. Information: 904-397-2192.

**FORT CLINCH STATE PARK**, Fernandina Beach—This Civil War fortification wasn't completed by that war's end, but was used as a training camp for soldiers during the Spanish-American War and again during World War II. It's a great spot for picnicking, camping, and exploring, and on the first weekend of each month, park rangers dress in Civil War–era clothing and reenact life at Fort Clinch circa 1864. Information: 904-261-4212.

**THE FLORIDA THEATRE**, Jacksonville—Symphonies, dance, concerts, and comedy are all on the calendar (but call ahead for schedules) in a newly restored, circa-1920s Mediterranean-style palace. Corner of Forsyth and Newnan Streets; Jacksonville 32202 (904-358-3600).

**ST. AUGUSTINE WALKING TOURS**—A free map of the nation's oldest city—founded in 1565, 42 years before Jamestown—is available at the Visitor Information Center (10 Castillo Drive) and provides a historic tour of the well-preserved city. The Visitor Center also offers stacks of brochures describing the various attractions, some of which, however, have entrance fees. On the tour, one finds the Mission of Nombre de Dios, the Oldest House, the Cathedral of St. Augustine, and many other sites of interest. The very best time to visit, however, is Palm Sunday, for the ceremony of the blessing of the fleet, and its attendant arts festival. Information: 904-829-5681.

---

*Travel Tip:* **DRIVING?**

Be sure to remember your driver's license, automobile registration, proof of insurance, gasoline credit cards, auto club card, and an extra set of car keys. Other important items include maps, flashlight, extra batteries, emergency flasher or flares, and a basic first-aid kit.

# CENTRAL FLORIDA

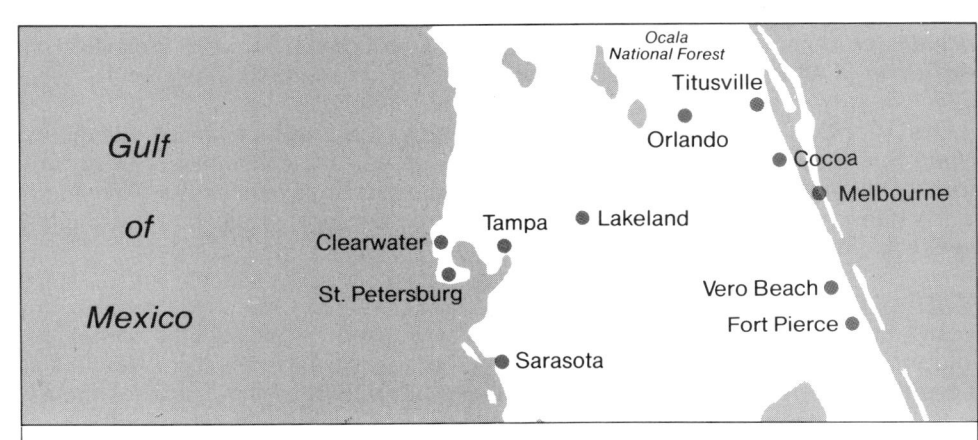

From the purely wacky (an optical illusion that makes cars appear to roll uphill) to the genuinely wonderful (a dawn lift-off at Cape Canaveral), the Sunshine State's midsection is amply endowed with things to see and do on a tight budget.

**CROWN HOTEL**, Inverness—This elegant Victorian grande dame, about 60 miles north of Tampa, was built during the 1880s and renovated in 1980. A beauty of the period with a distinctly British accent, its name comes from the replica Crown Jewels in the foyer. Open daily. 109 North Seminole Avenue; Inverness 32650 (904-344-5555).

**ROGER'S CHRISTMAS HOUSE**, Brooksville—So what if it's July? Roger's, about 40 miles north of Tampa, has one of the largest collections of Christmas decorations, gifts, and trinkets under one roof. Twinkling lights, Christmas trees, bells, angels, wreaths, and even non-Christmas items—such as collectibles and crystal sets—are on display. Open daily 9:30 A.M. to 5 P.M. 103 Saxon Avenue; Brooksville 33512 (904-796-2415).

**ST. NICHOLAS GREEK ORTHODOX CATHEDRAL**, Tarpon Springs—It was at this church, a replica of St. Sophia's in Istanbul, that a cleaning woman claimed she saw a statue of St. Nicholas shed a tear. You'll have to judge for yourself, but with its stunning stained-glass windows and marble interior, this sanctuary is well worth a visit. Open weekdays. 6 North Pinellas Avenue; Tarpon Springs 33589 (813-937-3540).

**TAMPA'S SUPERVISED PLAYGROUNDS**—The city recreation department runs several playgrounds that have a variety of specially organized programs—for sports, arts and crafts, and creative dramatics—and field trips. Two of the most popular playgrounds are **Riverfront Park;** 1000 North Boulevard (813-251-3742) and **Perry Harvey Sr. Park;** 1200 North Orange Avenue (813-228-8921). For additional information about specific parks and programs: City of Tampa Recreation Department; 1420 North Tampa Street; Tampa 33602 (813-223-8615).

**SAFETY VILLAGE**, Tampa—At this miniature village, children are taught about crossing streets, watching for cars, and other safety rules. Open Mondays through Saturdays by appointment. Located at the north end of Lowry Park at Sligh Avenue and North Boulevard. Tampa Parks Department; 7525 North Boulevard; Tampa 33612 (813-933-3103).

**TAMPA INTERNATIONAL AIRPORT**—An airport? Well, not just any old aerodrome. Tampa International has been called the best airport in the country and with its Star Wars–like shuttle cars (that whisk people from the main terminal to gates and various interesting shops), it's a fun place to visit even if you don't have a plane to catch. Open daily 24 hours. U.S. Highway 19 and State Road 60; Tampa 33622 (813-883-3400).

**UNIVERSITY OF SOUTH FLORIDA PLANETARIUM**, Tampa—Programs change with the seasons and the stars, but university staff is always on hand to answer visitors' questions. Call ahead to make a reservation. Fowler Avenue; Tampa 33620 (813-974-3010).

**FLORIDA STRAWBERRY FESTIVAL**, Plant City—About 20 miles east of Tampa is the city known as the world's winter strawberry capital. The annual Strawberry Festival, first held in 1936, is usually slated for late February and lasts through early March; activities include a grand parade, a strawberry cook-off, the coronation of the strawberry queen, and all sorts of evening entertainment. Information: Drawer 1869; Plant City 33566 (813-752-9194).

**SPOOK HILL**, Lake Wales—The corner of Fifth Street and North Avenue in Lake Wales is a popular place to park. Here motorists turn off their cars at the bottom of the hill and watch as an optical illusion seems to make their autos roll back up the hill. Open anytime. To get there take I-4 west to U.S. Highway 27 exit 23, and follow the signs on Route 17A east. Lake Wales Chamber of Commerce; Box 191; Lake Wales 33859 (813-676-3445).

**BOB WHITE AIRFIELD**, Zellwood—It's not the landing strip, a 3,300-foot grass field about 20 miles southwest of Orlando, that is of interest so much as the collection of some 2 dozen restored vintage planes headquartered here, most of which are the loving work of owner White. Open anytime Bob is around, so call ahead. West Jones Avenue; Zellwood 32798 (305-886-3180).

**COLBY MEMORIAL TEMPLE**, Cassadaga—The "home of the mystics and the mediums" refers both to the temple and the town it serves, both founded by George P. Colby in 1894. From September through May, psychics from all over the world gather for a series of events that are usually open to the public. The temple is also open to visitors the rest of the year. Box 152; Cassadaga 32706 (904-228-2880).

**HONTOON ISLAND STATE PARK**, DeLand—Ride the free ferry across the St. Johns River from DeLand to this 1,800-acre park, which marks the ceremonial grounds of the Timucuan Indians. Self-guided nature walks, camping, freshwater fishing, boating, and picnicking are all available, as are rental cabins for overnight stays. Ferries run from 9 A.M. to an hour before dusk. 2309 River Ridge Road; DeLand 32720 (904-734-7158).

**CENTRAL CHRISTIAN CHURCH**, Orlando—The stained-glass windows here are said to be the only faceted glasswork by French artist Jean Lesquibe in the Western Hemisphere. Open Mondays through Fridays 7 A.M. to 3 P.M. 250 West Ivanhoe Boulevard; Orlando 32803 (305-425-6611).

**HYATT REGENCY GRAND CYPRESS**, Orlando—Wandering around the lobby and grounds of this elegant, world-class resort makes a terrific afternoon diversion. The 200-foot atrium lobby is decorated with lush greenery and pieces from the hotel's $1 million art collection. A pianist plays in the lobby lounge every afternoon. The hotel's free-form swimming pool is one of the largest in the state. One Grand Cypress Boulevard; Orlando 32819 (305-239-1234).

**MONUMENT OF THE STATES**, Kissimmee—This step pyramid, 50 feet tall with 21 tiers, was constructed during the 1940s from concrete and stones donated by Americans in every state of the union, not to mention the contributions from 22 other countries. The names of those people who donated one or more bags of cement are imprinted at the base of the pyramid. Open 24 hours a day. Monument Street at Lake Front Park (305-847-3174).

**ORLANDO INTERNATIONAL ARTSFEST**—Orlando's annual peforming arts festival, usually held in April, features dance, music, and drama performances on three stages set up downtown on the city's main drag. The side streets are also closed to traffic and each is devoted to the food, arts, and culture of a different ethnic group. The festival draws some 150,000 visitors. Information: Council of Arts and Sciences for Central Florida; 1900 North Mills Avenue, Suite 2; Orlando 32803-1465 (305-843-2787).

**WINTER PARK SINKHOLE**—The tony suburban town (of Orlando) made headlines in 1980 when a sinkhole swallowed up a home, a foreign-car repair shop, portions of 2 local streets, part of the municipal pool, and 6 cars. The hole is now about 350 feet across and 100 feet deep—about the size of a small lake. Sinkholes are not so unusual in the state, but they are rarely as ambitious as this behemoth. Comstock and Denning Avenues. Winter Park Chamber of Commerce; Box 280; Winter Park 32790 (305-644-9860).

**TURTLE MOUND HISTORICAL SITE**, Titusville—This Indian shell mound on the Canaveral National Seashore in New Smyrna Beach is one of the highest points in this area, and offers a great view of both the Atlantic Ocean and Mosquito Lagoon. On Route A1A. Canaveral National Seashore; Box 6447; Titusville 32782 (305-867-0634).

**FLORIDA SOLAR ENERGY CENTER**, Cape Canaveral—A prototype of a solar-powered home and several solar water heaters are part of the display at this center, which explores the latest technology for capturing the sun's power. Special programs feature solar-powered toys and other new inventions. Open Mondays through Fridays 8 A.M. to 5 P.M. 300 State Road 401; Cape Canaveral 32920 (305-783-0300).

**NASA LAUNCHES**, Kennedy Space Center—Space shuttle launches are an exciting and frequent occurrence these days. Shuttles go up about once a month and almost any place along the coast offers a fine view of these spectacular events. NASA publishes a list of scheduled launches. For a copy call 305-867-2468.

**NASA SPACEPORT, USA**, Kennedy Space Center—Moon rocks, a Lunar Rover set on a simulated moon surface, and a Viking spacecraft set on a simulated Mars surface are among the fascinating and free displays in the Gallery of Spaceflight. Open daily 8 A.M. to dusk. (305-867-1566).

**DESERET RANCH**, Melbourne—The 300,000-acre spread, owned by the Church of Jesus Christ of Latter Day Saints, produces beef cattle, timber, and citrus fruit. Visitors must call ahead for tours. Open for group tours only. Star Route; Box 1250; Melbourne 32901 (305-892-3672).

## Travel Tip: TIPPING

Some things don't change. Porters in Florida receive the standard 50¢ to 75¢ per suitcase; waiters and waitresses, 15 percent to 18 percent of the restaurant bill; and hairdressers and manicurists, 15 percent.

# SOUTHERN FLORIDA

The world of space centers and spiritualist churches gives way to nature itself in Florida's southernmost reaches. There are enough eccentricities and manmade wonders to keep one's sense of humor honed, but the real grabbers belong to nature—the peculiar natural phenomenon known as the Gulf Stream and the sunsets at Key West. Some pass within minutes, testaments to life's fleeting pleasures; others can keep you mesmerized for hours.

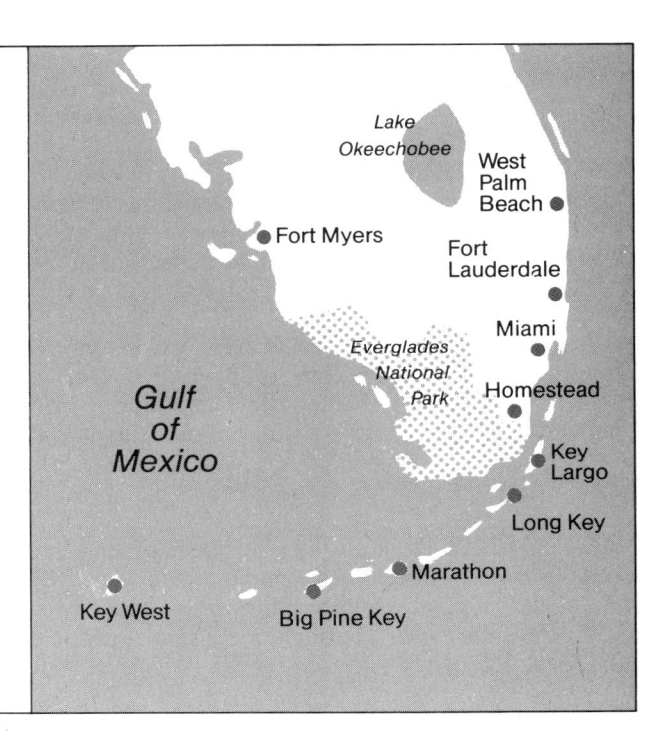

**THE OLD WELL**, Punta Gorda—The water from this well, located at the corner of Taylor Street and Marion Avenue, tastes far superior to city tap water and is rumored to be life-extending (though no proof exists). And it's free.

**WATERMELON CAPITAL**, Immokalee—Florida produces an average of 30 million watermelons each year, and this rural area in the northeastern corner of Collier County is the state's most productive area. Bring your own salt.

**WORLD'S LARGEST CHRISTMAS TREE**, Lantana—In keeping with its commitment to overstatement, the *National Enquirer* puts up the world's largest Christmas tree each year outside its Lantana offices. The tree is at least 100 feet tall and does its part to give balmy Lantana an extra dose of Christmas spirit. 600 Southwest Coast Avenue; Lantana 33464 (305-586-1111).

**THE GULF STREAM**, Delray Beach—The stream is a warm natural current that flows like a river within the Atlantic Ocean. It is indigo in color and flows close enough to the Florida coast here actually to be seen from the shore. It begins in the Gulf of Mexico and ends across the Atlantic in Europe's North Sea.

**GOODYEAR BLIMP**, Pompano Beach—The home base of Goodyear's *Airship Enterprise* is 1500 Northeast Fifth Avenue, Pompano Beach. Rides in the blimp's gondola are by invitation only, but it's quite an awesome sight even when tethered to the ground. Call 305-946-8300 to find out if it's grounded before visiting.

**FARMERS MARKET**, Pompano Beach—This huge fruit and vegetable bazaar draws buyers from major supermarket chains around the country. A 1,000-foot-long platform holds some 200 truckloads of the freshest produce around. Just come in and breathe in all the exotic aromas. Hammondville Road; Pompano Beach (305-946-6570).

**NEW RIVER**, Fort Lauderdale—Several urban rivers run through southern Florida cities, and this is perhaps the prettiest. Graceful sailboats, many with live-aboard families, dot the coconut palm–graced stream. An especially nice place to catch a glimpse of the serene sight is around 101 North New River Drive East.

**CITY CEMETERY**, Key West—Many victims of the sinking of the USS *Maine* (during the Spanish-American War) are buried here. Open daily sunrise to sunset. Windsor Lane; Key West.

**PINECREST**, Key West—Al Capone built a large house here during the 1930s, presumably as headquarters for his smuggling operations. Not much remains of the house (or of Capone, for that matter)—just its foundations and some scrub oaks. Six miles west of the 40 Mile Bend off the Tamiami Trail on State Road 94.

**KEY WEST SUNSETS**—About an hour before the sun actually goes down, a crowd gathers at Mallory Square at the western tip of Duval Street for a nightly ritual known appropriately enough as "The Sunset." Vendors, mimes, jugglers, and singers set up shop and compete for the crowd's attention. The sun sets in all its glory as the crowd murmurs approvingly, applauds, and then departs.

---

*Travel Tip:* **VISITORS: F.Y.I.**

The Florida Division of Tourism has a vast array of materials FYI—for your information—and free for the asking. Write the Division of Tourism; Collins Building; Tallahassee, FL 32301 (904-487-1462).

**COCONUT PALMS**—Except for the sun, there is no symbol more identifiable with Florida than the coconut palm tree. Unfortunately, a disease has killed many of the state's trees during recent years, but they are still quite abundant in Palm Beach, Coconut Grove, and Key West. A few bits of trivia: the average coconut palm produces about 50 nuts a year and a coconut is most likely to fall from a tree between the hours of 2 A.M. and 5 A.M. Early-morning joggers beware.

## Travel Tip: AUTOMOBILE CLUBS

If you plan to tour extensively by car, joining a reputable travel or automobile club is a good idea. Choose one that offers these basic services:

- Travel and vacation planning, including routing and maps
- Round-the-clock emergency breakdown service
- Insurance that covers road accidents, personal injury, bail bond, even lawyer's fees when necessary

(Specific policies and programs vary from club to club, and most charge between $25 and $50 a year for membership. Shop around to find the one that best suits your needs.)

Some of the best-known and largest auto clubs are:

- *American Automobile Association*—Join through local chapters (listed under "Automobile Club of . . ." in the telephone book); information from national office; 8111 Gatehouse Rd.; Falls Church, VA 22047 (703-222-6000).
- *Amoco Motor Club*—Join through Amoco's office; 3700 Wake Forest Rd.; Raleigh, NC 27609 (919-872-4000 or 800-334-3300).
- *Allstate Motor Club*—Run by Allstate Insurance; join through any Allstate agency; information from the Club; 3701 West Lake; Glenview, IL 60025 (312-291-5461).
- *Ford Auto Club*—Membership Services Division; Box 224688; Dallas, TX 75222 (800-348-5220).
- *Gulf Auto Club*—Join by writing Box 4189; South Bend, IN 46634 (800-348-5126; 800-342-5666 in Indiana).
- *JTX Travel Club*—Run by the Insurance Company of North America; Box 13901; Philadelphia, PA 19101 (215-241-4000; 800-262-5213 in Pennsylvania; 800-523-1965 elsewhere).
- *Montgomery Ward Auto Club*—Join through credit manager at any Montgomery Ward store; national office, 2020 W. Dempster; Evanston, IL 60202 (800-621-5151; 800-572-5577 in Illinois; 312-570-5006 in Alaska).
- *Motor Club of America*—Open to residents of 30 states (protection extends to members traveling in all states); national office, 484 Central Ave.; Newark, NJ 07107 (201-733-1234).

# SPORTS

It could be said that Florida is a state specifically designed for sports enthusiasts. The right combination of land and water makes almost all active and athletic things possible, save for skiing and mountain climbing. It's a fisherman's paradise, a watersports lover's delight, and a haven for hikers and bikers.

There are tennis courts and golf courses enough to keep any hacker or duffer blissfully happy, but unfortunately most of these facilities assess some fee. We have, however, discovered one court where tennis (complete with lessons) is free, plus a couple of other sporty surprises.

Major-league baseball teams, clearly seeing the light, have made Florida the spring-training capital of the country. It's an annual ritual—one that allows fans a peek at players warming up for the season ahead. Tickets for exhibition games are inexpensive and the practice sessions are absolutely free; both offer a chance to see the pros loosening up their winter-weary muscles, stretching their hamstrings in the hope that they won't pull them later in the year, and having an all-around good time before the official season gets under way. Spring training also offers fans a great opportunity to snag autographs from favorite players—the atmosphere is usually quite relaxed.

There are plenty of sporting activities to entertain both spectator and participant. From fishing in the world's bass capital and pitching a few horseshoes to watching a competitive crew race and enjoying an exciting polo match, it's all here—and it needn't cost a cent.

# NORTHERN FLORIDA

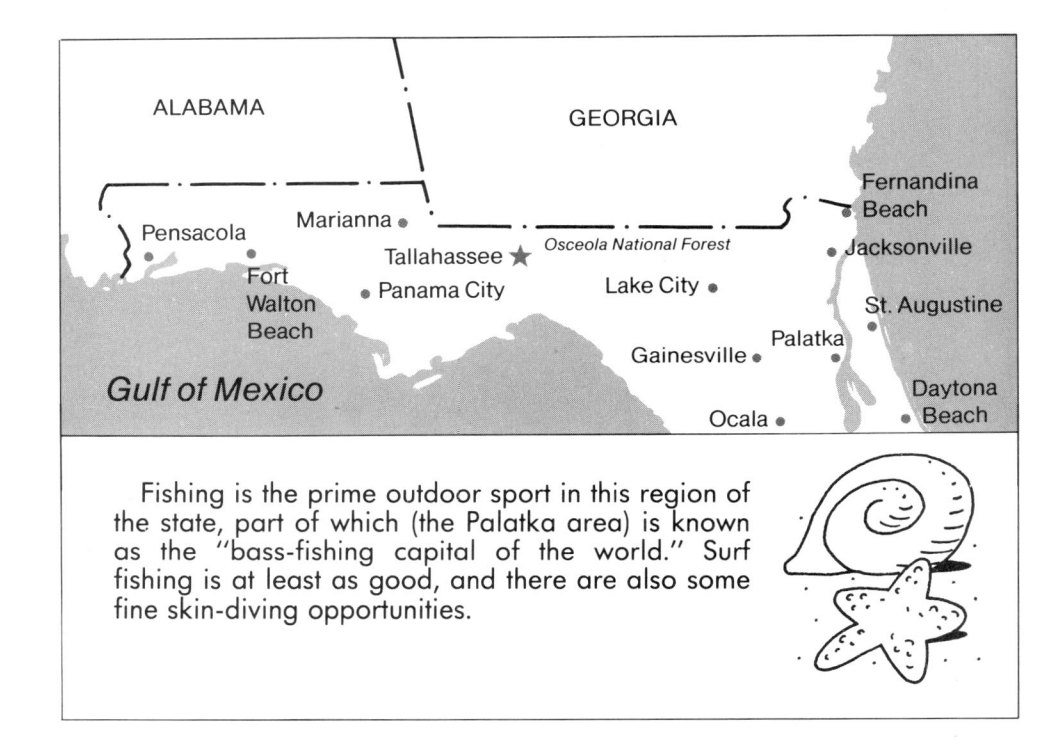

Fishing is the prime outdoor sport in this region of the state, part of which (the Palatka area) is known as the "bass-fishing capital of the world." Surf fishing is at least as good, and there are also some fine skin-diving opportunities.

**FRESHWATER FISHING**—Folks "gone fishin'" are a common sight on most of northern Florida's lakes and rivers, but the Palatka area, known as the "bass capital of the world," and the Oklawaha River and the Rodman Reservoir are the best spots for hooking 'em—or at least trying to. Also great for largemouth bass is Lake Jackson near Tallahassee. For additional information about fishing in Florida contact the Florida Department of Natural Resources; 3900 Commonwealth Boulevard; Tallahassee 32303 (904-488-7326).

**SURF CASTING**—Fine surf and pier fishing is abundant and accessible up and down both the Gulf and Atlantic coasts. Most notable is Destin, which bills itself as the "World's Luckiest Fishing Village." Destin Chamber of Commerce; Box 8; Destin 32541 (904-837-6241).

**SKIN DIVING**—There are great skin-diving opportunities all around northern Florida. Some of the best spots include the Wakulla River, near Tallahassee, where the river silt hides riches such as Indian relics and prehistoric fossils;

nearby Wakulla Springs; the Blue Grotto, near Gainesville; the Crystal River area; and Juniper and Salt springs in the Ocala National Forest; plus several offshore sites on the Atlantic coast such as the wreck of the *Gulf of America* near Amelia Island and a 9-mile-long reef east of Jacksonville. For detailed information about these sites and other spectacular skin-diving spots, contact Florida Skindivers Association; 4201 13th Lane Northeast; St. Petersburg 33703 (813-522-8885).

# CENTRAL FLORIDA

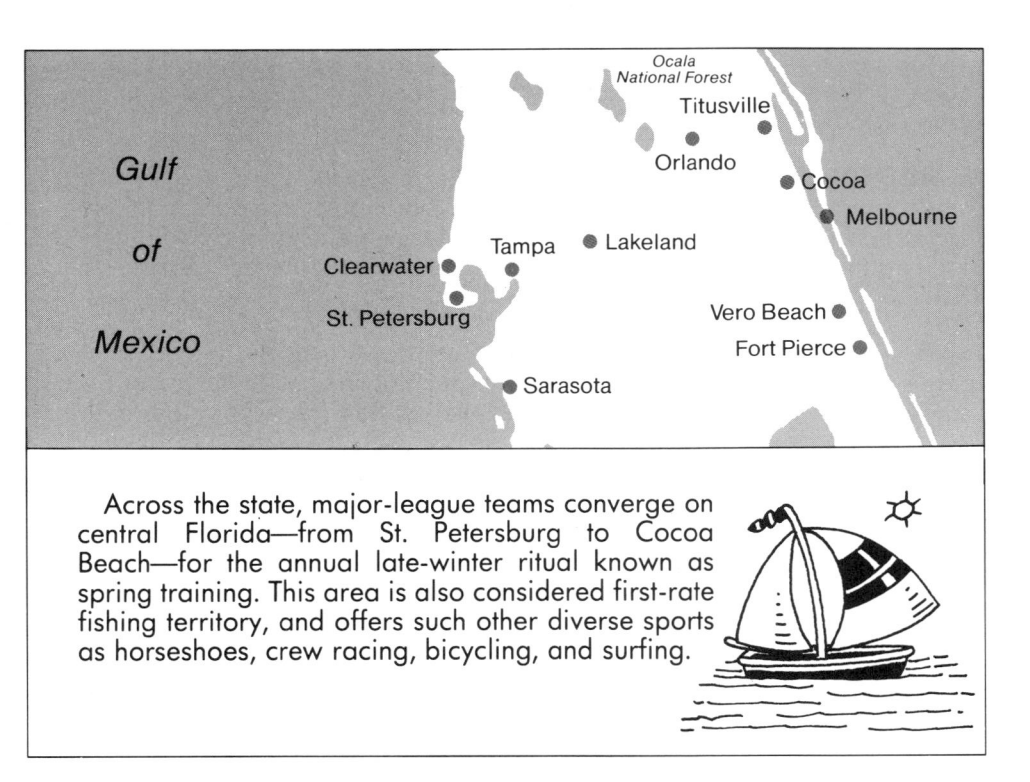

Across the state, major-league teams converge on central Florida—from St. Petersburg to Cocoa Beach—for the annual late-winter ritual known as spring training. This area is also considered first-rate fishing territory, and offers such other diverse sports as horseshoes, crew racing, bicycling, and surfing.

**PHILADELPHIA PHILLIES SPRING TRAINING**, Clearwater—You'll see the pros huffing down the running track, slogging through their push-ups and sit-ups, and getting the winter kinks out on the diamond at practices held from mid-February to mid-March, weekdays 10 A.M. to 1 P.M. The practices offer an opportunity to get a close-up look at your favorite players, plus a chance to grab a few autographs. Jack Russell Stadium; Clearwater 33517 (813-441-8638).

**CLEARWATER HORSESHOE CLUB**—Regular day-long tournaments—sometimes featuring reigning world champions—are held here during the season, from the first week in October through the end of April. Weekends are busiest. Ed Wright Park; 1908 Nugget Drive; Clearwater 33515 (813-443-2892).

**LAKE PARK**, Lutz—About 10 miles north of Tampa on 600 acres of parkland are an archery range, a bicycle motorcross (BMX) track, and rodeo grounds (but you must bring your own horse). There's also boating and fishing on the park's 5 lakes. Open daily sunrise to sunset. 17302 North Dale Mabry Highway; Lutz 33549 (813-961-4226).

**CINCINNATI REDS SPRING TRAINING**, Tampa—A great opportunity to see big-name stars and up-and-coming players getting their games—and bodies—into top shape for the long summer season ahead. The Reds practice daily mid-February through April 10 A.M. to 1 P.M. at Al Lopez Field; Dale Mabry Highway; Tampa 33607 (813-876-3943).

**PRESIDENT'S CUP REGATTA**, Tampa—Some of the biggest names in college crew racing, including teams from Yale and Dartmouth, compete in this event, sponsored by the University of Tampa. The race is usually held during the first weekend in April on Tampa Bay. 401 West Kennedy Boulevard; Tampa 33606 (813-253-3333).

**TAMPA BAY BUCCANEERS**—Practice sessions for Tampa's National Football League team are held during July and August and are open to the public free of charge (and may give viewers some indication of how the team will fare during the coming season). Practices are usually held from 9:15 A.M. to 11:15 A.M. but call ahead for exact times. One Buccaneer Place; Tampa 33607 (813-870-2700).

**TAMPA RECREATION DEPARTMENT TENNIS LESSONS**—The city offers free tennis lessons for children and adults at various municipal courts around town. Regular clinics are part of the program. For more information: 15 Columbus Drive; Tampa 33606 (813-253-3997).

**WILDERNESS PARK**, Tampa—Hiking, fishing, and canoeing at Dead River are popular at this huge 16,000-acre park. Open daily dawn to dusk. Dead River Road and Highway 301. Hillsborough County Parks and Recreation Department; 1101 East River Cove Drive; Tampa 33604 (813-272-5840).

**EDWARD MEDARD PARK**, Dover—This 1,284-acre reservoir is one of the most popular freshwater fishing spots in Hillsborough County. The most common catch here, from a fishing pier on the reservoir, are bass, brim, and speckled perch. There's also a boardwalk leading to an observation tower on a small island. Open daily 6 A.M. to sunset. Turkey Creek Road, south of Highway 60. Route 1; Box 444; Dover 33527 (813-681-8862).

**FESTIVAL OF STATES**, St. Petersburg—Swimming races and unusual sporting events—bed races?—are a large part of this annual 2-week festival held around Easter. New events are added each year. Suncoasters of St. Petersburg; Box 1731; St. Petersburg 33731 (813-898-3654).

**FORT DE SOTO COUNTY PARK**, St. Petersburg—There's good fishing at this 880-acre park; other facilities include picnic tables, grills, a playground, and boat ramps. Open daily sunrise to sunset. State Road 679; St. Petersburg 33730 (813-866-2484).

**PIER PLACE**, St. Petersburg—Fishermen line this half-mile public fishing pier, which also offers an excellent view of the yacht basin and Tampa Bay. The structure, which looks like an upside-down pyramid, houses a bait shop, restaurants, and several stores. Open daily. 800 Second Avenue Northeast; St. Petersburg 33701 (813-893-7437).

**WORLD'S CHICKEN PLUCKIN' CHAMPIONSHIP**, Spring Hill—It may be less popular than football, but this annual sporting event draws big crowds to watch chicken pluckers compete for new world records. Some of the performances here, in fact, have been included in the *Guinness Book of World Records*. Held the first Saturday in October. VFW Post No. 10209; 7504 Spring Hill Drive; Spring Hill 33526 (904-796-0398).

**DETROIT TIGERS SPRING TRAINING**, Lakeland—Detroit's finest pitchers and hitters get warmed up for the season from late February through early April, weekdays 10 A.M. to 1 P.M. Joker Marchant Stadium; 2301 Lakeland Hills Boulevard; Lakeland 33802 (813-682-1401).

**ORANGE CUP REGATTA**, Lake Hollingsworth—This Lakeland lake has been the site of so many powerboat speed records that it has come to be known as the "fastest lake in the world." The Orange Cup Regatta, held each March, features a day of high-speed powerboat races, waterskiing shows, and ski-jumping contests. Information: 813-683-3762.

**BOSTON RED SOX SPRING TRAINING**, Winter Haven—The atmosphere at spring warm-ups is usually casual enough to allow visitors to grab a few autographs from team favorites. Mid-February to late March, daily 10 A.M. to 1 P.M. Chain o' Lakes Park; Winter Haven 33880 (813-293-3900).

**WATER SKI MUSEUM AND HALL OF FAME**, Winter Haven—This is probably the world's most complete collection of information on this popular Florida sport. Various publications on the subject are indexed and maintained in the library, and the displays in the Hall of Champions showcase the style of various world champs. Open weekdays 10 A.M. to 5 P.M. 799 Overlook Drive; Winter Haven 33880 (813-324-2472).

**GOLDEN AGE GAMES**, Sanford—Senior citizens compete in 37 events, including bicycle races, bowling matches, archery, bridge, swimming, dancing, dominoes, and croquet, at this annual event held during the second week in November. Greater Sanford Chamber of Commerce; Jack Horner; Drawer CC; Sanford 32772-0868 (305-322-2212).

**DENMARK'S SPORTING GOODS STORE**, Orlando—Denmark's has a long-standing reputation for expert advice, which it doles out free of charge to any fisherman who calls for up-to-date tips on where they're biting. 141 North Magnolia Street; Orlando 32801 (305-425-2525).

**FLORIDA FREEWHEELERS**, Orlando—Different bicycle rides are scheduled each weekend along scenic trails in Orange, Seminole, and Lake counties. To join the experts' trips, you must be able to keep up a pace of 25 miles an hour; beginners' tours go at a much slower clip. Information: 683 Parati Lane; Orlando 32817 (305-647-5353 or 305-277-2693).

**LANGFORD CITY PARK**, Orlando—There's tennis, basketball, and other sports facilities at this 19-acre park and nature center. Other highlights include lovely walking trails. Open daily, dawn to dusk. 1808 East Central Street; Orlando 32800 (305-849-2283).

**MINNESOTA TWINS SPRING TRAINING**, Orlando—The Twins flee the bitter cold of Minnesota to start their preseason practices in mid-February; training lasts till late March, every weekday from 10 A.M. to 1 P.M. Tinker Field; Church Street and Tampa Avenue; Orlando 32755 (305-849-6346).

**WINDY ACRES POLO CLINICS**, Orlando—Here's a chance to sample the sport of kings, and you don't even need your own horse. Horses and mallets are provided and lessons are given by Norman Taylor. Spectators are also welcome. Saturdays noon to 2 P.M. Windy Acres, Damon Road off McCormick Road. Information: Norman Taylor; 333 McGuire Boulevard; Orlando 32803 (305-894-8221).

**SENIOR AEROBIC EXERCISE**, Orlando—Aerobic dance classes are offered for senior citizens by Orlando's Bureau of Recreation; 649 West Livingston Street; Orlando 32801 (305-849-2288).

**HOUSTON ASTROS SPRING TRAINING**, Cocoa—It's only fitting that the Astros get into shape for the summer season near the Kennedy Space Center. Practices run from mid-February through mid-March on weekdays from 10 A.M. to 1 P.M. Cocoa Stadium; Cocoa 32922 (305-632-5200).

**SURFING CONTESTS**, Cocoa Beach—Thousands of spectators convene for various surfing competitions held at the Canaveral Pier. The most important competitions are usually held during Easter and Labor Day weekends. There are also Hobie Cat regattas and other boat races. 401 Mead Avenue; Cocoa Beach 32931 (305-783-7549).

**MARINA PARK**, Titusville—Softball and football fields, children's playgrounds, a fishing area, and a public boat ramp are offered at this 12-acre park. Open dawn to dusk. Brevard County Recreation and Parks Division; 475 North Williams Avenue; Titusville 32796 (305-269-8170).

**SPACECOAST FREEWHEELER TEN-SPEED BIKE CLUB**, Merritt Island—Every weekend, 10-speed cyclists take off on rides of up to 50 miles. Some go along the beach and others trace countryside roads. Information: Irv Hayes; 166 North Atlantic Avenue; Cocoa Beach 32931 (305-783-1196).

**HARBOR CITY ROWING CLUB**, Melbourne—Rowing is a fairly popular sport in the Sunshine State, and spectators gather at the Melbourne Causeway on spring weekends to watch daylong events in various classes of races. 2900 Riverview Drive; Melbourne 32901 (305-723-1814).

---

## Travel Tip: FINDING THE LOWEST FLORIDA AIRFARE

It is an absolute necessity to comparison shop for flights to Florida. There is no more competitive market in America, and the airlines that serve Florida destinations from around the country compete in a constantly changing array of low promotional fares—many available even at the height of the traditional winter "high" tourist season. Watch local newspapers for promotional ads, and call each airline that serves your desired destination, stressing that you are interested in economy. (And remember that the lowest fares will almost always carry certain restrictions—advance purchase and payment, minimum or maximum lengths of stay, specific days when flying is prohibited, etc.—so be flexible). Having found an acceptable fare, pay for the ticket as soon as possible; this guarantees the price even if fares go up—as they can at any time—before your departure date. When it is necessary to take more than one flight to reach your destination, try to book them through only one airline. This will help keep connections as simple as possible.

# SOUTHERN FLORIDA

The major-league teams that couldn't find homes in the central segment of the state found perfect playing places down south. Some other highlights of the free sporting scene in southern Florida include polo matches at the Palm Beach Polo and Country Club, snorkeling trips in Biscayne Bay, and a couple of other purely pleasant surprises.

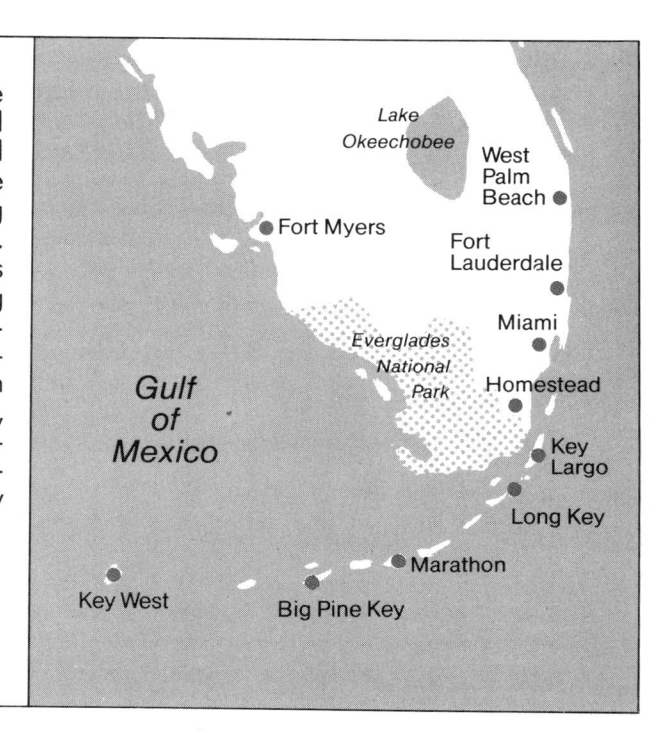

**PITTSBURGH PIRATES SPRING TRAINING**, Bradenton—Catch some rising stars and see the established sluggers loosen up and get into shape for the long season. Mid-February through mid-March on weekdays from 10 A.M. to 1 P.M. Pirate City; Bradenton (813-747-3031).

**CHICAGO WHITE SOX**, Sarasota—It's windy in the Windy City in winter, so the Sox head for sunnier and warmer climes to get into the proper frame of mind (and body) for the 6-month season ahead. Late February to mid-March. Payne Park; Ringling Boulevard and Washington Street; Sarasota (813-957-3191).

**KANSAS CITY ROYALS SPRING TRAINING**, Fort Myers—The Royals ramble down here from Missouri to get their game in gear. Mid-February through mid-March. Terry Park; Fort Myers (813-337-1624).

**SNORKELING**, Homestead—At Biscayne National Park, a particularly fine spot for underwater exploration, there's a free 2½-hour introductory snorkeling trip that offers a lesson in Biscayne Bay's ecology, as well as the sport of snorkeling. The trips are usually held Wednesdays, Saturdays, and Sundays, but call ahead for exact schedules. In addition, you must make a reservation on the day you wish to join a trip (between 9 A.M. and 10 A.M.) by calling 305-247-7275. At Convoy Point on Biscayne Bay; Box 1369; Homestead 33030.

**LOS ANGELES DODGERS SPRING TRAINING**, Vero Beach—We're not entirely sure why the Dodgers choose Florida as the place to train (after all, southern California isn't such a bad place in which to winter), but choose it they did, mostly because they've been coming here since the Dodgers' roots were firmly planted in Brooklyn. Late February through mid-March. Holman Stadium; Vero Beach (305-569-4900).

**TEXAS RANGERS SPRING TRAINING**, Pompano Beach–Even Texans head for the Sunshine State for their rites of spring. Late February through mid-March. Municipal Stadium; 1601 Northeast Eighth Street; Pompano Beach (305-943-4873).

**PALM BEACH POLO AND COUNTRY CLUB**, West Palm Beach—There's no royal fee charged to watch the sport of kings when you pull up for a match played on the backfields of the club. During the regular season, which runs from December through May and again in summer, polo matches played on these fields outside the main stadium are free. So bring a picnic lunch, pull up a patch of grass, and have a look at a sport that has been said to be as difficult as trying to play chess while bobsledding. Palm Beach Polo and Country Club; 13198 Forest Hill Boulevard; West Palm Beach 33414 (305-793-1113).

**MONTREAL EXPOS SPRING TRAINING**, West Palm Beach—Last year's stars, rookies with high hopes, and all the old standbys are getting ready for the long season ahead. Late February through mid-March. Municipal Stadium; West Palm Beach (305-684-6801).

**NEW YORK YANKEES SPRING TRAINING**, Fort Lauderdale—The Bronx Bombers head south for spring to get into the swing and, usually, the tabloid headlines. Mid-February through mid-March. Fort Lauderdale Stadium; 5301 Northwest 12th Avenue; Fort Lauderdale (305-776-1921).

**COLUMBUS DAY SAILBOAT REGATTA**, Coconut Grove—The annual regatta is quite a spectacle, with a rainbow of sails heading off in a race for the finish. One of the best spots for spectators is at Alice Wainwright Park; 2845 Brickell Avenue; Coconut Grove (305-579-6900).

**THE BIKE TRAIL**, Coconut Grove—There is an ever-growing number of scenic bike trails throughout the southern portion of the state, but one particularly long and beautiful route runs from the Coconut Grove area of Miami, through the estates of Coral Gables, by the Matheson Hammock and the Fairchild Tropical Gardens. For those who prefer to enjoy the sport of bicycling from a spectator's point of view, most cities and towns hold bike races and tours during the year. For information about local activities, contact the Chamber of Commerce in the area you're visiting (see **INFORMATION SOURCES**).

**BALTIMORE ORIOLES SPRING TRAINING**, Miami—Baltimore's baseball team follows the other teams migrating south for spring workouts. Late February through mid-March. Miami Stadium; 2301 Northwest Tenth Avenue; Miami (305-635-5395).

**FISHING**—Fleets of charter boats happily take fishermen out for the catch, but unhappily take big bites out of their wallets, too. Fear not. No license is required for saltwater fishing, and you can usually do just as well from the many piers, jetties, or bridges as you can from a boat. Many of the bridges are equipped with catwalks. An especially good spot is the Card Sound Bridge on the Dade County–Monroe County line. (The Overseas Highway that leads to the Keys also has many good fishing bridges.) For additional information about fishing in Florida contact the Florida Department of Natural Resources; 3900 Commonwealth Boulevard; Tallahassee 32303 (904-488-7326).

**SHUFFLEBOARD**—Although the Shuffleboard Hall of Fame is in central Florida, the sport's popularity extends down south. Courts are located in a wide variety of places, including municipal parks, where they are often sheltered by a roof to shade players or protect them from frequent afternoon thunderstorms. Despite its image as the sport of the retired set, there's a lot of skill and energy required to play the game well. Sarasota, Fort Myers, Port Charlotte, Hollywood, and Miami have many free courts open to the public. Contact their respective parks departments for more information.

---

## *Travel Tip* · BIKING SAFETY

Florida bicycle riders are required to follow the same rules and regulations as motor vehicle drivers. Stay to the right side of the road. Ride no more than 2 abreast, or single file where traffic is heavy. Keep 3 bike lengths between you and the bike in front. Stay alert to potential danger spots, such as potholes, wet surfaces, sand, or gravel. Wear bright clothing and a helmet. Equip your bike—and your body—with reflectors for night riding.

SAVVY TRAVELER

# INDUSTRIAL TOURS

**F**lorida is not known as an industrial state and, in fact, its largest commercial industry is tourism. But the state hasn't been entirely overlooked during the past 15 years by the multitude of manufacturers building plants across the Sunbelt, and as a result Florida's business community has grown apace. In fact, several major corporations have set up their world headquarters in the state, particularly in Central Florida. Harcourt Brace Jovanovich, Westinghouse, and Martin Marietta all call Orlando home.

That's the good news, because the reigning philosophy of Florida manufacturers seems to have been that plant tours and public access were good for everybody. There has been, in the past, a rich variety of enterprises and companies to visit. The bad news is that in the most recent years industrial firms have become more security conscious, and in the process a lot of very interesting factory tours have been closed.

But that's not the end of the story. There are still quite a number of companies around the state that run regular tours of their premises, and the range is rather impressive—vineyards, newspapers, breweries, even the Tupperware factory in Orlando. These tours offer a view of Florida that most visitors rarely see—a state at work. Tourists can get an insight into what it's like to live and work in Florida by participating in one of these tours. The reason that most people don't see this side of the Sunshine State is because they don't know how to go about it. Some of the companies listed on the following pages offer scheduled tours while others require advance reservations. It is probably a wise idea to call before heading out to confirm hours and tour information.

# NORTHERN FLORIDA

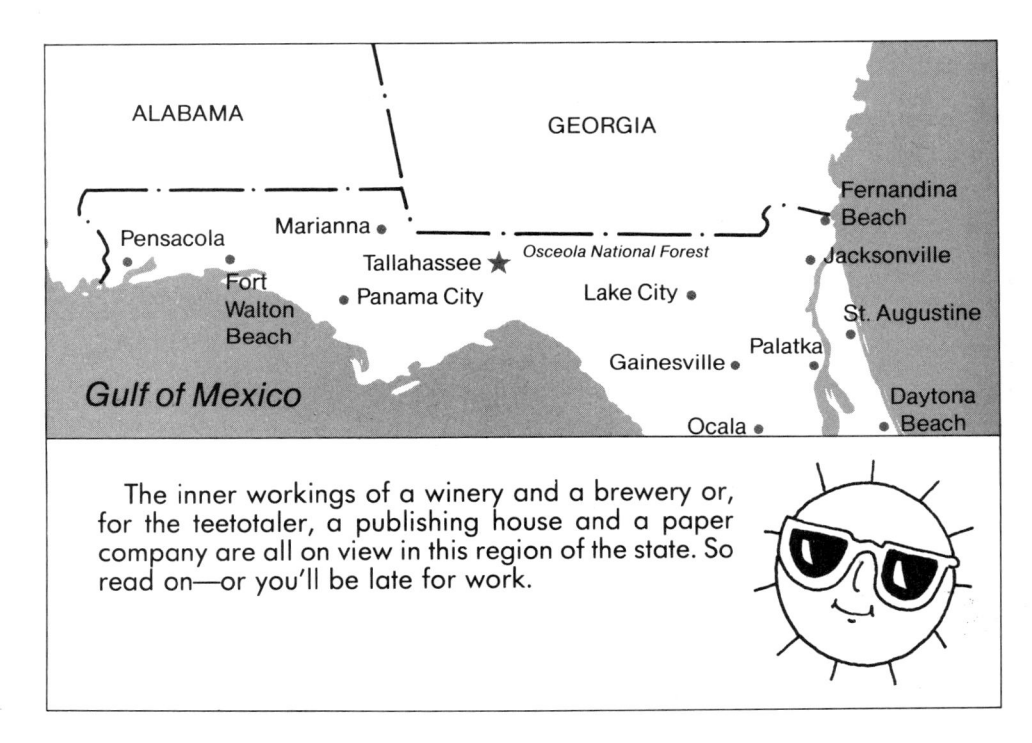

The inner workings of a winery and a brewery or, for the teetotaler, a publishing house and a paper company are all on view in this region of the state. So read on—or you'll be late for work.

**ALAQUA WINERY**, Freeport—Florida is not exactly famous for growing wine grapes, but there are a couple of spots where vines do quite well. Alaqua is located about 15 miles northeast of Niceville and produces 10 different varieties of wine. Tours and tastings are offered Wednesdays through Saturdays 10 A.M. to 5 P.M.; Sundays 1 P.M. to 5 P.M. Route 1; Box 97C4; Freeport 32439 (904-835-2644).

**THE FLORIDA PUBLISHING COMPANY**, Jacksonville—Tours for groups of from 10 to 60 can be arranged at this plant, which prints both the *Florida Times Union* and the *Jacksonville Journal*. Monday through Thursday mornings. One Riverside Avenue; Jacksonville 32207 (904-359-4111).

**ANHEUSER-BUSCH BREWERY**, Jacksonville—Nearly 7 million barrels of foamy stuff are produced here each year. Self-guided tours can be taken Mondays through Fridays 9:30 A.M. to 3:30 P.M. Guided tours are conducted on the hour from 10 A.M. to 3 P.M. There's also a gift shop. 111 Busch Drive; Jacksonville 32218 (904-751-0700).

**LIBERTY HOMES, INC.,** Ocala—To some they're RVs, to others mobile homes. This plant produces single-wide and double-wide models. Saturday tours of the factory can be arranged by appointment only. 495 Oak Road; Ocala 32670 (904-687-4141).

**ST. JOE PAPER COMPANY,** Port St. Joe—On the Gulf Coast, about 35 miles south of Panama City Beach, this factory produces paper from some 80,000 acres of surrounding timberland. Tours are available on request. Box 190; Port St. Joe 32456 (904-227-1171).

# CENTRAL FLORIDA

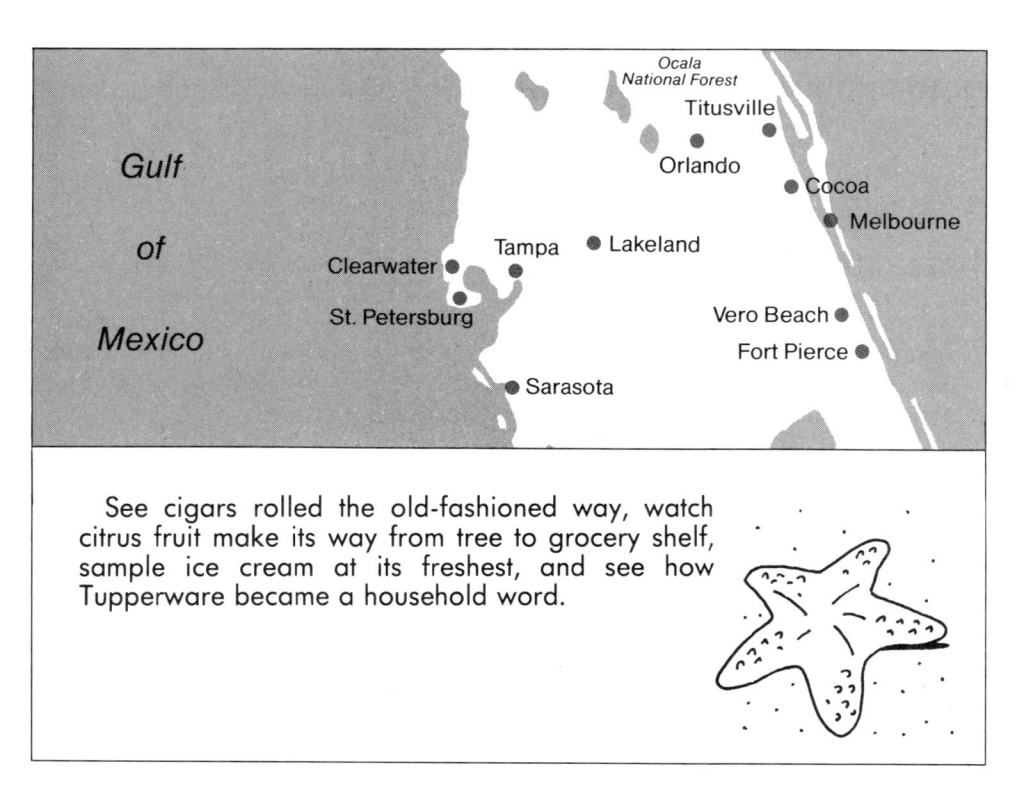

See cigars rolled the old-fashioned way, watch citrus fruit make its way from tree to grocery shelf, sample ice cream at its freshest, and see how Tupperware became a household word.

**FLORIDA POWER CORPORATION,** St. Petersburg—Several of the corporation's power facilities are open for group tours. Interested visitors should contact the company two weeks in advance. Florida Power Corporation; Public Information Department; Box 14042; St. Petersburg 33733 (813-866-5151).

**PABST BREWERY**, Tampa—Learn the art of making suds. Tours, followed by tastings (soft drinks for nonimbibers), are offered Mondays through Fridays every half hour from 10 A.M. to 3 P.M. 11111 North 30th Street; Box 9217; Tampa 33674 (813-971-7070).

**WINES OF ST. AUGUSTINE**, Ybor City—One of the more arcane products created at this winery is an orange-flavored wine. Tours are offered weekdays from 2 P.M. to 4 P.M. 8th Avenue and 13th Street; Ybor City 33605 (813-273-0070).

**VILLAZON AND COMPANY**, Tampa—Cigarmaking has become more or less mechanized in recent years, but at this traditional old factory visitors can see stogies being rolled and filled both by machine and by the old-fashioned hand method. Tours are available weekdays at 9:30 A.M. and at 2:30 P.M. The plant is closed from July 1 through 14 and from December 20 through January 15. 3104 North Armenia Street; Tampa 33607 (813-879-2291).

**DONALD DUCK CITRUS WORLD**, Lake Wales—The processing of citrus fruit, from tree to grocery store, is the subject of a 20-minute film at this facility in the heart of citrus country. There are also free tastings. Open Mondays through Fridays 9:30 A.M. to 3:30 P.M. from December through March. Highway 27 North; Lake Wales 33853 (813-676-1411).

**INTERNATIONAL MINERALS AND CHEMICAL CORPORATION, INC.**, Lakeland—Tours, designed for people in agriculture-related businesses, demonstrate the way in which phosphate is mined and processed. For information contact Joe Shaw; Manger of Business and Community Relations; International Minerals and Chemical Corporation, Inc.; Lakeland 33807 (813-646-8583).

**PUBLIX MILK AND ICE CREAM PLANT**, Lakeland—One of the state's largest supermarket chains opens its ice cream and milk factory. Refreshments are served after the tour. Yummy! Call or write to arrange a visit. Publix; 3045 New Tampa Highway; Lakeland 33802 (813-688-7150).

**DAVIDSON OF DUNDEE**—When plain citrus fruit in its natural state gets tiring, Davidson's creates candies made from oranges, grapefruits, lemons, and combinations thereof. For those with an incurable sweet tooth, there's also some delicious peanut butter fudge and a variety of chocolates. Free samples are offered after the tour. Open Mondays through Saturdays 8 A.M. to 6 P.M.; Sundays 9 A.M. to 6 P.M. Highway 27; Box 800; Dundee 33838 (813-439-2284).

**TUPPERWARE WORLD HEADQUARTERS**, Orlando—The plant that launched a thousand house parties is located in a campuslike setting, surrounded by lakes and gardens. Tours, which last 20 to 30 minutes, take in a pictorial display of the Tupperware manufacturing process and a gallery of food containers representing the evolution of food storage from ancient times to the present. Open Mondays through Fridays 9 A.M. to 4 P.M. U.S. Highway 441; Box 2353; Orlando 32802 (305-847-3111).

**CENTRAL FLORIDA REGIONAL HOSPITAL**, Sanford—Tours conducted here are tailored to the special interests of each group. One area of particular interest is the hospital's poison plant garden (used for research), where visitors find that many of Florida's most common plants are quite poisonous. Go behind the scenes to get an idea of how a hospital is run. Physical therapy rooms are among the stops along the way. Free refreshments are available after the tour. 1401 West Seminole Boulevard; Sanford 32771 (305-321-4500, ext. 647).

**HALE INDIAN RIVER GROVES**, Wabasso—Another look at Florida's giant citrus industry at this plant, about 20 miles south of Melbourne. Free tastings. Open Mondays through Fridays 7:30 A.M. to 6 P.M. Indian River Plaza; Wabasso 32970 (305-589-4334).

## *Travel Tip:* PACKING POINTERS

The idea is to get everything into the suitcase and out again with as few wrinkles as possible. Put heavy items on the bottom toward the hinges of the suitcase so that they do not wrinkle other clothes. Candidates for the bottom layer include shoes (stuff them with small items to save space), toiletry kit, handbags (stuff them to help keep their shape), and alarm clock. Fill out this layer with things that will not wrinkle or will not matter if they do, such as socks, bathing suit, and underwear.

If you get this first, heavy layer as smooth as possible with the fill-ins, you will have a shelf for the next layer of the more easily wrinkled items like slacks, jackets, shirts, dresses, and skirts. These should be buttoned or zipped and laid along the whole width of the suitcase, with as little folding a possible. When you do need to make a fold, do it on a crease (as with pants), along a seam in the fabric, or in a place where it will not show, such as shirttails. Alternate each piece of clothing, using one side of the suitcase, then the other, to make the layers as flat as possible. You'll be surprised how many extra pieces of clothing will fit in a suitcase.

On the top layer put the things you will want at once: nightclothes, an umbrella or raincoat, or a sweater. With men's two-suiter suitcases, follow the same procedure. Then place jackets on hangers, straighten them out, and leave them unbuttoned. If they are too wide for the suitcase, fold lengthwise down the middle, straighten the shoulders, and fold the sleeves in along the seam.

# SOUTHERN FLORIDA

Many Southern Florida plants and factories have discontinued tours, but it is still possible to watch the teams of professionals who put the *Miami Herald* and the *Palm Beach Post and Times* on the newsstands each day.

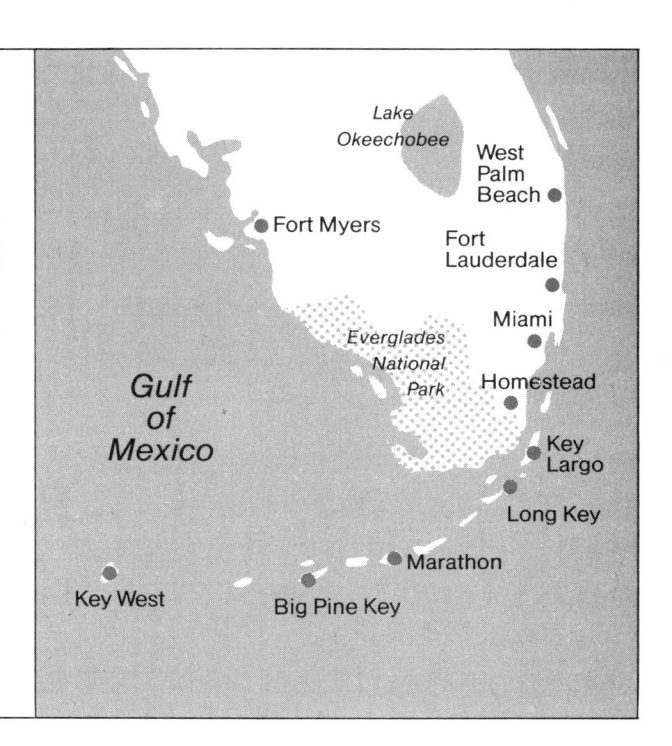

**SHELL FACTORY**, Fort Myers—See shells cleaned, polished, and made into lamps, ashtrays, and other decorative items. The factory also has one of the world's largest shell and coral collections. Tours are offered weekdays every hour on the hour from 10 A.M. to 6 P.M. 2787 Tamiami Trail; North Fort Myers 33902 (813-995-2141).

**PALM BEACH POST AND TIMES**, West Palm Beach—The newsroom, composing room, pressroom, and plate-making areas are included on tours that last about an hour and are offered on Thursdays and Fridays from 9 A.M. to 3 P.M. Reservations must be made in advance. 2751 South Dixie Highway; West Palm Beach 33405 (305-837-4272).

**THE MIAMI HERALD**—Florida's most widely read newspaper is headquartered in a bayside building that was once called the Taj Mahal of journalism. A free tour takes in all major departments. Mondays, Wednesdays, and Fridays 10 A.M. and 2 P.M. 1 Herald Plaza; Miami 33101 (305-376-2909).

# LIBRARIES, COLLEGES, AND UNIVERSITIES

Some of Florida's colleges and universities are set in such lovely surroundings that it's a wonder students ever manage to get to class at all. There are campuses where just strolling around the grounds is a pleasure in itself, and others where the architecture is the compelling attraction. And many Florida schools have interesting museums, galleries, and well-stocked libraries that are open to students and the general public alike. It would probably surprise most travelers to learn that the world's largest single collection of Frank Lloyd Wright-designed buildings is on the campus of one of Central Florida's colleges. And there's one college with its very own zoo.

Along with its universities, visitors should pay special attention to Florida's extensive public library system, where everything from the latest John D. MacDonald thriller to storytelling hours for toddlers can be found at no cost. With programs of lectures, films, and special exhibitions, Florida's local libraries can add immeasurably to a trip through the state. And when combined with stops at the universities along the way, a trip to Florida can be an education in itself.

# NORTHERN FLORIDA

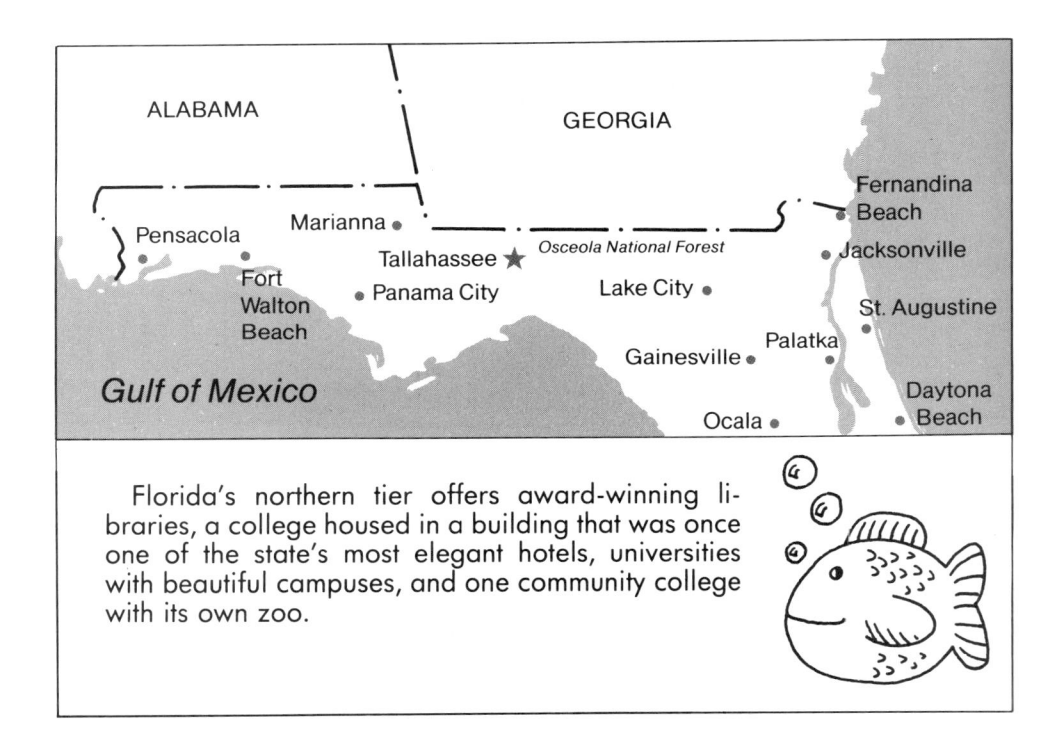

```
ALABAMA          GEORGIA
                                        Fernandina
                                        Beach
    Pensacola  Marianna
               Tallahassee ★  Osceola National Forest    Jacksonville
       Fort    Panama City      Lake City
       Walton                                  St. Augustine
       Beach
                              Gainesville  Palatka
Gulf of Mexico                                        Daytona
                                    Ocala             Beach
```

Florida's northern tier offers award-winning libraries, a college housed in a building that was once one of the state's most elegant hotels, universities with beautiful campuses, and one community college with its own zoo.

**WEST FLORIDA REGIONAL LIBRARY**, Pensacola—The major attraction is a large genealogy center, plus a section on local history. Open Mondays through Thursdays 8 A.M. to 8 P.M.; Fridays and Saturdays 8 A.M. to 5 P.M. 200 West Gregory Street; Pensacola 32501 (904-438-5479).

**NORTHWEST REGIONAL LIBRARY**, Panama City—There is a main branch, plus 12 affiliates throughout Bay County and the surrounding area. Open Mondays through Wednesdays 10 A.M. to 8 P.M.; Thursdays and Fridays 10 A.M. to 5 P.M.; Saturdays 11 A.M. to 3 P.M. 25 West Government Street; Panama City 32401 (904-785-3457).

**FLORIDA STATE UNIVERSITY**, Tallahassee—Northern Florida's long-standing educational institution was founded back in 1857. The Florida State Conference Center, which draws conventions and conferences from all over the world, is a recent addition to the campus. Copeland Street at College Avenue; Tallahassee 32611 (904-392-3261).

**FLORIDA A & M UNIVERSITY**, Tallahassee—Founded in 1887, this predominantly black institution houses the Black Archives and Research Center. South Martin Luther King Boulevard; Tallahassee 32307 (904-599-3000).

**UNIVERSITY OF FLORIDA**, Gainesville—Founded in 1853, the main campus spreads over 2,000 acres, with a 72,000-seat football stadium and the 3.6-acre O'Connell Center for student and community activities. Some 34,000 students attend classes in 20 different colleges within the university. 13th Street and University Avenue; Gainesville 32611 (904-392-3261).

**SANTA FE COMMUNITY COLLEGE**, Gainesville—An 8-acre zoo that's home for a great many exotic South American animals—and which is used as an on-campus teaching facility—is open to the public free of charge. Also of interest is the Santa Fe Community College Community Gallery of Art, which sometimes hosts traveling exhibits from such sources as the Smithsonian Institution and the National Gallery of Art. 3000 Northwest 83rd Street; Gainesville 32602 (904-395-5000).

**CENTRAL FLORIDA REGIONAL LIBRARY**, Ocala—You'll know you're deep in Florida's horse country when you visit the main Osceola Avenue branch, with its John Haxton Wallace Collection, a resource that offers information on the raising, riding, and breeding of horses—as well as pithy bits of horsey history. There are 15 affiliate libraries around the county. The main branch is open Mondays through Thursdays 9 A.M. to 9 P.M.; Fridays and Saturdays 9 A.M. to 6 P.M. 15 Southeast Osceola Avenue; Ocala 32670 (904-629-8551). For hours at the other branches, call the main library.

**JACKSONVILLE PUBLIC LIBRARY**—Includes the main library in downtown Jacksonville, plus 12 branches scattered around the city. The main branch features a mezzanine gallery where works by local artists are on display, and there's also a new Genealogy and Florida Collections room. Another highlight is the Frederick Delius collection; the composer was a longtime Jacksonville resident. Open Mondays through Fridays 9 A.M. to 9 P.M.; Saturdays 9 A.M. to 6 P.M. 122 North Ocean Street; Jacksonville 32202 (904-633-6870). For details about the other branches, contact the main library.

**UNIVERSITY OF NORTH FLORIDA**, Jacksonville—Set on an attractive, wooded, 1,000-acre campus, this university has 12 miles of nature trails, plus a nature and wildlife preserve. It recently won a 4-year operating status from the Florida Board of Regents. 4567 St. John Bluff Road South; Jacksonville 32216 (904-646-2450).

**JACKSONVILLE UNIVERSITY**—A beautiful waterfront campus, where the restored home of composer Frederick Delius can be visited. 2800 University Boulevard North; Jacksonville 32211 (904-744-3950).

**FLAGLER COLLEGE**, St. Augustine—Students here are constantly running into tourists because Flagler College, housed in what was once the elegant Hotel Ponce de Leon, built by tourism pioneer Henry Flagler, is one of St. Augustine's most popular tourist attractions. The ornate ceiling of the college's rotunda is particularly attractive. 74 King Street; St. Augustine 32085 (904-829-6481).

**VOLUSIA COUNTY PUBLIC LIBRARIES**, Daytona Beach—This library system (13 branches in all) has won several awards for community involvement programs, including volunteer services, endowment drives, and computer classes. The works of local artists are on display. Open Mondays, Fridays, and Saturdays 9 A.M. to 5 P.M.; Tuesdays, Wednesdays, and Thursdays 9 A.M. to 9 P.M. City Island; Daytona Beach 32014 (904-252-8374).

# CENTRAL FLORIDA

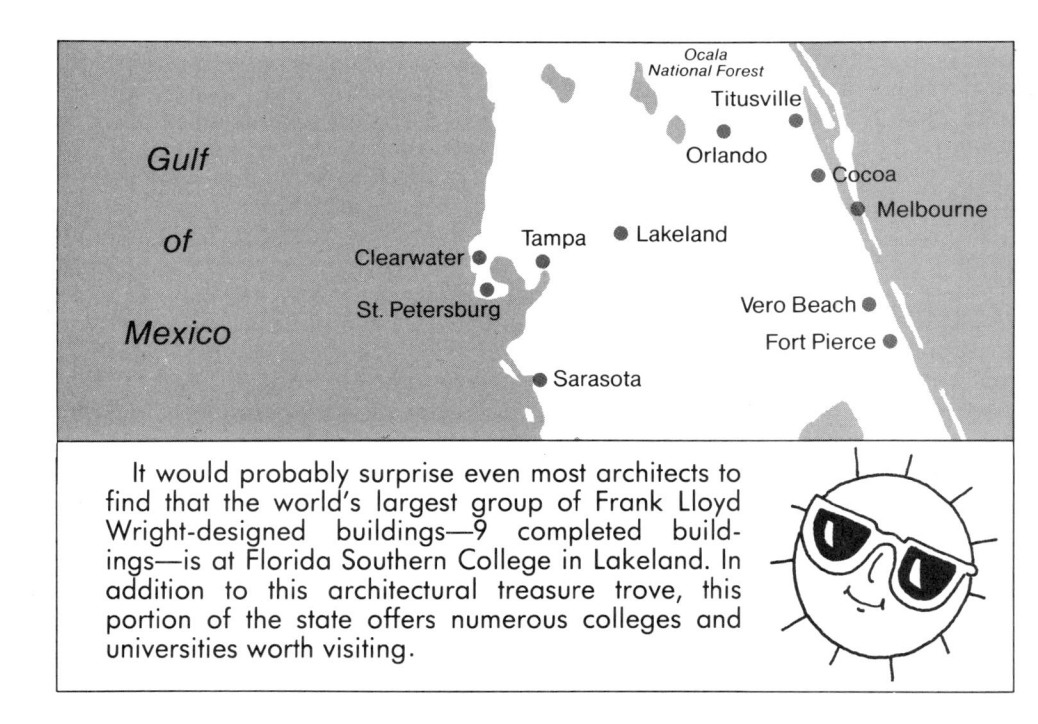

It would probably surprise even most architects to find that the world's largest group of Frank Lloyd Wright-designed buildings—9 completed buildings—is at Florida Southern College in Lakeland. In addition to this architectural treasure trove, this portion of the state offers numerous colleges and universities worth visiting.

**CLEARWATER PUBLIC LIBRARY SYSTEM**—More than half a million books, records, and art prints were borrowed from the 3 libraries in Clearwater last year. Special programs and films complete the wide menu of services. The main branch is at 100 North Osceola Avenue; Clearwater 33515 (813-462-6800). Open Mondays through Wednesdays 9 A.M. to 9 P.M.; Thursdays through Saturdays 9 A.M. to 5 P.M.; closed Sundays and holidays. There are also branches on Beach Street and North Greenwood Street, and another soon to open on Drew Street. Call the main branch for details.

**ST. PETERSBURG LIBRARY**—Books, films, videocassettes, and special senior citizen programs are among the services offered. Open Mondays through Thursdays 9 A.M. to 9 P.M.; Fridays and Saturdays 9 A.M. to 5:30 P.M.; closed Sundays and holidays. 3745 9th Avenue North; St. Petersburg 33713 (813-893-7724).

**TAMPA-HILLSBOROUGH COUNTY PUBLIC LIBRARY SYSTEM**—A wide assortment of audiovisual materials, as well as a series of special programs, are popular features of the county's extensive library system, which includes the large Central Library in downtown Tampa plus 13 branches. The Central Library is located at 900 North Ashley Street; Tampa 33602 (813-223-8945). Open Mondays through Thursdays 9 A.M. to 9 P.M.; Fridays 9 A.M. to 6 P.M.; Saturdays 9 A.M. to 5 P.M.; closed Sundays and holidays. Other locations include Ybor City, West Tampa, Seminole, East Gate, Brandon, Riverview, Ruskin, Peninsula, Port Tampa, Citrus Park–Keystone, Lutz, North Tampa, and West Gate. Specific locations, hours, and special facilities at each branch are available from the main library, as is "It's Your Library," a concise pamphlet describing the library's various operations and services.

**UNIVERSITY OF SOUTH FLORIDA**, Tampa—Various campus art galleries house original works, and the university's series of special programs and lectures are open to the public free of charge. 4202 East Fowler Avenue; Tampa 33620 (813-974-2848).

**FLORIDA SOUTHERN COLLEGE**, Lakeland—For architecture buffs (and even the simply curious) this campus boasts 9 Frank Lloyd Wright–designed buildings, the largest collection in any one place in the world. In the late 1930s, the then-president of FSC, Lud Spivey, challenged Wright, a friend of his, to design the first truly American university campus. Construction began late in 1938 and continued until the late 1950s, when Wright was quite ill. The most famous building, Annie Pfeiffer Chapel (one of two chapels), was completed in 1941. In addition to the chapels, Wright designed a library, an administration building, 3 small seminar buildings, the Ordway Arts Complex, and the Polk Science Building. Wright's apprentices, however, continued the theme of his designs—integrating the landscape and local building materials into the designs—and a dozen additional buildings have been erected since Wright's death. Self-guided walking-tour brochures are available. Plan to allot at least an hour to see it all. Open weekdays 8 A.M. to 5 P.M. Admissions Office; Lakeland 33802 (813-680-4116).

**ORANGE COUNTY LIBRARY SYSTEM**, Orlando—The 10 libraries have a combined collection of almost a million books, including publications using large-print. Other services include recordings, periodicals, pamphlets, films, framed art reproductions, talking books for the blind, and VHS videocassettes. There's also a wide variety of other reference materials. The main library, which was recently expanded, is at 101 East Central Boulevard; Orlando 32801 (305-425-4694). Open Mondays through Fridays 9 A.M. to 9 P.M.; Saturdays 9 A.M. to 6 P.M.; Sundays 1 P.M. to 5 P.M.; closed holidays. Call the main library for information about the library system.

**SAINT LEO COLLEGE**—A warm blend of Spanish baroque and contemporary architecture is reflected at this 4-year Catholic liberal arts institution, founded almost 100 years ago by the Order of Saint Benedict. The quiet, restful campus has orange groves and a mile-wide, spring-fed lake. Guided tours can be arranged, but the grounds invite leisurely strolls and the public is welcome. There are also daily masses during the school year. Open daily. To reach the campus take State Road 50 west to Interstate 75 south and exit at Route 52 east. The college is about 4 miles down the road. Admission Office; Box 2008; Saint Leo 33574 (904-588-8283).

**UNIVERSITY OF CENTRAL FLORIDA**, Orlando—Visitors are welcome to browse through the university library, which features displays and exhibits reflecting interests and achievements of the college community. There are also changing displays in the art department, and free student concerts (call 305-275-2869 for exact dates and times). Open Mondays through Thursdays 7 A.M. to 7 P.M.; Fridays 7 A.M. to 5 P.M.; Saturdays 10 A.M. to 5 P.M.; and Sundays 11 A.M. to 2 P.M. Office of Public Affairs; Box 25000; Orlando 32816 (305-275-2504).

**VALENCIA COMMUNITY COLLEGE**, Orlando—The wide variety of free offerings includes a national issues forum, taped information on more than 200 careers, individual career counseling, programs on parenting and infant care, a fitness trail, tennis courts, programs for the blind, and tuition-free courses for students over 55 years of age. Director of Communications; Box 3028; Orlando 32802 (305-299-5000, ext. 3368).

**WINTER PARK PUBLIC LIBRARY**—Fiction, nonfiction, newspapers, and periodicals to be checked out or read at the library. Open Mondays and Wednesdays 9:30 A.M. to 9 P.M.; Tuesdays, Thursdays, and Fridays 9 A.M. to 6 P.M.; Saturdays 9:30 A.M. to 5 P.M.; Sundays 1 P.M. to 5 P.M.; closed holidays. 460 East New England Avenue; Winter Park 32789 (305-647-1638).

**BREVARD COUNTY LIBRARIES**—There are more than a half-million volumes on the shelves of the Brevard County Library System's facilities. The libraries are tied by computer to other collections throughout the United States. There is a wide range of periodicals, as well as large-print books, records, films, projectors, videotape equipment, craft programs, children's events, and special displays. Here are some of the branches and their particular specialties:

**Cape Canaveral:** Special features include senior citizen services and a large collection of cookbooks. Open Mondays through Thursdays 9:30 A.M. to 6 P.M.; Fridays 9:30 A.M. to 5 P.M. 211 Carolyn Street; Cape Canaveral 32920 (305-783-1456).

**Cocoa:** Noted holdings include paintings, puzzles, records and audio cassettes, and genealogy books. Open Mondays through Wednesdays 9 A.M. to 9 P.M.; Thursdays through Saturdays 9 A.M. to 5 P.M. 430 Delannoy Avenue; Cocoa 32922 (305-636-7323).

**Cocoa Beach:** Art, music, and literature, plus Instamatic cameras for loan. Open Mondays through Wednesdays 10 A.M. to 9 P.M.; Tuesdays and Thursdays 10 A.M. to 6 P.M.; Saturdays and Sundays 10 A.M. to 5 P.M. 55 South Brevard Avenue; Cocoa Beach 32931 (305-783-7350).

**Melbourne:** Largest book collection in the system. Also records, audio cassettes, art prints, and the largest genealogy collection in the county. Open Mondays, Fridays, and Saturdays 8:30 A.M. to 5 P.M.; Tuesdays, Wednesdays, and Thursdays 8:30 A.M. to 9 P.M. 540 East Fee Avenue; Melbourne 32901 (305-723-0611).

**Palm Bay:** Children's services and special literacy programs are offered. Open Mondays, Tuesdays, and Thursdays 10 A.M. to 8:30 P.M.; Wednesdays and Fridays 9 A.M. to 5 P.M.; Saturdays 10 A.M. to 4 P.M. 1520 Port Malabar Boulevard Northeast; Palm Bay 32905 (305-725-1456).

**Satellite Beach:** Crafts programs and special services for the deaf. Open Mondays, Tuesdays, and Thursdays 9 A.M. to 9 P.M.; Wednesdays and Fridays 9 A.M. to 5 P.M.; Saturdays 10 A.M. to 2 P.M. 565 Cassia Boulevard; Satellite Beach 32937 (305-773-9411).

---

## *Travel Tip:* REDUCING RESTAURANT BILLS

Eating away from home is costly. To save pennies here and there, eat some meals in cafeterias rather than in restaurants with table service, where individual dishes are sure to cost more. But don't give up fancier places altogether; remember that very often entrées in good restaurants cost less at lunch than at dinner. And considering the bounty of fresh vegetables and fruits available at roadsides across Florida, no mealtime alternative is more attractive for the traveling family than an impromptu picnic. Pick up sandwich fixings along the way and stop at one of the state's great parks for lunch.

# SOUTHERN FLORIDA

Southern Florida's universities are known for their museums (see **MUSEUMS and GALLERIES** chapter), but music and dance performances as well as extensive library holdings are also part of the school scene here. In addition, the Broward County Library System has a new $39 million main library in downtown Fort Lauderdale that's both architecturally and intellectually impressive.

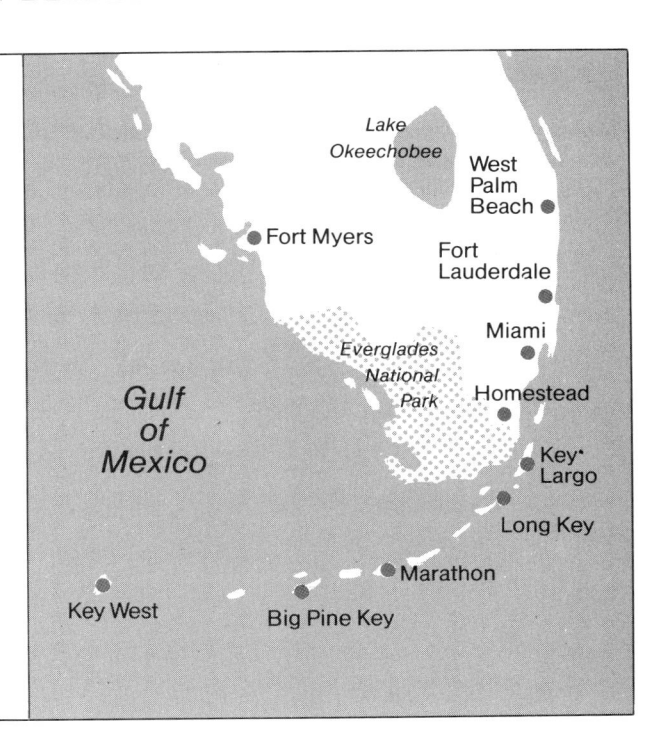

**UNIVERSITY OF MIAMI**—The School of Music here offers more than 200 concerts each year, and many of them are free. Performances are held at the modern Gusman Concert Hall. University of Miami Main Campus; South Dixie Highway; Coral Gables 33124 (305-284-5500).

**PORT CHARLOTTE CULTURAL CENTER**—More than 10,000 older citizens are enrolled in courses at this educational facility, where the campus motto is "If you can't find something to interest you here, check your pulse." The center is more commonly referred to as Port Charlotte U. Small fees are charged for most classes, but free offerings include dancing lessons, a library with more than 35,000 books, and a paperback book exchange. 2280 Aaron Street; Port Charlotte 33952 (813-625-4175).

**BROWARD COUNTY LIBRARY SYSTEM**—The new $39 million main library, located in downtown Fort Lauderdale, is a 6-story building that's winning accolades for its architectural innovation. The front of the structure has a facade of tiered glass and terraces that face a tiled plaza, which includes a reflecting pool and a small park. The first floor of the library has facilities for the blind and physically handicapped, plus a small section of best-sellers and a 300-seat auditorium. There are departments of business science and technology, fine arts, and government documents, and a sophisticated electronic system that includes a computerized interlibrary loan program and telephone reference services. The library is open Mondays and Thursdays noon to 9 P.M.; Tuesdays and Wednesdays 10 A.M. to 9 P.M.; Fridays and Saturdays 9 A.M. to 5 P.M.; and Sundays 1 P.M. to 5 P.M. There are also 22 branches, some of which have recently been renovated. The main library is located at 100 South Andrews Avenue; Fort Lauderdale 33301 (305-357-7444). For information about the other branches, call the main library.

## LIBRARY CARDS FOR VISITORS

By registering at any local library, visitors staying at least a week in a specific Florida county can obtain a County Library System courtesy card, good for the length of the visit at any branch library within the county's system. Cards take at least a week to process (and require proof of permanent residence and local address), but 2 books may be checked out at the time of application. Anyone staying in Florida for a year or longer is eligible for a permanent library card.

### Travel Tip · TRANSPORTATION: WAYS AND MEANS

A major factor in any travel budget is the means by which one gets to and around one's destination. Should you drive your own car or rent one, or take a bus, train, or plane? Some things to consider before deciding: the cost of driving based on the distance to be covered, your car's mileage average, current gasoline prices, and the cost of lodging and food en route.

If you decide to fly or take the train or bus, will you need to rent a car after arrival? Local chambers of commerce are good sources for information on the quality and frequency of local transportation, as well as the proximity of your accommodations to recreational facilities and shopping areas. It's not impossible that your own two feet will be all you'll need.

# BACK TO SCHOOL FOR FREE

The Florida legislature recently passed a law that may have older citizens flocking back to college—without charge. Florida residents 65 and over can now enroll in state universities and colleges without paying any fees, provided that the class they've chosen has at least 20 fee-paying students already enrolled, and if the course is being taken on a noncredit basis. For additional information about this enticing state-sponsored program, contact Office of the Registrar; Tigert Hall; Room 34; University of Florida; Gainesville 32611 (904-392-3261).

## Travel Tip: LOST TRAVELER'S CHECKS

Traveler's checks, accepted throughout Florida even in the tiniest towns and establishments, can nip travel-cash troubles in the bud because, unlike money, lost or stolen checks are refundable. Keep check numbers separate from the checks, so that in the event of their disappearance you can call with exact information, avoiding complications and ensuring a quick refund. (And remember that refund policies vary from company to company; ask about procedures and refund time before purchasing checks.)

Here are emergency and refund request numbers to America's major traveler's checks companies:

American Express—800-221-7282
Bank of America—800-227-3460
Citicorp—800-645-6556
Thomas Cook—800-223-7373
MasterCard—800-223-9920
Visa—800-227-6811

## Travel Tip: HEALTH PROBLEMS?

Keep prescriptions and medical insurance I.D. card with you at all times, as well as a brief summary of your medical history and present condition, a list of drugs to which you are allergic, and your personal doctor's name, address, and telephone number. If you have heart problems, consider carrying your most recent electrocardiogram.

# MILITARY AND GOVERNMENT SITES

**F**lorida is the site of several important naval and air force bases, from Pensacola in the north to Homestead in the south, and many of these are not only open to the public, but offer tours that allow a glimpse of the military in action—everything from test pilots putting new planes through their paces to dogs being trained for military duty. A visit to one of these facilities might include a look at the world's only climatic hangar, a walk around a giant aircraft carrier, or a chance to see how a flight simulator works. Note, however, that most military bases require advance reservations for tours, so be sure to plan ahead to avoid disappointment.

There are also quite a few interesting state and local government facilities where formal, free tours can reveal state-of-the-art energy-saving buildings, the oldest operating courthouse in the state, and the state capitol in Tallahassee, which sits quite appropriately on the city's highest hill. One very interesting government outpost is the Federal Aviation Administration's air traffic control facility near Jacksonville. It is one of the nation's major centers and tours allow visitors a look at controllers at work.

# NORTHERN FLORIDA

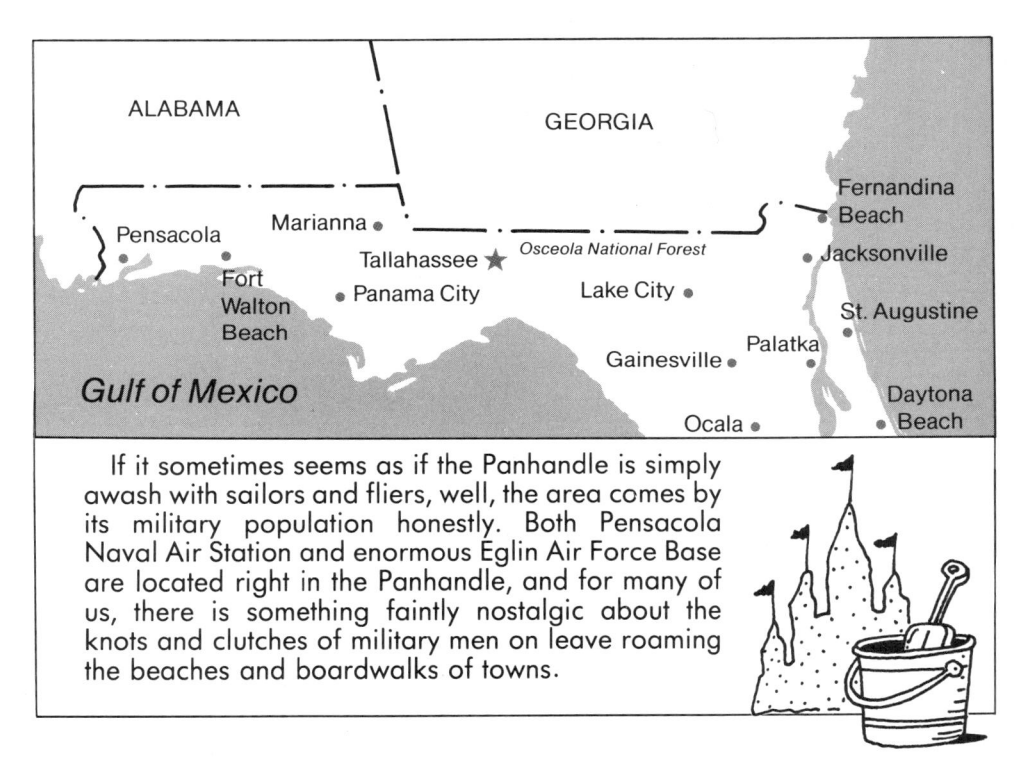

If it sometimes seems as if the Panhandle is simply awash with sailors and fliers, well, the area comes by its military population honestly. Both Pensacola Naval Air Station and enormous Eglin Air Force Base are located right in the Panhandle, and for many of us, there is something faintly nostalgic about the knots and clutches of military men on leave roaming the beaches and boardwalks of towns.

**UNITED STATES NAVAL AIR STATION**, Pensacola—Known as the "cradle of naval aviation," this was the nation's first naval air station, established in 1914. The 16,500 acres that make up this military base are home to 21,000 employees, both military and civilian. Tours of the base are available daily 9 A.M. to 5 P.M., and a don't-miss is the Pensacola Naval Aviation Museum (see the **MUSEUMS and GALLERIES** chapter). If you happen by on the right day you may even catch sight of the navy's precision flying team, The Blue Angels, who call this air station home. By the way, the Angels are always in Pensacola during the month of November. Also at the base is Fort Barrancas, a restored Civil War–era fort, and the Land Survival Exhibit that shows survival techniques used by soldiers who find themselves in a hostile environment. The entire base is closed to visitors on Thanksgiving Day, Christmas, and New Year's Day. Public Affairs Office; NAS Building 45; Pensacola 32508-5000 (904-452-2311).

**EGLIN AIR FORCE BASE**, Fort Walton Beach—Planes of all types can be seen taking off and landing in test maneuvers that are reminiscent of scenes from the film *The Right Stuff*, and the world's only climatic hangar is located at this testing facility. The hangar is used for testing new aircraft in controlled environments (temperatures in the hangar can be made to drop to 60 degrees below zero for test purposes). There's also a canine military training exhibit. Eglin is under the command of Andrews Air Force Base (in Silver Springs, Maryland), and employs more than 10,000 military and 5,000 civilians. Free tours are offered every Wednesday from 9 A.M. to noon, but reservations must be made well in advance by calling 904-244-8191.

**HURLBUT FIELD**, Fort Walton Beach—A tactical air force base where many top-secret operations are conducted. Tours of those areas of the base that are not off-limits are available by calling 904-244-8191.

**TYNDALL AIR FORCE BASE**, Panama City—The first Friday of every month is tour day, when visitors can observe pilot training sessions. There are great opportunities for good photos as the squadron of brilliant F-15 Eagle aircraft approaches the flight line, where the planes line up for take-off. Tour reservations must be made through the Public Affairs Office, 904-283-2965.

**NAVAL COASTAL SYSTEMS CENTER**, Panama City—This is the principal center for naval research, development, testing, and evaluation of mine, torpedo, and other underwater weapons systems. Tours are available for groups only. Contact the Public Affairs Office, 904-234-4420.

## Travel Tip: GETTING MAIL

To receive mail along your Florida route, have it sent to you care of General Delivery of any city, where it will be held at the main post office. Envelopes should be clearly marked HOLD FOR 30 DAYS. In addition, Automobile Association of America members may have mail held at any AAA office, and travelers with American Express traveler's checks can similarly use American Express offices on their route.

## Travel Tip: RESOURCE ALERT!

Florida is zealous in protecting its natural resources. If you see any abuse of them—someone damaging delicate sand dunes, starting unlawful fires, or feeding wildlife—report it by calling 800-342-1821.

**STATE CAPITOL**, Tallahassee—Though some rumors have it that the capital might move to Orlando, this building is currently the seat of state government. The capitol sits (appropriately) on the highest hill in the city, and its 22nd-floor observation deck affords a great view of the city and the surrounding countryside. While the state legislature is in session, visitors are welcome to watch the proceedings from various galleries. Guided tours of the building are also offered. The Capitol; Tallahassee 32301 (904-488-6167). The original state capitol (across the street from the more modern building) was built between 1839 and 1845, and has been restored to its original splendor. It is also open for visitor tours. For information call 904-487-1902.

**MAYPORT NAVY STATION**, Mayport—Located about 18 miles east of Jacksonville, this is one of the state's major navy bases, with aircraft carriers, destroyers, and missile cruisers—whatever happens to be in port at the time—open to the public for tours on weekends only. Saturdays 10:30 A.M. to 4:30 P.M. and Sundays 1 P.M. to 4:30 P.M. Building 213; Box 195; Mayport 32225 (904-246-5583).

**CECIL FIELD NAVAL STATION**, Jacksonville—On the 26,000 acres of this training base, navy pilots hone their skills. Tours must be arranged a month in advance and are designed around the interests of a particular group. Most tours include a look at the flight line, an in-depth description of an airplane on display, and slide presentations of pilot training procedures. Public Affairs Office; Building 199; Jacksonville 32215 (904-778-6055).

**AIR TRAFFIC CONTROL CENTER**, Hilliard—More than 300 air traffic controllers work at the center, about 40 miles north of Jacksonville. It is one of three south regional Federal Aviation Administration facilities for monitoring air traffic. Guided tours include a movie on air traffic control, plus a look at controllers at work in front of their radar screens. The action is viewed from a glass catwalk that runs around the inside of the control room, and the tour includes a look at the dynamic-simulation lab, where controllers are trained by following simulated flight programs. Tours last about an hour and a half, and must be prearranged by calling 904-791-2581.

*Travel Tip:*
## BEACHCOMBING
Allowed on all Florida public beaches! And spectacular on the Gulf Coast shores of Captiva and Sanibel islands.

# CENTRAL FLORIDA

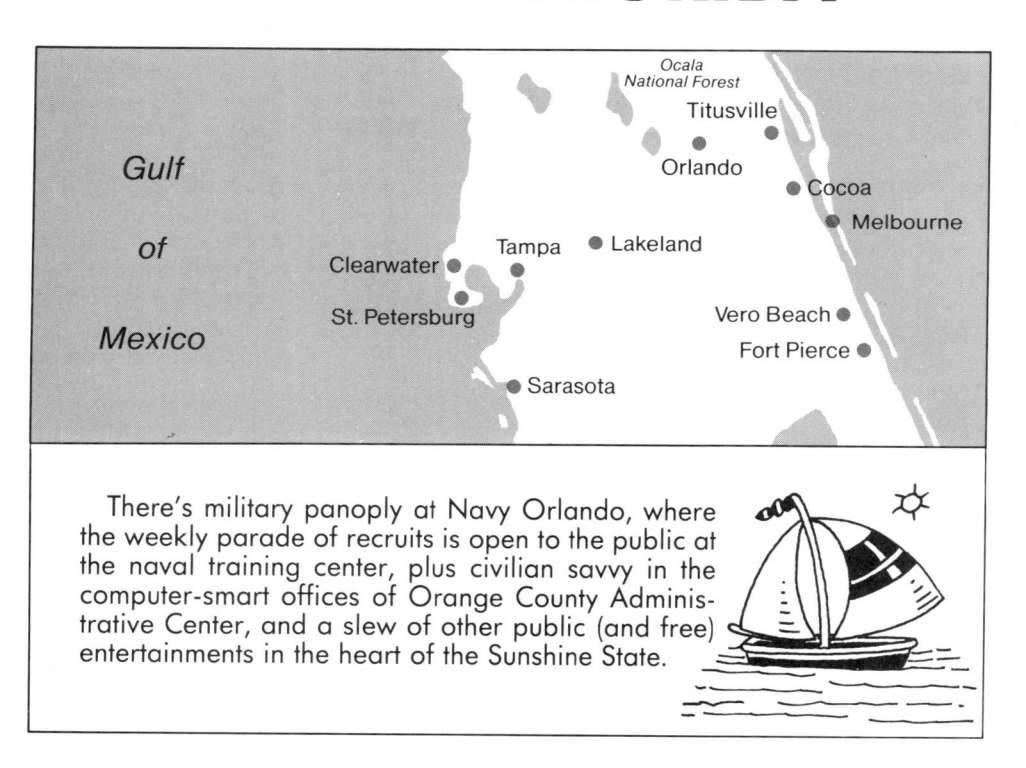

There's military panoply at Navy Orlando, where the weekly parade of recruits is open to the public at the naval training center, plus civilian savvy in the computer-smart offices of Orange County Administrative Center, and a slew of other public (and free) entertainments in the heart of the Sunshine State.

**CLEARWATER CITY HALL**—A beautiful view of the city can be had from the city manager's office, which he is generous enough to share with the public weekdays from 8 A.M. to 5 P.M. 112 South Osceola Street; Clearwater 33516 (813-462-6900).

**PINELLAS COUNTY COURTHOUSE**, Clearwater—Tours are available of both the civil and criminal courthouses. Trials here run the gamut from negligence cases to murder. The civil court is located at 315 Court Street and the criminal court at 5100 144th Avenue North. Both are open weekdays 8 A.M. to 5 P.M. For tour information contact Karleen F. DeBlaker; Clerk of the Civil Court; 315 Court Street; Clearwater 33516 (813-462-3341).

**MACDILL AIR FORCE BASE**, Tampa—Headquarters for the 56th Tactical Training Wing, United States Central Command, and United States Readiness Command. There are a variety of aircraft on display, including the dramatic F-16s. Tour requests must be made in writing well in advance of a visit; all correspondence should include name, address, and telephone number, and should be sent to: 56 TTW/PA; MacDill Air Force Base; Tampa 33608-5000 (813-830-2215).

**HILLSBOROUGH COUNTY COURTHOUSE**, Tampa—One-hour tours of this courthouse take in a historical museum. Open Mondays through Fridays 8:30 A.M. to 5 P.M. 419 Pierce Street; Tampa 33602 (813-272-5900).

**ST. PETERSBURG CITY HALL**—This WPA structure was built during the Depression. It has brass railings and marble steps. There are no organized tours, but visitors are welcome to visit on their own Mondays through Fridays 8 A.M. to 5 P.M. 175 Fifth Street North; St. Petersburg 33731 (813-893-7111).

**LAKELAND CITY HALL**—Old photographs offer a look at the evolution of this mid-state city. Open weekdays 8 A.M. to 5 P.M. 228 South Massachusetts Street; Lakeland 33802 (813-682-1141).

**NAVY ORLANDO**—Everybody loves a parade, so the naval training center here opens its gates every Friday morning and invites the public to watch the recruit review. Approximately 600 men and women pass in review each week, and graduates of this center go on to 32 different commands and activities in the U.S. Navy, Army, Air Force, and Coast Guard. Navy Orlando is one of the largest facilities of its kind in the world. Parades begin at 9:45 A.M. and last about an hour. Take Bennett Road to General Rees Road; turn right at the Navy Orlando gate; 305-646-4474.

**ORANGE COUNTY ADMINISTRATIVE OFFICES**, Orlando—Pneumatic blinds that open and close with the movement of the sun and bathroom lights that turn on and off in response to body heat are just 2 of the unusual aspects of this state-of-the-art government building. There are also lovely stained-glass windows. Visitors are welcome weekdays 8 A.M. to 5 P.M., but there are no organized tours. 201 South Rosalind Street; Orlando 32801 (305-236-7370).

**ORLANDO CITY HALL**—Tours of the seat of government of one of the nation's fastest-growing cities can be arranged in advance by contacting Kathy Russell; Bureau Chief of Special Services; 400 South Orange Avenue; Orlando 32801 (305-849-2169).

**OSCEOLA COUNTY COURTHOUSE**, Kissimmee—This century-old building, the oldest operating courthouse in the state, is still used for its original purpose. Visitors are welcome weekdays 8:30 A.M. to 5 P.M., but there are no organized tours. 12 South Vernon Street; Kissimmee 32741 (305-847-1300).

**MISSILE DISPLAY**, Satellite Beach—Ten-story high Titan and Atlas missiles are only part of the missile arsenal on view at an outdoor display in front of the

MILITARY AND GOVERNMENT SITES/Southern Florida 109

Eastern Test Range Technical Laboratory on Highway A1A, just south of Cocoa Beach. Chamber of Commerce of South Brevard; 1005 East Strawbridge Avenue; Melbourne 32901 (305-724-5400).

# SOUTHERN FLORIDA

Free for the looking down south is the bomb shelter built for John F. Kennedy in 1960 and tours of Homestead Air Force Base, home of the Thunderbirds, as well as a host of less martial sights.

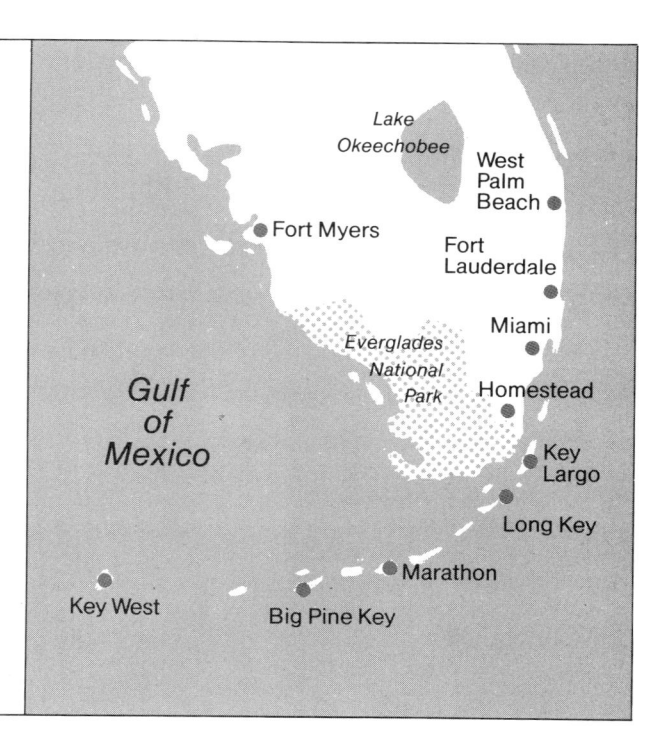

**PALM BEACH COUNTY OFFICE BUILDING/WEST PALM BEACH CITY HALL—** These 2 dramatic new structures, facing one another across Olive Street, add some high-tech glamour to old-fashioned Palm Beach. The interiors of the buildings have atria with walkways circling the perimeters to connect the floors. County Office: 301 North Olive Street; West Palm Beach 33402 (305-837-2040) and City Hall: 200 Second Street; West Palm Beach 33402 (305-659-8000).

**PEANUT ISLAND COAST GUARD INSTALLATION**, between Palm Beach and Lake Riviera—The Coast Guard facility here is small, but what brings visitors to tiny Peanut Island is a relic from the Kennedy administration. A bomb shelter with a full command post for the president's use was built here in 1960, close to

110 MILITARY AND GOVERNMENT SITES/Southern Florida

the Kennedy Palm Beach home. Although the equipment has been removed, the shelter remains and is open. Peanut Island (305-844-5030).

**OLD TOWN HALL**, Boca Raton—Built in 1925 by Addison Mizner, the founder of Boca Raton, this is one of only a few original Mizner structures left standing. It has been restored and the Boca Raton Historical Society has its offices on the second floor. Open weekdays 8 A.M. to 5 P.M. 71 North Federal Highway; Boca Raton 33432 (305-395-6766).

**PORT EVERGLADES**, Fort Lauderdale—This is a "liberty port" for the naval ships of the United States' foreign allies. British and Dutch fleets as well as a NATO fleet from the Caribbean have all been recent visitors. The port is open to the public from 6 A.M. to 6 P.M. For information about which ships will be open to visitors contact the Navy Services Office at 305-764-6289.

**U.S. COAST GUARD BASE/OLD GOVERNOR'S ISLAND**, Miami Beach—Although this base is small, it is the busiest search-and-rescue station in the country. There's a 210-foot cutter with a 50-person crew on board, plus 2 95-foot patrol boats, which cruise Miami waters searching for drug smugglers, in addition to their safety-at-sea functions. Tours are available for groups only. Call 305-672-2021.

**HOMESTEAD AIR FORCE BASE**, Florida City—Located 35 miles south of Miami, this training facility for F-4 crews is one of the most interesting bases in the state for a civilian visitor. It has more than 60 F-4 Phantoms, with new F-16s soon to arrive. Visitors can see the maintenance departments, the flight line, the control tower, the canine sentries, and, sometimes, a flight simulator. Homestead is also home to the Air Force's precision flying team, The Thunderbirds. Tours last 2 to 3 hours and are available for groups of 10 or more. Reservations must be made 3 to 4 weeks in advance by calling 305-257-8396.

---

## Travel Tip · WELCOME STATIONS

Florida's 6 Welcome Centers are open from 8 A.M. to 5 P.M. daily except Easter, Thanksgiving, and Christmas. Visitors arriving by car from a neighboring state are given a free sample of Florida orange juice or grapefruit juice, and staff members are on hand to answer questions and help in planning a stay in the Sunshine State. The Welcome Center locations are:
- I-95 near Yulee • U.S. 1/U.S. 301 near Hilliard
- U.S. 231 near Campbellton • I-75 near Jennings
- I-10 near Pensacola • Inside the Capitol Building in Tallahassee

# GREAT DRIVES

What's so great about driving around Florida? Well, for one thing, there's the variety. Most visitors—and residents, for that matter—are familiar with just one part of the state, whether it's the Panhandle, Tampa, Orlando, or Miami, and from that modest experience they imagine they know it all. Nothing could be further from the truth, so driving some of Florida's smaller roads provides an opportunity to discover the state's remarkable diversity firsthand.

In mapping the following routes, we've chosen those that traverse Florida's most spectacular and fascinating landscapes. In the north, for instance, our paths pass through salt marshes, along dune-bordered shores, and through little towns full of old-fashioned charm.

Hills in Florida? They're here, in the central tier, carpeted with citrus trees and dotted with typical "Cracker" houses. There are also hundreds of lakes, acres of woods, grazing cattle; and even a bit of the tropics. In southern Florida one immediately thinks of beaches, but the southernmost tip of the Florida peninsula also has just about everything found elsewhere in the state—and the Everglades and the Florida Keys besides. Nothing really compares with a loop through the wild Everglades with its magnificent water birds and stunning vistas.

All of which is to say that, despite some interstate routes that are best forgotten, and the overdevelopment of certain sections of its shores, Florida is really rural at heart. That alone would be cheering; more pleasing still is knowing that the way to the state's heart is along its roads. All you need is a car and a sense of adventure and discovery.

# NORTHERN FLORIDA

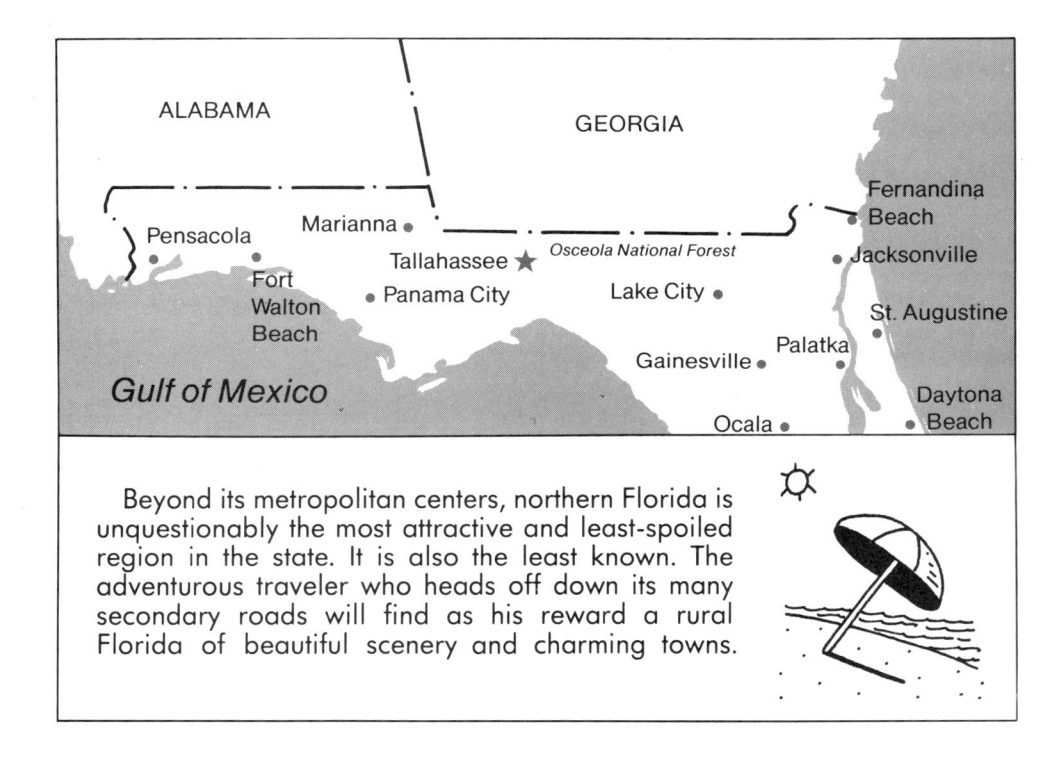

Beyond its metropolitan centers, northern Florida is unquestionably the most attractive and least-spoiled region in the state. It is also the least known. The adventurous traveler who heads off down its many secondary roads will find as his reward a rural Florida of beautiful scenery and charming towns.

**Navarre to Destin**—For vistas of sugar-white beaches and the sapphire waters of the Gulf of Mexico, this section of Highway 98, along the Emerald Coast, can't be beat. True, you can't always see the Gulf—commercial development and resorts sometimes block the view—but large stretches remain pristine, offering a fine opportunity to experience one of Florida's most beautiful stretches of coastline.

**Gainesville to Cross Creek**—Home of Marjorie Kinnan Rawlings, best known for her novel *The Yearling*, Cross Creek lies about 20 minutes east of Gainesville. To get there, travel east on Route 20 and then south on U.S. 325. Although some of the drive traverses less prosperous sections of the state's interior, the route will also take you past Lochloosha and Orange Lakes and sparsely populated towns. Cross Creek itself, with its lush vegetation and abundant wildlife, is positively irresistible.

**Gainesville to Micanopy and McIntosh**—Home to the University of Florida,

Gainesville is also the starting point for 2 short, pretty country drives. Micanopy is about 10 miles south of Gainesville on U.S. 441. A small, wooded town with a resident artists' colony and some enticing antique shops, Micanopy was once the site of a Timucuan Indian village. McIntosh, a few miles farther south, is a beautifully maintained, small southern town that derives its old-fashioned charm from lovely houses and, again, shops selling antiques.

**Jacksonville to Cedar Key**—The first half of this 3-hour drive—on I-10 west to Balwin and then U.S. 301 south to Waldo—is fairly unremarkable. But the landscape along Highway 24, from Waldo through Gainesville, Archer, and Bronson and on to Cedar Key, is considerably more interesting. This is the state's so-called Cracker country, agricultural northern Florida at its most typical. This laid-back landscape provides a fascinating contrast to the waterfront charm of Cedar Key, with its historic houses, fine restaurants, and lively festivals.

**Jacksonville to White Springs**—From Jacksonville, travel west on I-10, about which there is nothing too remarkable until it cuts through Osceola National Forest. Then, rather than exiting onto I-75 and following it all the way to White Springs, choose instead to drive on more scenic U.S. 41, traveling north from Lake City. The whole trip takes 2 hours, and at trail's end is a pretty town (once a resort renowned for its sulfurous waters), best known today for the Stephen Foster Center, its proximity to the Suwanee River, and the annual Florida Folk Festival.

**Jacksonville Beach to St. Augustine**—Easily the most scenic route from Jacksonville to the country's oldest settlement, Route A1A (Florida's first coast highway) passes between high, overgrown dunes on the Atlantic side and the primordial marshes of the Intracoastal Waterway. Although the dunes give way in places to single-family, oceanfront homes, most of the waterway side is designated as a wildlife refuge, and the vistas remain unchanged.

**Mayport to Fernandina**—Known as the "Buccaneer Trail," this stretch of Route A1A winds along the St. Johns River, providing wonderful salt-marsh vistas and glimpses of bird life on the way. Start at Mayport (18 miles east of Jacksonville) and take the automobile ferry across the river; the drive north to Fernandina Beach takes about 45 minutes, unless you stop at Kingsley Plantation, built in 1792 and Florida's oldest, and at Little Talbot Island State Park, neither of which should be missed.

**St. Augustine to Daytona Beach**—Hugging the coastline, Route A1A parallels one of Florida's least developed oceanfront stretches. The drive takes about an hour (more if the traffic is heavy) and passes Marineland, Flagler Beach, and Ormond Beach. Along the way one catches glimpses of dune formations, broad ocean vistas, and some of the state's vintage coastal settlements.

# CENTRAL FLORIDA

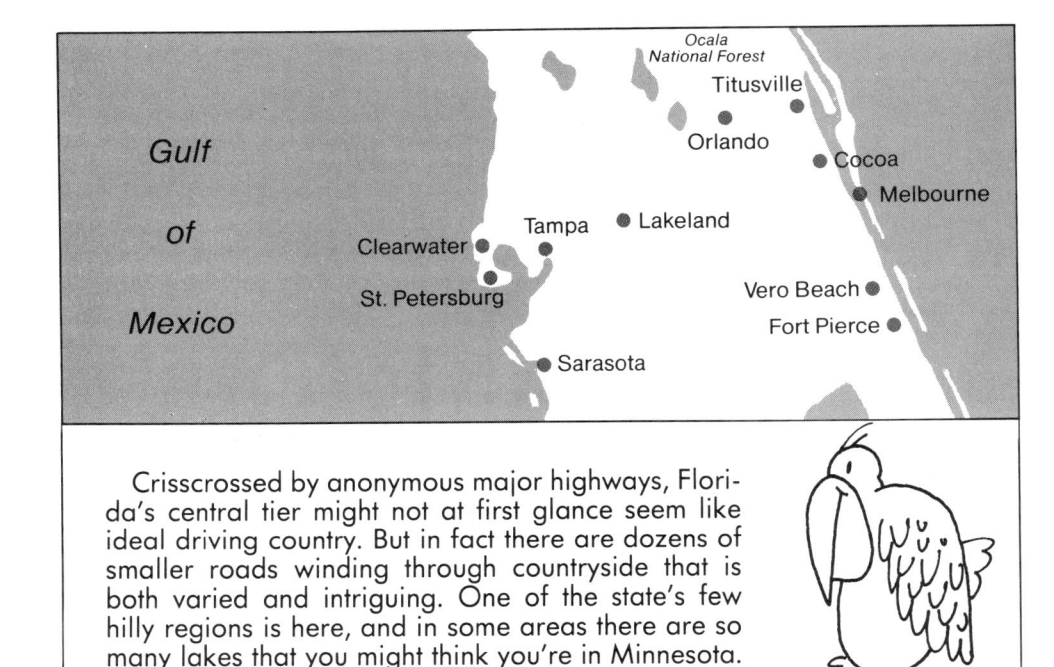

Crisscrossed by anonymous major highways, Florida's central tier might not at first glance seem like ideal driving country. But in fact there are dozens of smaller roads winding through countryside that is both varied and intriguing. One of the state's few hilly regions is here, and in some areas there are so many lakes that you might think you're in Minnesota.

**U.S. 27**—Between Leesburg and I-4, this road passes through one of the few hilly sections of the state. Despite recent freezes and disease problems, citrus trees still blanket the rolling countryside, and few housing developments mar its beauty. All this is particularly striking in the late afternoon, when the sun is low in the sky.

**Florida 44**—Punctuated here and there by small towns, this road winds its way from Crows Bluff, on Lake Woodruff, through a less developed part of Florida. The 2 lanes are edged with pine forest and, heading west, lead to Eustis, Leesburg, and Wildwood. A nice country drive.

**Florida 19**—South off of U.S. 441, this route leads to the town of Howie-in-the-Hills, which should easily win any competition for best town name in the state. There are no billboards here, and no neon; just narrow red-clay roads and modest houses perched high on rounded hilltops. As the road crosses Lake Harris, the view from the bridge includes chimneys peeping out of the woods along the shore. Past an old white church, the route finally comes to a dead end at the world-famous Mission Inn Golf and Tennis Resort, nestled in the hills.

**Florida 44**—Turn east off U.S. 19 about a mile south of Crystal River, on the Gulf Coast, and you'll be driving through a landscape of primitive beauty. Broad expanses of black needle rush, a type of grass that really is nearly black, line both sides of the road; the view over the flat countryside is broken only by distant clusters of towering palms. At Lecanto, pick up Florida 491 and take it down to Brooksville.

**Dogwood Trail**—The dogwood blossoms are at their best during the last 2 weeks of March, but the trees are splendid any time of the year. From Brooksville, take U.S. 41 north past Florida 476; turn left on McKethan Lake Road, a graded dirt road that forks about 250 yards farther on. Follow either fork; they're each fine.

**Courtney Campbell Causeway**—This is surely the most scenic route between Tampa and sparkling Clearwater Beach, on the Gulf of Mexico. From this section of U.S. 60, motorists can gaze at all the sun, sand, and water they could possibly desire, as well as an impressive flotilla of fishing craft gathered in the Gulf of Mexico.

**Lake Hollingsworth Drive**—One of the most beautiful routes in the Lakeland area, this 3-mile drive circles Lake Hollingsworth. Along the lake's northern shore, the road passes Florida Southern College, which has the single greatest concentration of Frank Lloyd Wright buildings in the world. (Free pamphlets outlining walking tours are available at the administration building.) From Tampa, take I-4 to the Memorial Boulevard exit; turn right on Florida Avenue, then follow it through town (about 2½ miles) and turn left onto Patten Heights; Patten comes to a dead end at Lake Hollingsworth Drive.

**Windermere**—A stone's throw from Walt Disney World, this sheltered enclave is well worth the drive for a glimpse of the stately homes set along the shores of Lakes Butler and Down and along shady, quiet streets. From Florida 50 or the turnpike, pick up Florida 437 going south; then follow the signs to Windermere.

**New Smyrna Beach**—Cars are allowed to drive on much of this 8-mile stretch of sand—just like at better-known Daytona Beach. The difference is that New Smyrna is less crowded and more relaxed than its northern neighbor.

**Melbourne**—A driving tour of this Atlantic coast city takes in stately old homes, the yacht club and basin, and many notable landmarks. The best way to be sure to see them all is to pick up a copy of the city's centennial historical map from the Chamber of Commerce of South Brevard; 1005 East Strawbridge Avenue; Melbourne 32901 (305-724-5400).

**South Tropical Trail**—From this winding road (Florida 3) south through Merritt Island, the views are of citrus, mango, and avocado groves and, on either side, the Indian and Banana rivers; it's tropical all right, and highly scenic. The route leads to Mather's Bridge, a favorite picnic spot, though some prefer lunch at *Mather's Bridge Restaurant*.

**Melbourne to St. Cloud**—If it's off-the-beaten-track you want, take U.S. 192 west through what is largely an agricultural region: barbed wire fences, grazing cattle, and the quiet towns of Deer Park and Holopaw. This drive also skirts the Bull Creek wildlife management area where, if you're lucky, you might spot an armadillo, among other animals.

# SOUTHERN FLORIDA

Think of southern Florida and beaches probably come most quickly to mind. They are there all right, and they're splendid. But take to the road and you'll discover a whole new side to the state—coastal roads for sweeping views of the Gulf and lush tropical forests; inland routes for a glimpse of "cow country," the nation's second-largest lake, and the spectacular Everglades. And the Overseas Highway is the region's "Key" drive.

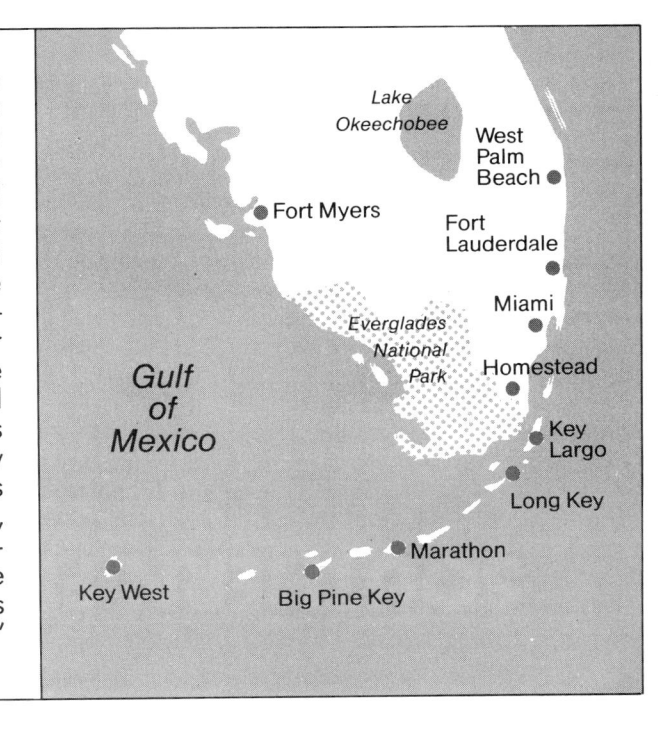

**Arcadia to Okeechobee**—This 60-mile stretch of Florida 70 must be the straightest in the state, and it's relaxing to drive, especially after the interstates.

The road passes through wide open, empty spaces—"cow country"—and in fact you are likely to see some local cowboys along the way. Pack a lunch, though, because you won't see much else.

**Around Lake Okeechobee**—The drive circling the second-largest body of fresh water in the United States is about 100 miles long, but it's well worth your time. Start at Clewiston, "America's Sweetest City," and drive west on U.S. 27 to the excellent fishing town of Moore Haven. Continue north along the shore on Florida 78, past the Brighton Seminole Reservation to Okeechobee, as pretty a little country town as you could hope to find; turn south on U.S. 98-441 and head down through Upthegrove Beach (a good picnic spot), Belle Glade, and Bean City.

**Charlotte Harbor**—The last of the Gulf Coast's wide open spaces (and they won't be there for long) are best viewed from U.S. 41 or from the new I-75. Between Port Charlotte and Punta Gorda the sweeping harbor vistas are particularly magnificent, and Punta Gorda itself, the Charlotte County seat, is still very much old Florida, with tin roofs and ancient cabbage palms. What's more, there are many good seafood restaurants along the way.

**Easy Street**—Some people really do live on Easy Street—in Port Charlotte, that is. It may be worth the trip just to see this 2-mile-long road and comfort yourself knowing that you too might live on Easy Street someday.

**Loop Road, Everglades**—Going west on the Tamiami Trail, turn left at the Indian Baptist Church; 24 miles and some of the worst potholes south of Georgia later, you'll come out at Monroe Station. The road passes through backwoods Florida, scruffy and mean, but you'll be rewarded by the sight of huge owls hunting in daylight; soft-shelled turtles the size of large dogs; and bottle-green canals crawling with new litters of chirping alligators.

**Fort Myers to West Palm Beach**—The best section of this route, a pleasant, 125-mile-long country drive between two increasingly large coastal cities, is along Florida 80. It runs just south of the Caloosahatchee River, the favorite Florida stream of Henry Ford and Thomas Edison. Near La Belle, the road passes stands of huge live oaks strung with Spanish moss and groves of cabbage palms, the state tree, which, by the way, are edible.

**Old Cutler Road**—Southern Florida's premier tropical route begins just south of the Cocoplum Circle, near the Coral Gables-Coconut Grove line, and ends some 20 miles later in Cutler Ridge, a pioneer town named for a knife sharpener. Its 2 lanes wind through a landscape that is mostly agricultural (mango and avocado groves) and junglelike (Matheson Hammock Park is worth a stop: the beach costs $1.50; the jungle is free). Either way, it's also some of southern Florida's most scenic countryside.

**The Treasure Coast**—This 80-mile stretch of A1A—from Tequesta (where it is called The Gold Coast) to Fort Pierce—gets its name from the many Spanish galleons that were wrecked on its shores. Most of the route passes over Hutchinson Island, whose beauty remains unfaded, despite a new nuclear power plant. Just about any spot along here is perfect for a seaside picnic.

**Key Largo to Key West**—Beyond dispute, the "Overseas Highway" is Florida's most stunning drive. Many of the old foundations for what was originally Henry M. Flagler's "Railroad That Went To Sea" have been replaced in the past few years, and now soaring new bridges span this tropical dream of islands. Florida's government considers the Keys a state treasure; drive these 105 miles, the Atlantic on one side and the Gulf of Mexico on the other, and you will understand why.

## Travel Tip: RENTING WHEELS

Renting a car is sometimes the most logical way to get around, but exploring the widely varying charges companies assess for the exact same make and model—and checking out the latest promotions—is the only way to assure yourself of the lowest possible price. One car-rental agency may be more reasonable in one city; another in another. Always ask about any special midweek or weekend rates, and verify that there is no mileage charge. Some agencies now charge for the gas they provide with the car initially, but you may then return the car with an empty tank—a real time-saver if you're rushing to catch a plane and have to drop off a rental car first.

Some major national rental companies with toll-free telephone numbers are:
*Alamo*—800-327-9633
*Avis Rent A Car*—800-331-1212, except Oklahoma
*Budget Rent a Car*—800-527-0700, except Nebraska
*Dollar Rent A Car*—800-421-6868, except California
*Hertz*—800-654-3131; 800-522-3711 in Oklahoma City
*National Car Rental*—800-328-4567; 800-862-6064 in Minnesota
*Thrifty Rent A Car*—800-367-2277

In the fall, just before the Florida "season" begins, look for the extraordinary promotional fares offered by the major national carriers to encourage renters to drive rental cars from northeast and midwest locations to specified Florida cities. These promotional deals can include very low weekly rates and free airfare from Florida back to your point of origin, all designed to get the companies' fleets of rental vehicles into the Florida market for the heavy season. In late spring the promotional fares reappear in reverse, to get the fleets to more northerly markets.

# ALMOST FOR FREE

While there are clearly enough free things to see and do in Florida to fill a book (like this one), there really should be a whole second volume devoted to the things available for next to nothing. But since we have only a limited number of pages on which to deal with this near-free phenomenon, we must provide only a hint of the inexpensive opportunities that dot the Florida landscape.

The justification for this companion guide is simply that there is a vast inventory of first-rate attractions available in the Sunshine State for only nominal sums. For example, many of the state parks that fill the Florida map open their expansive and peaceful grounds for only 50¢; several museums harboring priceless collections and absolutely irresistible exhibits ask for only $1 at their doors; and fascinating historic sites can often be explored for a song. See what we mean?

In addition, there are aquariums (including the world's first oceanarium), where dolphins and porpoises frolic to the delight of visitors; stunning gardens where a leisurely stroll is an absolute pleasure; an alligator farm where men wrestle the mighty reptiles; the oldest house in the nation's oldest city; state recreation areas where Seminole Indians once fought; and state parks where crystal-clear springs flow at a constant 72 degrees. And this only begins to scratch the slight-cost surface.

Below you'll find the most compelling and exciting of these "almost for frees"—a good basic guide to have in hand when a few of the best things in Florida life turn out to carry modest price tags.

# NORTHERN FLORIDA

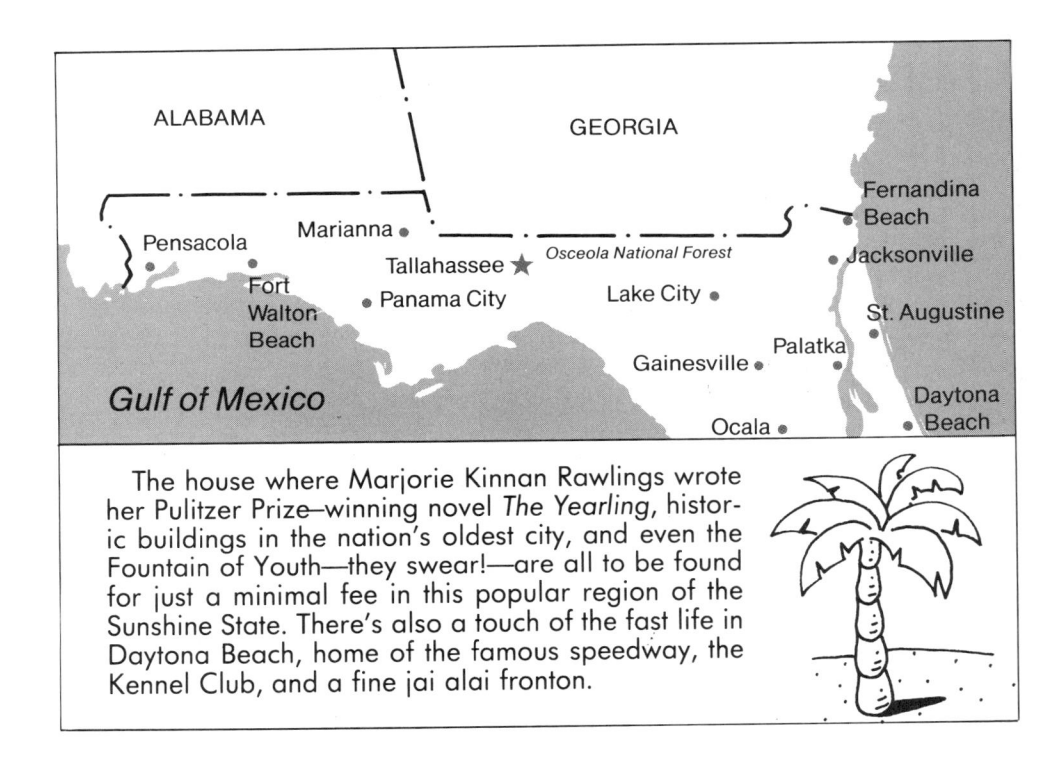

The house where Marjorie Kinnan Rawlings wrote her Pulitzer Prize–winning novel *The Yearling*, historic buildings in the nation's oldest city, and even the Fountain of Youth—they swear!—are all to be found for just a minimal fee in this popular region of the Sunshine State. There's also a touch of the fast life in Daytona Beach, home of the famous speedway, the Kennel Club, and a fine jai alai fronton.

**THE ZOO**, Gulf Breeze—About 10 miles south of Pensacola are 20 acres of zoological park and botanical gardens, including a wildlife rehabilitation area and bird sanctuary. Open daily 10 A.M. to dusk. Admission is $5 for adults; $3 for children. 5801 Gulf Breeze Parkway; Gulf Breeze 32561 (904-932-2229).

**GULFARIUM**, Fort Walton Beach—Highlights are a porpoise show and a sea lion exhibition. Open daily 9 A.M. to 4 P.M. October through April; 9 A.M. to 6 P.M. May through September. Admission is $6 for adults; $3 for children. Highway 98 East; Fort Walton Beach 32548 (904-244-5169).

**GULF WORLD**, Panama City Beach—Another aquarium (they're understandably popular in the Sunshine State) with regular shows of dolphins and sea lions. Other attractions include a scuba show, bird exhibits, and a shark tank. Open daily June through September 9 A.M. to 7:30 P.M. Hours vary the rest of the year, so call ahead for exact times. Admission is $6.75 for adults; $4.75 for children. 15412 Highway 98 West; Panama City Beach 32407 (904-234-5271).

**ALFRED B. MACLAY STATE GARDENS**, Tallahassee—A masterpiece of floral architecture, with huge pines and oaks towering over smaller flowering dogwoods and redbuds. Azaleas and camellias are the predominant bloomers. Open daily 8 A.M. to sunset. Admission from May 1 through December 31 is 50¢; from January 1 through April 31, $2. 3540 Thomasville Road; Tallahassee 32308 (904-893-4232).

**MARJORIE KINNAN RAWLINGS STATE HISTORIC SITE**, Hawthorne—The home of the Pulitzer Prize–winning author, just north of Cross Creek, has been restored to look just the way it did when Marjorie (all the locals called her by her first name only) wrote The Yearling and subsequent books. Even her old manual typewriter is in its original place. There are guided tours available. Open daily 9 A.M. to 5 P.M. Admission is $1. Route 3; Box 92; Hawthorne 32640 (904-466-3672).

**JACKSONVILLE ZOOLOGICAL PARK**—The largest zoo in northern Florida features more than 400 animals. Special exhibits include a birds of prey aviary and an elephant show. There's also a safari train and children's rides. Open daily 10 A.M. to 5:45 P.M. from Memorial Day through Labor Day; 9 A.M. to 4:45 P.M. the rest of the year. Closed Thanksgiving, Christmas, and New Year's Day. Admission is $2.75 for adults; $1.25 for children. 8605 Zoo Road; Jacksonville 32218 (904-757-4463).

**OLDEST HOUSE**, St. Augustine—An appropriate name for the oldest structure in the nation's oldest city. Archaeological studies indicate that the first floor was built in the early 1600s by the Spaniards and made of coquina from nearby Anastasia Island. The wooden second story was added later by the English. The house is furnished with authentic antiques and there are costumed guides on hand to answer questions. The St. Augustine Historical Society has its headquarters here and runs a library with 7,500 books about Florida's history; souvenirs are also on sale. The house is open daily 9 A.M. to 5 P.M.; the Historical Society is open weekdays 9 A.M. to 5 P.M. Admission is $2. 14 St. Francis Street; St. Augustine 32084 (904-824-2872).

**CASTILLO DE SAN MARCOS**, St. Augustine—This massive masonry fort, the oldest in the country, was begun in 1672 and took 15 years to complete. It was never taken in battle—not too surprising considering its impenetrable walls, 30 feet high and 9 to 12 feet thick, plus the 40-foot-wide moat that surrounds it. Open daily 9 A.M. to 5:45 P.M. in summer; 8:30 A.M. to 5:15 P.M. the rest of the year. Admission is 50¢. 1 Castillo Drive; St. Augustine 32084 (904-829-6506).

**ST. AUGUSTINE ALLIGATOR FARM**—Billed as the "world's original alligator attraction." Hourly alligator-wrestling shows are just part of the fun. There are also raccoons, snakes, and waterbirds to be seen, plus "Snapping Sam," a demonstration of just how strong an alligator's jaws really are. Open daily

9 A.M. to 5:30 P.M. Admission is $4.50 for adults; $2.50 for children. Highway A1A; St. Augustine 32084 (904-824-3337).

**MARINELAND**, St. Augustine—When Marineland opened in 1938 it was the world's first oceanarium. Now it has grown to include 2 huge oceanariums housing porpoises, sharks, manatees, and barracudas, among other creatures of the sea. There's an electric-eel show, seal and whale shows, a spectacular 3-D film, and a porpoise performance. Visitors can also peer through thick glass windows as divers feed the fish by hand. Open daily 9 A.M. to 6 P.M. Admission is $6 for adults; $3.50 for children. Highway A1A; St Augustine 32086 (904-471-1111).

**FOUNTAIN OF YOUTH**, St. Augustine—Ponce de Leon never found it, but that hasn't stopped hundreds of others, inspired by the famed story of the explorer's search for eternal youth. Visitors can drink from the fountain and take a gander at a statue of Florida's founder. Open daily 9 A.M. to 4:45 P.M. Admission is $3 for adults; $1.50 for children; and $2.50 for senior citizens. 155 Magnolia Avenue; St. Augustine 32084 (904-829-3168).

**POTTER'S WAX MUSEUM**, St. Augustine—One of the oldest such establishments in the United States, with more than 240 recognizable figures on display. Open daily 9 A.M. to 9 P.M. in summer; 9 A.M. to 5 P.M. the rest of the year. Admission is $3.75 for adults; $2 for children. 1 King Street; St. Augustine 32084 (904-829-9056).

**DAYTONA INTERNATIONAL SPEEDWAY**, Daytona Beach—Called the "world's fastest track," and home to the world-renowned Daytona 500 every February, the speedway hosts stock car and motorcycle races year-round. Tours are available when the speedway is not being used for testing or a race. Seating capacity is 100,000. Admission is $1. Highway 92; Daytona Beach 32014 (904-253-6711).

**DAYTONA BEACH KENNEL CLUB**—Speed of another sort is the attraction here. Greyhounds compete from May through October in 13 races nightly (except Thursdays and Sundays) beginning at 8 P.M. There is pari-mutuel betting. Admission is $1. Junction of Highway 92 and I-95; Box 2360; Daytona Beach 32015 (904-252-6484).

**DAYTONA BEACH JAI ALAI**—It's yet another game of speed. Players, called *pelotari*, with baskets known as *cestas* attached to their arms, compete in this fast and furiously difficult Basque game. There's pari-mutuel betting and admission is $1; $2 for reserved seats. All matinee seats are $1. Open nightly (except Sundays and Tuesdays) February through August from 7:15 P.M.; matinees Mondays and Saturdays at noon. Highway 92; Daytona Beach 32015 (904-255-0222).

# CENTRAL FLORIDA

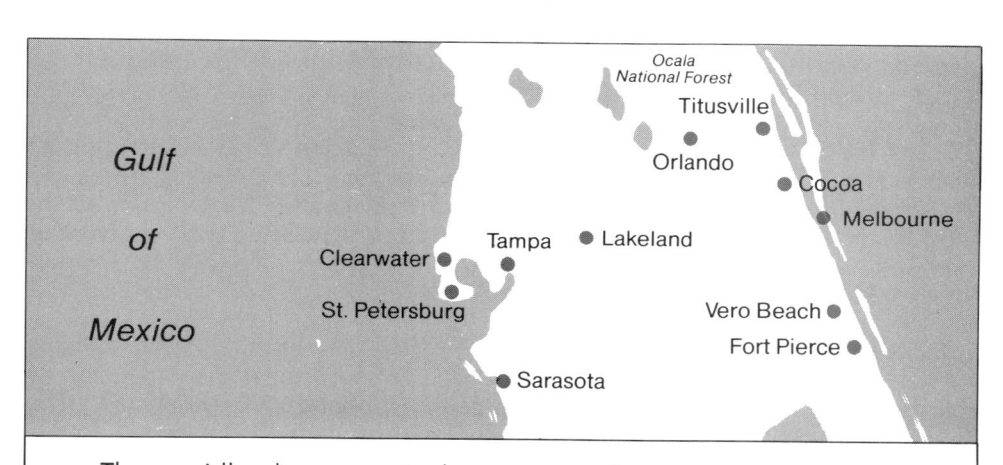

These midlanders seem to love a spot of green, and they've got the spots—glorious state parks and a lush botanical garden—splashed all across their section of the Sunshine State. The best news of all is that by and large it doesn't take more than a pocketful of change to join the frolic with Mother Nature.

**FORT COOPER STATE PARK**, Inverness—A pioneer fort built to protect sick and wounded soldiers during General Winfield Scott's withdrawal in the second Seminole Indian War. Guided tours are available. There's also picnicking, shelters, grills, swimming, fishing, and nature trails. Admission is 50¢; children under 6 free. Open daily 8 A.M. to sunset. 3100 Old Floral City Road; Inverness 32650 (904-726-0315).

**BAY BEACH**, St. Petersburg—There's a nominal 10¢ charge for this beach, which has shelters, showers, and beautiful snow-white sands. Located at North Shore Drive and 13th Avenue Northeast. Information: 813-867-3972.

**BOYD HILL NATURE TRAIL**, St. Petersburg—Two hundred and sixteen acres of nature, with 6 miles of trails and boardwalks. A nature center features displays and exhibits of native wildlife, and guided tours are available. Open daily (except Thursdays) 9 A.M. to 5 P.M.; until 8 P.M. on Tuesdays and Fridays. Admission is 75¢ for adults; 35¢ for children. 1101 Country Club Way South; St. Petersburg 33705 (813-893-7326).

**LITHIA SPRINGS PARK**, Tampa—This popular park is a landing spot for canoeists on the Alafia River. Amenities include a natural spring for swimming and snorkeling, picnic facilities, campgrounds, and, in summer, various concession stands. The natural spring keeps water temperature at a constant 72 degrees year-round. Open 8 A.M. to sunset. Admission is 50¢. Lithia Springs Road; Tampa 33547 (813-689-2139).

**YBOR CITY STATE MUSEUM**, Tampa—Exhibits depict the city's history, housed in the former Ferlita Bakery, in the heart of Tampa's Latin section. There are mementos from the 1930s, when the area was known as the "cigar capital of the world," as well as displays of early Tampa history. Open daily 9 A.M. to noon and 1 P.M. to 5 P.M. Admission is 50¢; children under 6 free. 1818 Ninth Avenue; Tampa 33605 (813-247-6323).

**BOK TOWER GARDENS**, Lake Wales—One of Florida's most famous landmarks, these 28 acres of flowers and plants provide seasonal vistas of color against a lush green background of ferns, palms, oaks, and pines. The nature observatory, called Window by the Pond, provides a vantage point for contemplation, and Bok Tower itself is actually a 53-bell carillon. (The bells range in weight from 17 pounds to nearly 12 tons, and recitals are given daily at 3 P.M.; the bells also chime all day long on the hour.) There's a fee of $2.50 per car when entering the garden's gate, but there is not an additional charge for individuals. Open daily 8 A.M. to 5:30 P.M. Drawer 3810; Lake Wales 33853 (813-676-1408).

**BLUE SPRING STATE PARK**, Orange City—Approximately 104 million gallons of crystal-clear water flow from this spring every day. Several dozen manatees find winter homes here and there's also swimming for humans, as well as camping, hiking, canoeing, boating, fishing, and picnicking facilities. Open daily 8 A.M. to sunset. Admission is 50¢; children under 6 free. 2100 West French Avenue; Orange City 32763 (904-775-3663).

**WEKIWA SPRINGS STATE PARK**, Apopka—Cool underground springs, averaging 70 degrees year-round, make for great swimming. There are also hiking trails, especially beckoning because wildlife abounds here and it's easy to spot otters, raccoons, turtles, herons, and egrets. Open daily 8 A.M. to sunset. Admission is 50¢; children under 6 free. 1800 Wekiwa Circle; Apopka 32703 (305-889-3140).

**TURKEY LAKE CITY PARK**, Orlando—One of Central Florida's most popular parks, for the best of reasons: its 774 acres include picnic facilities, bicycle and roller-skating trails, swimming facilities, a petting zoo, and ecology exhibits. Open daily 9:30 A.M. to 6 P.M. Admission is $1; under 2 free. An annual pass is available for $75, which admits a family of 5. 3401 Hiawassee Road; Orlando 32811 (305-299-5594).

# SOUTHERN FLORIDA

See where the famed Seminole Wars finally ended; visit the homes of some of the early southern Florida pioneers; and stretch out on the most beautiful beach in all the Keys. It's all here—and almost for free.

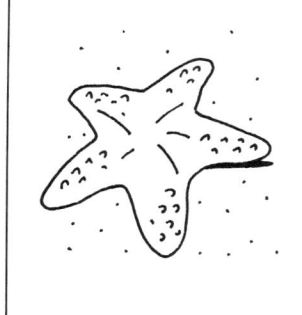

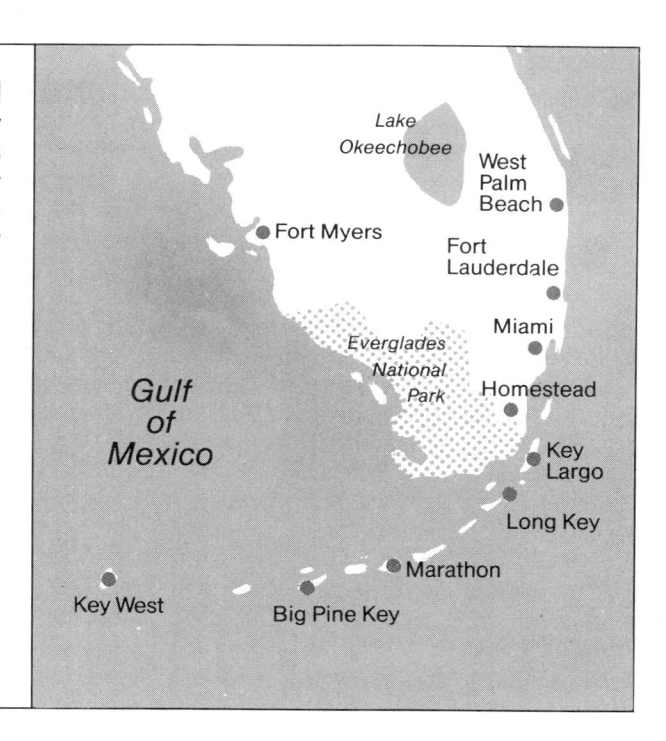

**HIGHLANDS HAMMOCK STATE PARK**, Sebring—These 3,800 acres have some of the best hiking trails in the state. There are scenic driving tours for the relatively sedentary and a museum for the curious. Open daily 8 A.M. to sunset. Admission is 50¢. Six miles west of Sebring off Highway 27; 813-385-0011.

**KORESHAN STATE HISTORIC SITE**, Estero—Religious pioneer Cyrus Teed settled here with a group of followers. He taught that the earth was hollow and that we live *inside* the world. Being a celibate society, it didn't last too long, but this restored village shows how Teed and his believers fared. Open daily 8 A.M. to sunset. Admission is 50¢. Near Fort Myers off Highway 41; 813-992-0311.

**COLLIER-SEMINOLE STATE PARK**, 17 miles south of Naples—A pristine spread of 6,423 acres of marshland where the Everglades meet the Big Cypress. This is said to be the spot where the Seminole Wars ended. There's canoeing, camping, and fishing. Open daily 8 A.M. to sunset. Admission is 50¢. Junction of Highways 92 and 41; 813-394-3397.

**DREHER PARK AND ZOO**, West Palm Beach—One of the area's most peaceful spots. There's a small zoo, a botanical garden, and a nature trail. Open daily 9 A.M. to 5 P.M. Admission is $2 for adults; $1 for children and senior citizens. 1301 Summit Boulevard; West Palm Beach 33405 (305-585-2197).

**SCIENCE MUSEUM OF PALM BEACH COUNTY**, West Palm Beach—Exhibits feature chemistry, physics, marine sciences, and anatomy. There's also a good planetarium. Open Tuesdays through Saturdays 10 A.M. to 5 P.M.; Sundays 1 P.M. to 5 P.M.; Fridays 6:30 P.M. to 10 P.M. Admission is $2 for adults; $1 for children and senior citizens. 4801 Dreher Trail North; West Palm Beach 33405 (305-832-1988).

**STRANAHAN HOUSE**, Fort Lauderdale—The oldest existing structure in Broward County was constructed in 1901 as the home of early pioneers Frank and Ivy Stranahan. Open Wednesdays, Fridays, and Saturdays 10 A.M. to 4 P.M.; Fridays 5:30 P.M. to 8:30 P.M.; Sundays 1 P.M. to 4 P.M. Admission is $3. Las Olas Boulevard; Fort Lauderdale 33303 (305-524-4736).

**BARNACLE STATE HISTORIC SITE**, Coconut Grove—The restored home of Commodore Ralph Munroe, an early Miami pioneer, was originally constructed of materials he found from shipwrecks. The naval architect and photographer later put the building's first story on stilts and built a new first floor beneath it. Open Wednesdays through Sundays for tours at 9 A.M., 10:30 A.M., 1 P.M., and 2:30 P.M. Admission is 50¢. 3485 Main Highway; Coconut Grove 33133 (305-448-9445).

**HAULOVER BEACH FISHING PIER**, Miami Beach—Extending 1,100 feet into the Atlantic, this is southern Florida's best wooden pier. It's between Bal Harbour and Motel Row, and the 500,000 visitors who visit the pier each year must agree on its appeal. There's great fishing, and tackle can be rented; or just pull up a bench and enjoy the stunning view. Open 24 hours daily. Admission is $2. 10500 Collins Avenue; Miami Beach 33160 (305-947-6767).

**CHEKIKA STATE RECREATION AREA**, 17 miles northwest of Homestead—Smack in the middle of the Everglades, this sawgrass prairie and tropical hammock was named for a Seminole chief. There's swimming, fishing, camping, and a nature trail. Open daily 8 A.M. to sunset. Admission is 50¢. Take Krome Avenue in Miami to 168th Street Southwest; Chekika is about 6 miles west (305-253-0950).

**BAHIA HONDA STATE PARK**, Big Pine Key—The most beautiful beach in all the Keys is found at this recreation area. There are nature trails, swimming, skin and scuba diving, fishing, and camping. Open daily 8 A.M. to sunset. Admission is 50¢. Reservations for campsites should be made well in advance. Route 1; Box 782; Big Pine Key 33043 (305-872-2353).

# DISCOUNT SHOPPING

**S**hopping, unlike sunbathing, swimming, and other such assorted amusements, is never as much fun when it costs absolutely nothing; buying almost always beats looking. But then, shopping isn't much fun when it leans toward the other extreme, either; no one wants to waste money for no reason.

Happily, Florida provides a rare balance between the joys of consumerism and the sorrows of high prices. The state is a virtual maze of factory outlets, discount fashion stores, and outlet malls, where savvy shoppers can buy everything from Bass boots to Carter's children's clothing to Dansk dishes, all at significant savings.

To help shoppers get the most for their money, here's a guide to the best of Florida's myriad bargain-shopping opportunities. In each of the 3 regions of the state, discount shopping stores are listed alphabetically, city by city. The first time a store is listed in each region, it is briefly described. Because so many of the stores are parts of chains and, therefore, have branches in several cities within a given region, subsequent listings include only addresses, phone numbers, hours, and a reference to previous store descriptions of stock. Unless specifically stated otherwise, stores accept major credit cards; however, it is probably a wise idea to call ahead and check the forms of payment accepted by individual stores.

# NORTHERN FLORIDA

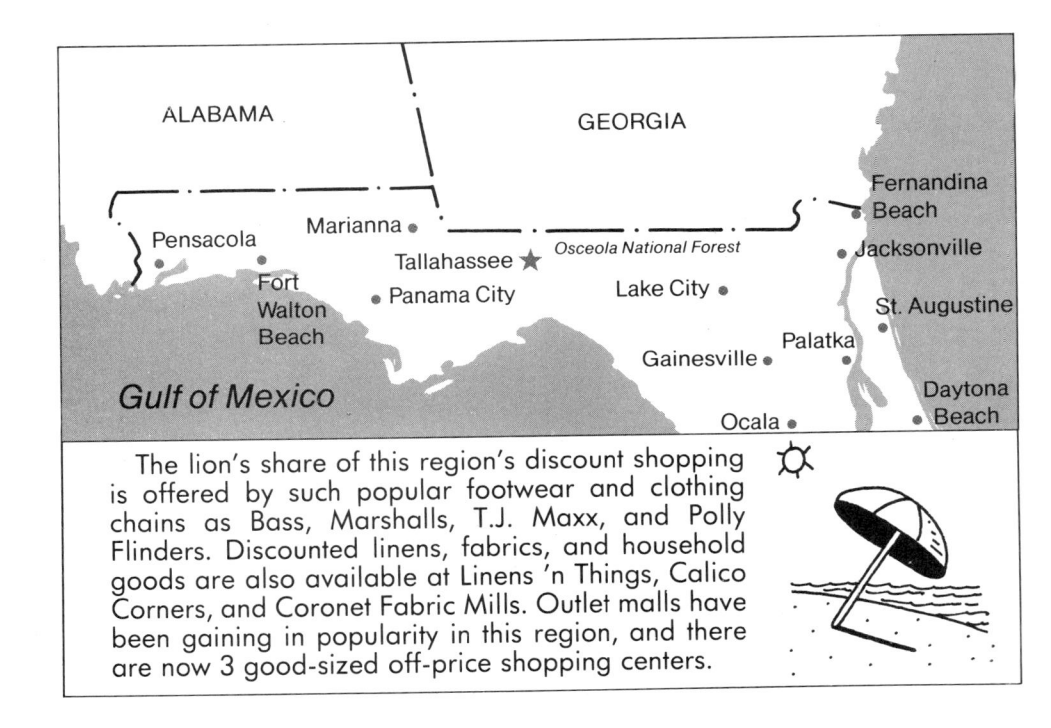

The lion's share of this region's discount shopping is offered by such popular footwear and clothing chains as Bass, Marshalls, T.J. Maxx, and Polly Flinders. Discounted linens, fabrics, and household goods are also available at Linens 'n Things, Calico Corners, and Coronet Fabric Mills. Outlet malls have been gaining in popularity in this region, and there are now 3 good-sized off-price shopping centers.

## PENSACOLA

**BANKER'S NOTE**—Designer labels such as Liz Claiborne, Evan Picone, Villager, and Sasson fill the racks of this popular chain store, where savings on women's sportswear range from 20 to 35 percent. 29 North Palafox Place (904-434-3578). Open Mondays through Fridays 9:30 A.M. to 5:30 P.M., Saturdays 9:30 A.M. to 4:30 P.M. Closed Sundays. *University Mall*, Davis Highway (904-478-3747). Open Mondays through Saturdays 10 A.M. to 9:00 P.M. and Sundays 12:30 P.M. to 5:30 P.M.

## FORT WALTON BEACH

**BANKER'S NOTE** (see above)—*Santa Rosa Mall* on Mary Esther Cutoff (904-243-3133). Open Mondays through Saturdays 10 A.M. to 9 P.M. and Sundays noon to 5 P.M.

**FLORIDA POTTERY**—A one-of-a-kind housewares store with everything from china, glassware, and stainless tableware to flowers—fresh and silk. Famous name brands include Oneida and Ewing (flatware); Pyrex and Select Brands (cooking ware); and International and United (china). Prices are generally 20 percent lower than normal retail. 224 Eglin Parkway (904-863-5181). Open 9 A.M. to 9 P.M. Mondays through Saturdays and noon to 6 P.M. Sundays.

**VAN HEUSEN OUTLET STORE**—Not only Van Heusen labels, but also Halston, Stanley Blacker, and Geoffrey Beene men's and women's first-quality sportswear. Outerwear, pajamas, and sweaters are also available. Prices are usually about 50 percent lower than normal retail. *Sun Plaza*, 41D Mary Esther Cutoff (904-243-7001). Open Mondays through Saturdays 9 A.M. to 6 P.M.; closed Sundays.

## TALLAHASSEE

**BANKER'S NOTE** (see Pensacola entry)—1414 Apalachee Parkway (904-878-7131). Open Mondays through Fridays 10 A.M. to 9 P.M., Saturdays 10 A.M. to 6 P.M., and Sundays 12:30 P.M. to 5:30 P.M.

**BASS SHOE FACTORY OUTLET**—You can't go wrong with the Bass label, and you can't go wrong with the prices at Bass factory outlets. Shoes, boots, clogs, athletic wear, and sports clothing, all Bass or Bear Trap, cost 30 percent less than in most conventional retail stores. 1201 Apalachee Parkway (904-878-5825). Open Mondays through Saturdays 10 A.M. to 9 P.M. and Sundays 11 A.M. to 6 P.M.

**CAPITAL MENSWEAR**—One of the few off-price stores to carry tall and big men's clothes and short men's sizes. The complete line of men's clothing and accessories is all first quality, and personal tailoring is done on the premises. Discounts run 20 to 30 percent. 1885 North Boulevard (904-385-6866). Open Mondays through Saturdays 10 A.M. to 6 P.M. and, in December only, Sundays 1 P.M. to 6 P.M.

**CAPITAL OUTLET MALL**—Anchored by *Winston's* (see below) and *U.S. Factory Outlet*, which is a small, off-price department store, this 25-store mall offers a good selection of men's and women's apparel, including *Amy Stoudt* for large women's sizes. There's also a *Linens 'n Things*, a *Nutrition Outlet*, and a *Hunt and Peck*. 5050 West Tennessee Street (904-576-7172). Open Mondays through Saturdays 10 A.M. to 9 P.M. and Sundays noon to 5:30 P.M.

**POLLY FLINDERS FACTORY STORE**—Polly Flinders's hand-smocked dresses for girls are the main event at one of Florida's most popular outlets, which carries only Polly Flinders's merchandise. Prices are 40 to 60 percent lower than normal retail. 3491-7 Thomasville Road (904-893-3730). Open Mondays through Saturdays 10 A.M. to 6 P.M.; closed Sundays.

**WINSTON'S**—Large and attractive department-type stores with merchandise at 20 to 50 percent off. Gloria Vanderbilt, Anne Klein, Botany 500, Arrow, Pierre Cardin, Health-tex, Stride-Rite, Freeman, and Bandolino are among the names men, women, and children will find on apparel and footwear. In *Capital Outlet Mall*, 5050 West Tennessee Road (904-575-9694). Open Mondays through Saturdays 10 A.M. to 9 P.M. and Sundays 12:30 P.M. to 5:30 P.M.

## GAINESVILLE

**BASS SHOE FACTORY OUTLET** (see Tallahassee entry)—Opposite *Butler Plaza* on Archer Road (904-372-5987). Open Mondays through Saturdays 10 A.M. to 9 P.M. and Sundays noon to 5 P.M.

**CORONET FABRIC MILLS**—More than a thousand patterns in slipcovers, draperies, and upholsteries, all available at discounts of 50 to 70 percent. Manufacturers include Waverly, Schumacher, Bloomcraft, Cohama, and Cyrus Clark. No credit cards. On State Road 441 North (904-373-3666). Open Mondays through Fridays 10 A.M. to 6 P.M. and Saturdays 10 A.M. to 4 P.M.

**POLLY FLINDERS FACTORY STORE** (see Tallahassee entry)—In *Westgate Regency Shopping Center*, University Boulevard and 34th Street (904-376-7282). Open Mondays through Saturdays 9:30 A.M. to 5:30 P.M.; closed Sundays.

## JACKSONVILLE

**CALICO CORNERS**—Seconds and irregulars of designer fabrics, for home decorating, especially upholstery and drapery materials. Intelligent courteous service and sizable savings distinguish stores in this chain. 4725 San Jose Boulevard (904-737-6930). Open Mondays through Saturdays 9:30 A.M. to 6 P.M. and Sundays noon to 5 P.M.

**CARTER'S CHILDREN'S OUTLET**—Durable, comfortable, and attractive apparel, underwear, and pajamas for boys and girls in sizes that range from layette to 14 (girls) or 16 (boys). First-quality and irregular garments carry price tags 30 to 60 percent below normal retail. No credit cards. 5868 Ramona Boulevard (904-783-0411). Open Mondays through Saturdays 10 A.M. to 6 P.M. and Sundays noon to 5 P.M.

**LINENS 'N THINGS**—Famous brand towels, sheets, comforters, blankets, and other household merchandise, with discounts of 40 to 50 percent on first quality

Lady Pepperell, West Point-Pepperell, and Martex, among other brands. Seconds and irregulars are priced even lower. 5840 Ramona Boulevard (904-783-1145). Open Mondays through Saturdays 10 A.M. to 9 P.M. and Sundays noon to 5 P.M.

**MARSHALLS**—High-quality, name-brand apparel for men, women, and children have earned the chain a national reputation for excellence. The stores also carry accessories, shoes, gifts, home fashions, and luggage, all at prices as much as 50 percent below retail. In *Argyle Forest Mall*, I-295 and Blanding Boulevard (904-777-1072). Open Mondays through Saturdays 9 A.M. to 9:30 P.M. and Sundays noon to 6 P.M.

**THE OLD MILL**—Moderate to better women's sportswear in sizes 4 to 16. Discounts on the first-quality Country Miss and other name-brand merchandise can be as much as 70 percent. In *Outlets Limited*, I-295 and I-10 at Lane Avenue (904-743-7000). Open Mondays through Saturdays 10 A.M. to 9 P.M. and Sundays 11 A.M. to 6 P.M.

**OUTLETS LIMITED**—More than 10 off-price and outlet stores, ranging from *Handy City* for building supplies to *Vogue* women's fashion store. The minimum discount at the mall, located on the west side of the city, is 20 percent. I-295 and I-10 at Lane Avenue (904-743-7000). Open Mondays through Saturdays 10 A.M. to 9 P.M. and Sundays 11 A.M. to 6 P.M.

**POLLY FLINDERS FACTORY STORE** (see Tallahassee entry)—9776 Atlantic Boulevard (904-721-3665). Open Mondays through Saturdays 9:30 A.M. to 5:30 P.M.; closed Sundays.

**T. J. MAXX**—The whole family can be outfitted with name-brand clothes, shoes, gifts, and dinnerware at discounts of 20 to 60 percent. Typical of the Maxx chain, 90 percent of the merchandise at this large, supermarket-style store is first quality. 9822 Atlantic Boulevard (904-721-1349). Open Mondays through Saturdays 9:30 A.M. to 9:30 P.M. and Sundays noon to 6 P.M.

## DAYTONA BEACH

**CARTER'S CHILDREN'S OUTLET** (see Jacksonville entry)—In the *Daytona Beach Outlet Mall*, 2400 South Ridgewood Avenue (904-788-4772). Open Mondays through Wednesdays 10 A.M. to 6 P.M., Thursdays through Saturdays 10 A.M. to 9 P.M., and Sundays noon to 6 P.M.

**DAYTONA BEACH OUTLET MALL**—Recently redecorated with cedarwood paneling, overhead bank lights, skylights, and indoor trees, this 46-store mall has the typical assortment of big-name, discount clothing, shoe, and accessory stores. 2400 South Ridgewood Avenue on U.S. 1 (904-767-8353). Open Mondays through Saturdays 10 A.M. to 9 P.M. and Sundays noon to 6 P.M.

**HAPPY FOOT**—Freeman, Air Step, and Naturalizer are just a few of the well-known makers of men's and women's footwear represented here at discounts of 30 to 50 percent. Hanes Hosiery is available at prices 75 percent below retail. 1294 Ocean Shore Boulevard, Ormond Beach (904-441-3211). Open Mondays through Saturdays 9 A.M. to 6 P.M. and Saturdays noon to 5 P.M.

# CENTRAL FLORIDA

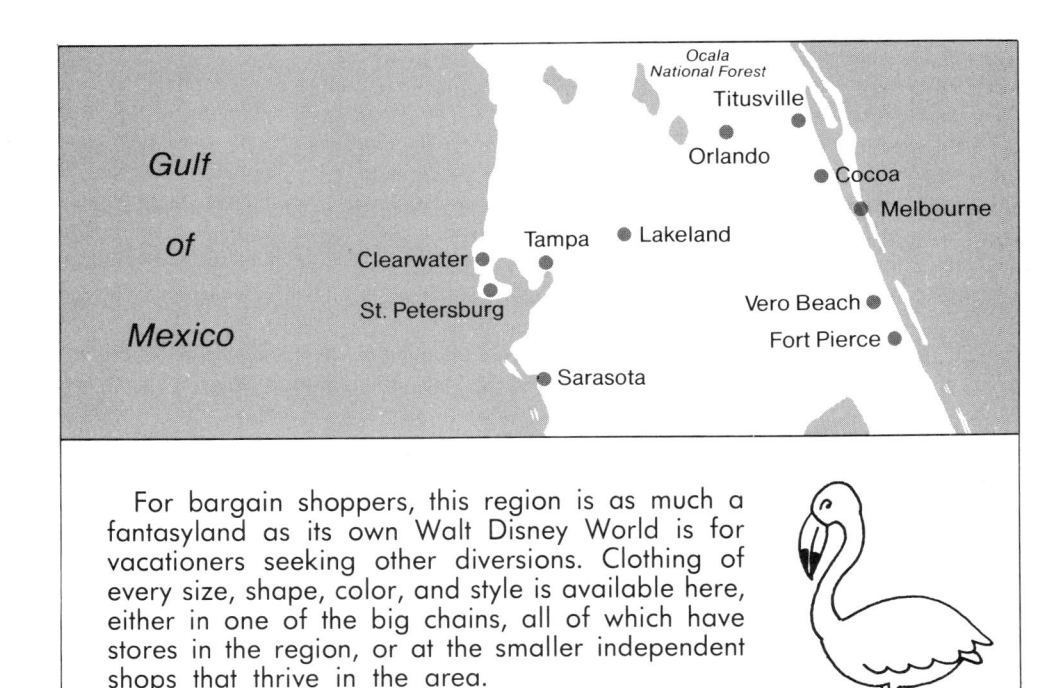

For bargain shoppers, this region is as much a fantasyland as its own Walt Disney World is for vacationers seeking other diversions. Clothing of every size, shape, color, and style is available here, either in one of the big chains, all of which have stores in the region, or at the smaller independent shops that thrive in the area.

## CLEARWATER

**BASS SHOE FACTORY OUTLET**—You can't go wrong with the Bass label, and you can't go wrong with the prices at Bass outlet stores. Shoes, boots, clogs, athletic wear, and sports clothing, all Bass or Bear Trap, cost 30 percent less than in retail stores. In *Bay Outlet Mall,* 15525 U.S. 19 South (813-530-1252). Open Mondays through Saturdays 10 A.M. to 9 P.M. and Sundays noon to 6 P.M.

**BAY AREA OUTLET MALL**—More than 20 factory outlet and discount stores, offering an excellent assortment of clothing, footwear, and accessories. Along with the well-known names, there are also some smaller bargain shops, including the *Publisher's Book Outlet,* which offers first-quality and closeout books and calendars at savings up to 70 percent. 15525 U.S. 19 South at Roosevelt Avenue (813-535-2337). Open Mondays through Saturdays 10 A.M. to 9 P.M. and Sundays noon to 6 P.M.

**DANSK FACTORY OUTLET**—The fine Dansk china, glassware, stainless flatware, pots and pans, and teakwood items are available at prices 30 to 50 percent off regular retail. Though most of the merchandise is Dansk brand, some other well-known brands in household goods are also represented. 2790 Gulf-to-Bay Boulevard (813-797-4940). Open Mondays through Saturdays 10 A.M. to 7 P.M. and Sundays noon to 6 P.M.

**GENERAL SHOE FACTORY TO YOU**—Dress shoes, work shoes, casuals, tennis shoes, and running shoes for men and women are all available here at 20 to 40 percent discounts. Famous name manufacturers include Johnston & Murphy, Hardy's, After Hours, Kangaroo, and Puma. About a third of the selection is first quality. In *Bay Outlet Mall,* 15525 U.S. 19 South (813-535-1981). Open Mondays through Saturdays 10 A.M. to 9 P.M. and Sundays noon to 6 P.M.

**THE HOME DEPOT**—Probably the only discount chain that claims to sell everything one needs to build a house. A wide variety of brand names in tools and home repair merchandise, including Black and Decker, Wagner, Hitachi, Glidden, and GTE, is available at significant savings. 2351 U.S. 19 North (813-797-8755). Open Mondays through Saturdays 8 A.M. to 9:30 P.M. and Sundays 9 A.M. to 6 P.M.

**JUST LABELS**—Top-of-the-line in discount apparel in both merchandise and decor. Fully carpeted and attractively decorated, the store, like others in the chain, offers Pierre Cardin, Anne Klein, Oleg Cassini, Jones New York, and other famous makers of men's and women's clothes for 20 to 60 percent off normal retail prices. In *Bay Outlet Mall,* 15525 U.S. 19 South (813-530-3429). Open Mondays through Saturdays 10 A.M. to 9 P.M. and Sundays noon to 6 P.M.

**LOEHMANN'S**—Incredible bargains on some of the most famous names in women's fashion. Labels are removed, but the price tag codes usually provide good clues to the designers of the suits, dresses, sportswear, and evening wear offered at discounts of 30 to 60 percent. 1730 U.S. 19 North (813-799-4300). Open Mondays through Fridays 10 A.M. to 9 P.M., Saturdays 10 A.M. to 5:30 P.M., and Sundays noon to 5 P.M.

**MARSHALLS**—High-quality, name-brand apparel for men, women, and children has earned the chain a national reputation for excellence. The stores also carry accessories, shoes, gifts, home fashions, and luggage, all at prices up to 50 percent below retail. In *Cypress Point Mall*, 2367 U.S. 19 North (813-799-3667). Open Mondays through Saturdays 9 A.M. to 9:30 P.M. and Sundays noon to 6 P.M.

**NEWPORT SPORTSWEAR/SOUTHLAND SHIRTS**—All first-quality casual and formal menswear, with labels such as Directions, Clear Creek, Plainsmen, Chapel Hill, and Country Squire in the collection. Some women's apparel is also offered. Savings range from 30 to 50 percent. In *Bay Outlet Mall*, 15525 U.S. 19 South (813-536-7957). Open Mondays through Saturdays 10 A.M. to 9 P.M. and Sundays noon to 6 P.M.

**PEPPERIDGE FARM THRIFT**—As the commercial says, Pepperidge Farm remembers. In its outlet stores, it remembers that people like to save money—up to 60 percent on Pepperidge Farm and Campbell Soup (which owns the baked-goods company) brands. No credit cards. 19th Street and Gulf-to-Bay Boulevard (813-796-1474). Open Mondays through Saturdays 9:30 A.M. to 6 P.M. and Sundays 9:30 A.M. to 5:30 P.M.

**SHAPES ACTIVEWEAR OUTLET**—First quality and irregular exercise wear: leotards, dance clothes, sweats, and warm-up suits. Socks, tights, and hosiery are also available, all at 40 to 60 percent off. In *Cypress Point Mall*, 2365 U.S. 19 North (813-799-6026). Open Mondays through Saturdays 10 A.M to 9 P.M. and Sundays 12:30 P.M. to 5:30 P.M.

**T. J. MAXX**—Outfit the whole family with name-brand clothes, shoes, gifts, and dinnerware at discounts ranging from 20 to 60 percent. Ninety percent of the merchandise at these large, supermarket-style stores is first quality. In *Bay Outlet Mall*, 15525 U.S. 19 South (813-530-4783). Open Mondays through Saturdays 10 A.M. to 9 P.M. and Sundays noon to 6 P.M. Or, in *Country Village Shopping Center*, 2541 Countryside Boulevard (813-799-0776). Open Mondays through Saturdays 9:30 A.M. to 9:30 P.M. and Sundays noon to 6:15 P.M.

# TAMPA

**BANKER'S NOTE**—Designer labels such as Liz Claiborne, Evan Picone, Villager, and Sasson fill the racks at these popular stores, where discounts on women's sportswear range from 20 to 35 percent. In *Mission Bell Shopping Center*, North Dale Mabry Highway (813-962-6568). Open Mondays through Fridays 10 A.M. to 9 P.M., Saturdays 10 A.M. to 8 P.M., and Sundays noon to 5 P.M. Or, 4501 West Kennedy Avenue (813-879-8244). Open Mondays through Saturdays 10 A.M. to 7 P.M. and Sundays noon to 5 P.M.

**BASS SHOE FACTORY OUTLET** (see Clearwater entry for description)—In *Tampa Outlet Mall*, 3910 West Hillsborough Avenue, West Tampa (813-879-7053). Open Mondays through Saturdays 10 A.M. to 9 P.M. and Sundays noon to 5 P.M.; also at 2307 Fowler Plaza South (813-977-5662). Open Mondays through Saturdays 10 A.M. to 9 P.M. and Sundays noon to 5 P.M.; and in *Belz Factory Outlet Mall*, I-4 and Buffalo Avenue (813-626-6690). Open Mondays through Saturdays 10 A.M. to 6 P.M. and Sundays noon to 6 P.M.

**BELZ FACTORY OUTLET MALL**—Disney-like storefronts and a festive atmosphere further enliven the already hopping scene at the 40 stores in this gigantic and diverse mall. Just about every imaginable item is on sale somewhere here, and at significant savings. I-4 and Buffalo Avenue (813-621-6047). Open Mondays through Saturdays 10 A.M. to 9 P.M. and Sundays noon to 6 P.M.

**CALICO CORNERS**—Seconds and irregulars of fabrics for home decorating, especially upholstery and drapery. Smart shoppers will recognize designer names in the selection. Intelligent, courteous service and sizable savings distinguish the chain. 1711 South Dale Mabry Highway (813-251-2327). Open Mondays through Saturdays 9 A.M. to 5 P.M.; closed Sundays.

**CASUAL MALE**—From socks to suits, a complete line of menswear at 50 to 60 percent off retail prices. Mostly first-quality merchandise from well-known designers. Stock is very seasonal, with swimsuits in spring and summer and overcoats in winter. In *Tampa Outlet Mall*, 3910 West Hillsborough Avenue in West Tampa (813-879-9449). Open Mondays through Saturdays 10 A.M. to 9 P.M. and Sundays noon to 5 P.M.

**DRUG EMPORIUM**—Though discounts on pharmaceuticals vary widely, the chain's high-volume buying and selling almost always results in a lower markup than in retail drugstores. Greeting cards, sunglasses, and other beach items are also discounted, usually 40 to 50 percent. No credit cards. 4210 South Dale Mabry Highway (813-831-2973). Open Mondays through Saturdays 9 A.M. to 9 P.M. and Sundays 10 A.M. to 6 P.M.

**HASTINGS RECORDS AND TAPES**—Most records here sell for $2 below list price. Tapes, videocassettes, music books, and some boutique items sell at prices up to 25 percent below retail. In *University Square Mall* at Fowler Avenue and 22nd Street (813-977-2314). Open 10 A.M. to 9 P.M. Mondays through Saturdays and 12:30 P.M. to 5:30 P.M. Sundays. Or, *Eastlake Square Mall*, 5701 Hillsborough Avenue (813-626-1024). Open Mondays through Saturdays 10 A.M. to 9 P.M. and Sundays 12:30 P.M. to 5:30 P.M.

**THE HOME DEPOT** (see Clearwater entry)—Florida and Waters Avenues (813-935-3090). Open Mondays through Saturdays 8 A.M. to 9:30 P.M. and Sundays 9 A.M. to 6 P.M.

**LINENS 'N THINGS**—Famous brand towels, sheets, comforters, blankets, and other household merchandise, with discounts of 40 to 50 percent on first-quality Lady Pepperell, West Point-Pepperell, and Martex, among others. Seconds and irregulars are priced even lower. In *Tampa Outlet Mall*, 3910 West Hillsborough Avenue, West Tampa (813-875-7759). Open Mondays through Saturdays 10 A.M. to 9 P.M. and Sundays noon to 5 P.M.; also at 14805 North Dale Mabry Highway (813-962-8644). Open Mondays through Saturdays 9:30 A.M. to 9 P.M. and Sundays 11 A.M. to 6 P.M.

**NEWPORT SPORTSWEAR/SOUTHLAND SHIRT** (see Clearwater entry)—In *Tampa Outlet Mall*, 3910 West Hillsborough Avenue, West Tampa (813-870-6058). Open Mondays through Saturdays 10 A.M. to 9 P.M. and Sundays noon to 5 P.M. Also in *Belz Factory Outlet Mall*, I-4 and Buffalo Avenue (813-626-2576). Open Mondays through Saturdays 10 A.M. to 6 P.M. and Sundays noon to 6 P.M.

**PELTZ FAMOUS BRAND SHOES**—Just like the name says, well-known manufacturers' footwear for men and women. Discounts on first-quality Amalfi, Ferragamo, Revelations, Dexter, Bally, Freeman, and other well-known brand shoes range from 20 to 50 percent. The Peltz branch in St. Petersburg has the highest volume of business per square foot in the entire Southeast. 1916 South Dale Mabry Highway (813-253-5725). Open Mondays 10 A.M. to 8 P.M. and Tuesdays through Saturdays 10 A.M. to 6 P.M.; closed Sundays.

**POLLY FLINDERS FACTORY STORE**—Polly Flinders's hand-smocked dresses for girls are the main event at one of Florida's most poular outlets, which carries only Polly Flinders's merchandise. Prices are 40 to 60 percent lower than most retail stores. In *Northgate Shopping Mall*, 9017 North Florida Avenue (813-932-7935). Open Mondays through Saturdays 10 A.M. to 6 P.M.; closed Sundays.

**SHAPES ACTIVEWEAR OUTLET** (see Clearwater entry)—In *Belz Factory Outlet Mall*, I-4 and Buffalo Avenue (813-626-4050). Open Mondays through Saturdays 10 A.M. to 6 P.M. and Sundays noon to 6 P.M.

**SOCKS 'N SUCH**—Everything a foot could want, from socks, hosiery, and tights to casual and athletic footwear. Some brand names, such as Adidas, in addition to the chain's own no-label goods. Discounts of 20 to 40 percent. In *Tampa Outlet Mall*, 3910 West Hillsborough Avenue, West Tampa (813-875-0597). Open Mondays through Saturdays 10 A.M. to 9 P.M. and Sundays noon to 5 P.M. Also in *Belz Factory Outlet Mall*, I-4 and Buffalo Avenue (813-623-5050). Open Mondays through Saturdays 10 A.M. to 6 P.M. and Sundays noon to 6 P.M.

**TAMPA OUTLET MALL**—About 10 mintues beyond downtown Tampa and a mile north of the home of the NFL Buccaneers, this mall, with more than 15 stores, has everything from discount sneakers and socks to discount gems. There's also a *Book Hutch* and a *Discount Nutrition Center*. 3910 West

Hillsborough Avenue, West Tampa (813-879-7053). Open Mondays through Saturdays 10 A.M. to 9 P.M. and Sundays noon to 5 P.M.

## ST. PETERSBURG

**HASTINGS RECORDS AND TAPES** (see Tampa entry)—In *Tyrone Square Mall*, Tyrone Boulevard and 66th Street (813-344-3575). Open Mondays through Saturdays 10 A.M. to 9 P.M. and Sundays 12:30 P.M. to 5:30 P.M. Also in *Pinellas Square Mall*, U.S. 19 and Park Boulevard (813-522-6833). Open Mondays through Saturdays 10 A.M. to 9 P.M. and Sundays noon to 5 P.M.

**POLLY FLINDERS FACTORY STORE** (see Tampa entry)—38th Avenue North and 4th Street (813-821-2708). Open Mondays through Saturdays 9:30 A.M. to 5:30 P.M.

**PELTZ FAMOUS BRAND SHOES** (see Tampa entry)—226 Central Avenue (813-898-6374). Open Mondays and Fridays 9:30 A.M. to 8 P.M., Tuesdays through Thursdays and Saturdays 9:30 A.M. to 5:30 P.M.; closed Sundays.

**SWIMSUIT OUTLET**—Outdoor clothing for the sunstruck. All first-quality swimsuits and sportswear, with names like Rosemarie Reed, Maxine, Tultex, and Jantzen usually in the selection. Discounts are 20 to 60 percent. 7116 Gulf Boulevard (813-367-1545). From January to June, open 9:30 A.M. to 7 P.M. Mondays through Fridays and 12:30 P.M. to 4:30 P.M. Saturdays. From July to December, Mondays through Fridays, open 9:30 A.M. to 6 P.M. and Saturdays 9:30 A.M. to 5 P.M.

## ALTAMONTE SPRINGS

**BASS SHOE FACTORY OUTLET** (see Clearwater entry)—In *Loehmann's Plaza*, 995 State Road 434 North (305-774-1546). Open Mondays through Fridays 10 A.M. to 9 P.M., Saturdays 10 A.M. to 6 P.M., and Sundays noon to 5:30 P.M.

**DANSKIN FACTORY OUTLET**—The only Florida outlet of this famous dancewear company. All Danskin products in all sizes at 50 percent below retail prices. Halston, Max Factor, and Almay cosmetics, as well as Samsonite luggage, are also available. I-4 and State Road 436 (305-339-3840). Open Mondays through Saturdays 10 A.M. to 9 P.M. and Sundays 11 A.M. to 5:30 P.M.

**LOEHMANN'S PLAZA**—If the lush landscaping at this 50-store outdoor plaza does not lure you to sample its wares, the funny names of some of the stores might. Who could pass up discount footwear from *And Shoes to Boot*? Or decorator items from *A Chair in the Sun of Madrid?* Many of the stores offer discount apparel or accessories, but not every store is discount. 995 State Road 434 North (305-862-2929). Open Mondays through Fridays from 10 A.M. to 9 P.M., Saturdays from 10 A.M. to 6 P.M., and Sundays from noon to 5:30 P.M.

**LINENS 'N THINGS** (see Tampa entry)—In *Loehmann's Plaza*, 995 State Road 434 North (305-774-0524). Open Mondays through Saturdays 10 A.M. to 9 P.M. and Sundays noon to 5 P.M.

**LOEHMANN'S** (see Clearwater entry)—In *Loehmann's Plaza*, 995 State Road 434 North (305-774-1247). Open Mondays through Saturdays 10 A.M. to 9 P.M. and Sundays noon to 5 P.M.

**MARSHALLS** (see Clearwater entry)—293 East Altamonte Drive (305-834-2015). Open Mondays through Saturdays 9:30 A.M. to 9:30 P.M. and Sundays noon to 6 P.M.

## ORLANDO

**BANISTER SHOE COMPANY**—At least 50 percent off on designer men's and women's shoes, with makers such as Gloria Vanderbilt, Joyce, Liz Claiborne, Amalfi, Bandolino, Evan Picone, and Capezio. Socks and hosiery are also available. In *Belz Factory Outlet Mall*, 5401 West Oakridge Road (305-351-2391). Open Mondays through Saturdays 10 A.M. to 9 P.M. and Sundays noon to 9 P.M.

**BANKER'S NOTE** (see Tampa entry)—In *Belz Factory Outlet Mall*, 5401 West Oakridge Road (305-894-4600). Open Mondays through Saturdays 10 A.M. to 9 P.M. and Sundays noon to 9 P.M.

**BASS SHOE FACTORY OUTLET** (see Clearwater entry)—In *Belz Factory Outlet Mall*, 5401 West Oakridge Road (305-351-2588). Open Mondays through Saturdays 10 A.M. to 9 P.M. and Sundays noon to 9 P.M.

**BELZ FACTORY OUTLET MALL**—The oldest and biggest factory outlet shopping center in Florida, with a list of stores that goes on forever. All of the big names in discount shopping are here, along with some worthwhile smaller ones: *Bedspread Warehouse, Golf Manufacturers Warehouse, Everything but Water, Wood Times.* Two extra plusses: the air-conditioning, and the mall's proximity to Walt Disney World. 5401 Oakridge Road (305-352-9600). Open Mondays through Saturdays 10 A.M. to 9 P.M. and Sundays noon to 9 P.M.

**BRANDED CARGO**—Teenagers will love the casual clothes for young men and women. At 30 percent off retail are Guess and Gloria Vanderbilt jeans and separates, Izod shirts and sportswear, and the Jordache line of clothing. Some children's apparel is also offered. In *Belz Factory Outlet Mall*, 5401 West Oakridge Road (305-351-7088). Open Mondays through Saturdays 10 A.M. to 9 P.M. and Sundays noon to 9 P.M.

**CALICO CORNERS** (see Tampa entry)—3702 Edgewater Road (305-299-2200). Open Mondays through Saturdays 9:30 A.M. to 5:30 P.M., until 9 P.M. Wednesdays; closed Sundays.

**CASUAL MALE** (see Tampa entry)—In *Belz Factory Outlet Mall*, 5401 West Oakridge Road (305-351-9599). Open Mondays through Saturdays 10 A.M. to 9 P.M. and Sundays noon to 9 P.M.

**CREIGHTON MALE**—The factory outlet store for Creighton shirts. Discounts of 30 to 50 percent on the men's and women's casual and dress shirts. Pants, sweaters, jackets, ties, and belts are also available. In *Belz Factory Outlet Mall*, 5401 West Oakridge Road (305-351-3300). Open Mondays through Saturdays 10 A.M. to 9 P.M. and Sundays noon to 9 P.M.

**DANSK FACTORY OUTLET** (see Clearwater entry)—7000 International Drive (305-351-2425). Open 9 A.M. to 7 P.M. every day.

**FRYE BOOT OUTLET**—Frye boots are well known for stylish durability, and this factory outlet offers first-quality and irregular shoes and boots for men, women, and children at savings of 60 to 70 percent. Other leather goods, including handbags, are also available. In *Belz Factory Outlet Mall*, 5401 West Oakridge Road (305-351-3537). Open Mondays through Saturdays 10 A.M. to 9 P.M. and Sundays noon to 9 P.M.

**THE HOME DEPOT** (see Clearwater entry)—6130 East Colonial Drive (305-282-1010). Open Mondays through Saturdays 9 A.M. to 9 P.M. and Sundays 10 A.M. to 6 P.M.

**HUNT AND PECK**—Low overhead here translates into low prices on women's sportswear. Peck and Peck, Villager, Sasson, and Liz Claiborne are among the designers in the selection, which includes suits and dresses as well as casual separates. Discounts on first-quality and closeout merchandise range from 25 to 50 percent. In *Loehmann's Plaza* (305-774-1725). Open 10 A.M. to 9 P.M. Mondays through Fridays, 10 A.M. to 6 P.M. Saturdays, and noon to 5:30 P.M. Sundays.

**QUALITY OUTLET CENTER** and **VILLAGE INTERNATIONAL**—The whimsy of Disney seems to have rubbed off on these two unusual off-price shopping centers, located across the street from one another. **Quality Outlet Center** features great bargains in china, glass, pottery, and crystal. Stores have names such as *Carolina Gifts, Goose Creek Trading Company,* and *Petals Silk Flowers.* **Village International** includes *Candy International, Photo Lab,* and *Nature's Wonder.* Both are at International Drive and Oakridge Road. Open Mondays through Saturdays 9:30 A.M. to 9 P.M. and Sundays 11 A.M. to 7 P.M.

**LEADING LABELS**—Undergarments with style at 20 to 50 percent discounts. Brand-name women's lingerie and hosiery, men's underwear and socks, and children's underclothes. In *Belz Factory Outlet Mall,* 5401 West Oakridge Road (305-352-8111). Open Mondays through Saturdays 10 A.M. to 9 P.M. and Sundays noon to 9 P.M.

**SHAPES ACTIVEWEAR OUTLET** (see Clearwater entry)—In *Belz Factory Outlet Mall,* 5401 West Oakridge Road (305-351-1638). Open Mondays through Saturdays 10 A.M. to 9 P.M. and Sundays noon to 9 P.M.

**SOCKS 'N SUCH** (see Tampa entry)—In *Belz Factory Outlet Mall,* 5401 West Oakridge Road (305-345-8874). Open Mondays through Saturdays 10 A.M. to 9 P.M. and Sundays noon to 9 P.M.

**FACTORY OUTLET WORLD KISSIMMEE**—Famous brand names at nearly half price are the rule at this 15-store mall. Merchandise includes clothing, shoes, paper goods, flatware, and pecans. Route 192 at 4699 Space Coast Highway (305-396-2260). Open from 9 A.M. to 9 P.M. Mondays through Saturdays and 1 P.M. to 9 P.M. Sundays.

---

## *Travel Tip:* COMFY BUS TRAVEL

If you plan to travel for long distances by bus, dress accordingly, in comfortable, loose-fitting clothes. Keep a sweater or jacket handy to wrap around you at night or when the air-conditioning gets too efficient, or to use as a pillow. Loosen your shoestrings, or slip into lounge shoes for the trip, putting on street shoes only for pit stops. Get off the bus every chance you have to stretch your legs and to avoid swollen ankles and achy muscles. Take these opportunities to wash up a bit and splash some cold water on your face.

A seat in the front near the driver affords the best view; the middle between the front and rear wheels, the smoothest ride. Take along a thermos and some snacks unless you have a propensity for bus-stop fare.

# SOUTHERN FLORIDA

Though Miami is the capital of discount shopping in this region, there are some interesting discount stores well worth investigating in other southern Florida cities. Try *Odd-Lot Trading* in Fort Lauderdale, or Fort Myers's *Jersild Factory Outlet*, or *Funtime Fashions* in Sarasota. In Miami, check out the mini-garment district on Northwest Fifth Avenue and 24th, 25th, and 26th Streets, where shoppers can revel in a variety of smaller, discount boutiques.

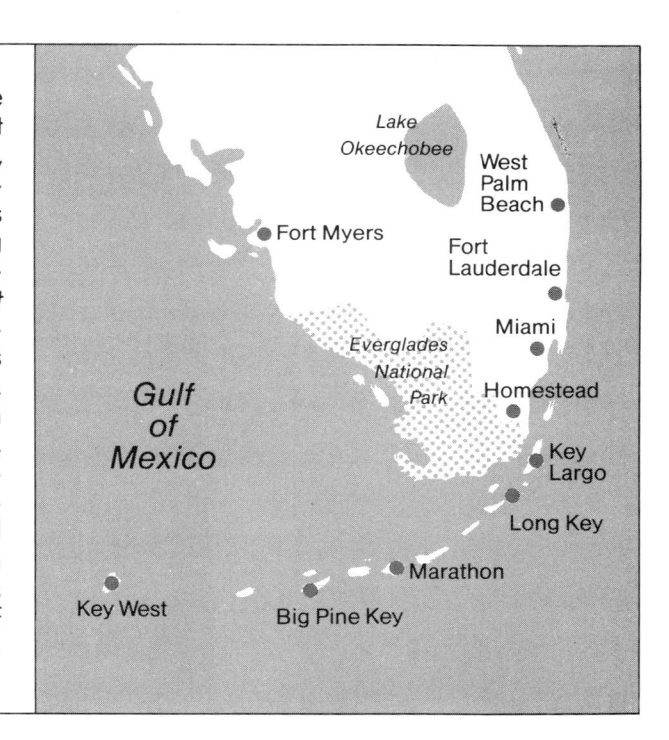

## SARASOTA

**BASS SHOE FACTORY OUTLET**—You can't go wrong with the Bass label, and you can't go wrong with the prices at Bass outlet stores. Shoes, boots, clogs, athletic wear, and sports clothing, all Bass or Bear Trap, cost 30 percent less than retail prices. 3756 Bee Ridge Road (813-923-3978). Open Mondays through Saturdays 10 A.M. to 9 P.M. and Sundays noon to 5 P.M.

**FUNTIME FASHIONS**—Women's sportswear and coordinated separates at 20 to 60 percent off. The selection includes bathing suits and golf wear, but not tennis clothes. 7204 South Tamiami Trail (813-924-4461). Open Mondays through Fridays 9 A.M. to 5 P.M.; closed Sundays.

**MARSHALLS**—High-quality, name-brand apparel for men, women, and children has earned the chain a national reputation for excellence. The stores also carry accessories, shoes, gifts, home fashions, and luggage, all at prices up to

50 percent below retail. In *Gulf Gate Mall*, Stickney Point Road and U.S. 41 (813-921-6641). Open Mondays through Saturdays 9:30 A.M. to 9:30 P.M. and Sundays noon to 6 P.M.

**POLLY FLINDERS FACTORY STORE**—Polly Flinders's hand-smocked dresses for girls are the main events at one of Florida's most popular outlets, which carries only Polly Flinders's merchandise. Infant clothing and home-sewing goods are also sold throughout the chain. Prices are 40 to 50 percent lower than retail. Bee Ridge and MacIntosh Roads (813-371-7742). Open Mondays through Saturdays 10 A.M. to 6 P.M.

**SWIMSUIT OUTLET**—Outdoor clothing for the sunstruck. All first-quality swimsuits and sportswear, with names like Rosemarie Reed, Maxine, Tultex, and Jantzen usually in the selection. Suntan products, rompers, T-shirts, and cover-ups are also avilable. Discounts are 20 to 60 percent. 1913 South Osprey Avenue (813-366-1781). Open Mondays through Fridays 9:30 A.M. to 6 P.M. and Saturdays 9:30 A.M. to 5 P.M.

## FORT MYERS

**BASS SHOE FACTORY OUTLET** (see Sarasota entry)—U.S. 41 South at Cleveland Avenue (813-936-2595). Open Mondays through Saturdays 10 A.M. to 9 P.M. and Sundays noon to 5 P.M.

**JERSILD FACTORY OUTLET**—Not only men's and women's Jersild sweaters, but also Osh Kosh b'Gosh children's (even those cute little overalls) and maternity clothes. All merchandise is first quality, and the discounts on Osh Kosh items range from 20 to 25 percent, while the sweaters cost 30 percent less than retail. 11751-17 Cleveland Avenue (813-936-0004). Open Mondays through Saturdays 10 A.M. to 5 P.M. during the summer; Mondays through Saturdays 9:30 A.M. to 6:30 P.M. during the winter; closed Sundays.

**MARSHALLS** (see Sarasota entry)—4429 South Cleveland Avenue (813-939-9900). Open 9:30 A.M. to 9:30 P.M. Mondays through Saturdays and noon to 6 P.M. Sundays.

**POLLY FLINDERS FACTORY STORE** (see Sarasota entry)—On U.S. 41 a mile north of the *Bell Tower Mall* (813-936-5998). Open Mondays through Saturdays 9:30 A.M. to 5:30 P.M.

**SWIMSUIT OUTLET** (see Sarasota entry)—2062 Beacon Manor Drive (813-936-3447). Open Mondays through Fridays 9:30 A.M. to 6:30 P.M. and Saturdays 9:30 A.M. to 5 P.M.; closed Sundays.

## FORT LAUDERDALE

**COHEN'S FASHION OPTICAL**—Ten to 20 percent discounts on prescription eyeglasses and prescription and nonprescription sunglasses. 2594 East Sunrise Boulevard (305-564-1999). Open Mondays through Saturdays 10 A.M. to 9 P.M., Sundays noon to 5:30 P.M.

**ODD-LOT TRADING**—The selection is diverse, to say the least, but the savings on shoes, toys, housewares, cosmetics, furniture, and electronics are substantial. 1437 Commercial Boulevard, Oakland Park (305-772-8357). Open Mondays through Wednesdays and Saturdays 10 A.M. to 6 P.M., Thursdays and Fridays 10 A.M. to 9 P.M., and Sundays 11 A.M. to 5 P.M.

**PEPPERIDGE FARM THRIFT**—As the commercial says, Pepperidge Farm remembers. In its outlet stores, it remembers that people like to save money—up to 60 percent on Pepperidge Farm and Campbell Soup (which owns the baked-goods company) brands. No credit cards. 957 East Cyprus Creek Road (305-772-5292). Open Mondays through Fridays 9:30 A.M. to 6 P.M. and Saturdays 9:30 A.M. to 5:30 P.M.; closed Sundays.

**POLLY FLINDERS FACTORY STORE** (see Sarasota entry)—1521 East Las Olas Boulevard (305-463-6807). Open Mondays through Saturdays 9 A.M. to 5 P.M.

**SYMS**—Everything for men, from tuxedos to loafers, is available at prices 30 to 50 percent below normal retail. The names are famous—John Weitz, Christian Dior, and Calvin Klein among many others—and the selection is abundant, but the decor is no-frills. Some women's clothing is also available. 5300 Powerline Road (305-772-0775). Open Mondays through Wednesdays 10 A.M. to 7 P.M., Thursdays and Fridays 10 A.M. to 8:30 P.M., and Saturdays 9 A.M. to 6 P.M.; closed Sundays.

**T. J. MAXX**—Outfit the whole family with name-brand clothes, shoes, gifts, and dinnerware at discounts ranging from 20 to 60 percent. Ninety percent of the merchandise at these large, supermarket-style stores is first quality. In *Coral Ridge Mall*, Oakland Park Boulevard and Federal Road (305-563-0313). Open Mondays through Saturdays 9:30 A.M. to 9:30 P.M. and Sundays noon to 6 P.M.

## MIAMI

**CALICO CORNERS**—Seconds and irregulars of fabrics for home decorating, especially upholstery and drapery. Smart shoppers will recognize designer names in the selection. Intelligent, courteous service and sizable savings distinguish the chain. 16810 South Dixie Highway (305-253-5400). Open Tuesdays through Saturdays 9 A.M. to 5 P.M. and Mondays 9 A.M. to 9 P.M.

**FASHION CLOTHIERS**—Men's suits, coats, pants, and shirts for less at this high-quality store in Miami's discount district. All first-quality and mostly designer merchandise. 2650 Northwest Fifth Avenue (305-573-5890). Open Mondays through Saturdays 9 A.M. to 5:30 P.M.

**GABRIELLE IMPORTS**—Leather handbags, belts, and accessories in a large, attractively decorated shop. All of the imported bags in this large store are first quality, and all of the makers, including Mario Columbetti, Capri, and Supreme, are first rate. Discounts are 20 percent. 415 Northwest 27th Street (305-576-3150). Open Mondays through Saturdays 10:30 A.M. to 5 P.M.; closed Sundays.

## Travel Tip: WEATHER CHART

Even in January Florida's weather is mild, ranging from about 55 degrees in the northern part of the state to almost 70 degrees in Key West. The average temperatures and rainfall given here are based on Central Florida statistics, but they give a good indication of what the weather is likely to be, month by month, throughout the state.

|  | Temperature Average high | Average low | Mean | Average rainfall |
|---|---|---|---|---|
| January | 70 | 50 | 60 | 2.28 |
| February | 72 | 51 | 62 | 2.95 |
| March | 76 | 56 | 66 | 3.46 |
| April | 82 | 61 | 71 | 2.72 |
| May | 87 | 66 | 76 | 2.94 |
| June | 89 | 71 | 80 | 7.11 |
| July | 90 | 73 | 81 | 8.29 |
| August | 90 | 74 | 82 | 6.73 |
| September | 88 | 72 | 80 | 7.20 |
| October | 82 | 66 | 74 | 4.07 |
| November | 76 | 57 | 67 | 1.56 |
| December | 72 | 52 | 62 | 1.90 |

## Travel Tip: $62...

That's what the average American traveler spends per day, staying in hotels and motels, eating three meals a day in moderately priced restaurants, and doing a little sightseeing along the way.

SAVVY TRAVELER

**THE HOME DEPOT**—Probably the only discount chain that claims to sell everything one needs to build a house. A wide variety of brand-name tools and home repair merchandise, including Black and Decker, Wagner, Hitachi, Glidden, and GTE, is available at significant savings. 1650 Northeast 183rd Street (305-947-9600). Open Mondays through Fridays 9 A.M. to 9 P.M., Saturdays 9 A.M. to 7 P.M., and Sundays 10 A.M. to 6 P.M. Also at 16051 South Dixie Highway (305-251-9200). Open Mondays through Fridays 9 A.M. to 9 P.M., Saturdays 9 A.M. to 7 P.M., and Sundays 10 A.M. to 6 P.M. Also, 1700 West 48th Street, Hialeah (305-823-6490). Open Mondays through Fridays 9 A.M. to 9 P.M., Saturdays 9 A.M. to 7 P.M., and Sundays 10 A.M. to 6 P.M.

**LINENS 'N THINGS**—Famous brand towels, sheets, comforters, blankets, and other household merchandise, with discounts of 40 to 50 percent on first-quality Lady Pepperell, West Point-Pepperell, and Martex, among others. Seconds and irregulars are priced even lower. 8603 Southwest 40th Street (305-559-0353). Open 9:30 A.M. to 9 P.M. Mondays through Fridays, 10 A.M. to 9 P.M. Saturdays, and noon to 5 P.M. Sundays. Also at 11561 North Kendall Drive (305-274-1880). Open Mondays through Saturdays 10 A.M. to 9 P.M. and Sundays 10 A.M. to 6 P.M.

**LOEHMANN'S**—Incredible bargains on some of the most famous names in women's fashion. Labels are removed, but the price tag codes usually provide good clues to the designers of the suits, dresses, sportswear, and evening wear offered at discounts of 30 to 60 percent. 18701 Biscayne Boulevard (305-932-4207). Open Mondays through Fridays 10 A.M. to 9 P.M., Saturdays 10 A.M. to 5:30 P.M., and Sundays noon to 5 P.M.

**NEW ENGLAND DIVERS, INC.**—Diving and snorkeling equipment reduced as much as 20 percent. Most major manufacturers, such as US Divers and Seatech, are represented in the selection. The chain also offers a short pool training course in which students earn diving certificates. 9820 South Dixie Highway (305-667-4622). Open Mondays through Thursdays 9 A.M. to 6 P.M. and Fridays and Saturdays 9 A.M. to 7 P.M.

**PETER KENT**—An elegant store with elegant American and European men's suits, sportswear, formal dress, outerwear, and accessories. Pierre Cardin, Yves St. Laurent, Nino Cerruti, Botany 500, Calvin Klein, Arrow, Van Heusen, Eagle, and London Fog are among the famous names represented. All merchandise is first quality, and discounts range from 25 to 40 percent. The store offers free overnight alterations as well as free alterations of its goods at any time after purchase. 560 Northwest 27th Street (305-576-2915). Open 8:30 A.M. to 6:15 P.M. Mondays through Saturdays.

**POLLY FLINDERS FACTORY STORE** (see Sarasota entry)—23rd Street and Biscayne Boulevard (305-895-1256). Open Mondays through Saturdays 9 A.M. to 5 P.M.; closed Sundays.

**SHAYNE OF MIAMI**—All first-quality better sportswear for women. Current styles of designer names in accessories, dresses, and sportswear. The atmosphere is boutique-like, but the discounts are 25 to 60 percent. 8801 Southwest 132nd Street (305-232-2404). Open Mondays through Saturdays 10 A.M. to 6 P.M. and Sundays noon to 5 P.M. Also at 2535 Northwest Fifth Avenue (305-576-2404). Open Mondays through Saturdays 10 A.M. to 5:30 P.M.; closed Sundays. Also 3618 Northwest 19th Street, Lauderdale Lakes (305-931-2404). Open Mondays through Saturdays 10 A.M. to 5 P.M. and Sundays noon to 5 P.M.

**T. J. MAXX** (see Fort Lauderdale entry)—18439 South Dixie Highway (305-233-7002). Open Mondays through Saturdays 9:30 A.M. to 9:30 P.M. and Sundays noon to 6 P.M. Also at 260 Southwest 117th Avenue (305-271-1443). Open Mondays through Saturdays 9:30 A.M. to 9:30 P.M. and Sundays noon to 6 P.M.

**WINSTON'S**—Large and attractive department-type stores with merchandise at 20 to 50 percent off. Gloria Vanderbilt, Anne Klein, Botany 500, Arrow, Pierre Cardin, Health-tex, Stride-Rite, Freeman, and Bandolino are among the brand names. 5739 Northwest 167th Street (305-624-3906). Open Mondays through Saturdays 9 A.M. to 6:30 P.M.; closed Sundays.

## THE DELICATE ART OF DISCOUNT SHOPPING

Discount shopping is a lot like a sport; it has its own rules, its own playing fields, and its own winners and losers. Luckily, just about anyone who knows the rules can be a winner. The first thing to understand is the variation in the quality of merchandise. Discount stores and factory outlets can offer as many as 3 grades of goods; *first-quality*, which, like the items in conventional retail stores, are flawless; *irregulars*, which have slight flaws but are considered to be near perfect; and *seconds*, which are more flawed than irregulars. Not all discount outlets mark goods as to quality, so the operative principle is *caveat emptor*—buyer beware. And even those goods that are marked as seconds or irregulars must be carefully inspected to locate imperfections. Otherwise one can end up with less than he or she has bargained for.

Though some stores sell designer goods with the labels left on, others, including *Loehmann's*, cut labels off. Often, however, designers can be identified by the store tags that remain on any item. At Loehmann's, for example, a price tag marked CK usually means the piece is a Calvin Klein creation.

Finally, remember that most discount stores operate with very low overhead. They do not, in general, look like department stores.

# INFORMATION SOURCES

**P**lanning a trip properly takes time, but most travelers find that the increased enjoyment is well worth the effort. There is no better place to start planning a trip to Florida than with the enormous amount of information available free from state tourism organizations and individual city chambers of commerce. By specifying your special travel interests and the areas you'll be visiting, you can receive dozens of relevant brochures, pamphlets, and listings that can meaningfully enhance your trip—and save money as well. The people who work at these organizations can also help travelers decide the best time of year to visit and offer calendars of special events around which you may want to plan your trip. For travelers who are not quite detail-oriented enough to send for information before their trip, these tourism organizations can still provide a wealth of free material right on the spot. Most chambers of commerce are located on the main streets in their particular cities and towns and are equipped to answer questions and help you make the most of your visit. Using this list in conjunction with a detailed Florida map—one that notes county boundaries and names—can be especially productive since you will be able to contact all the information sources that exist along the way. The tourist offices that serve the entire state are listed first, and the chambers of commerce are alphabetized within each region.

# STATE INFORMATION SOURCES

**Bureau of Visitor Services**
Florida Department of Commerce
Tallahassee 32301
904-488-7300

**Florida Department of Natural Resources**
Division of Recreation and Parks
Marjory Stoneman Douglas Building
3900 Commonwealth Boulevard
Tallahassee 32303
904-488-7326

**Florida Division of Tourism**
Visitor Inquiry Section
Department GM
126 Van Buren Street
Tallahassee 32301
904-488-5606

**Florida Game and Freshwater Fish Commission**
Farris Bryant Building
620 South Meridian Street
Tallahassee 32301
904-488-4066

**Florida's Emerald Coast Tourist Development Council**
Box 4204
Fort Walton Beach 32549
904-862-7263

**Florida Trail Association**
Box 13706
Gainesville 32604
904-378-8823

## NORTHERN FLORIDA

**Amelia Island/Fernandina Beach Chamber of Commerce**
Box 472
Fernandina Beach 32034
904-261-3248

**Bay County Chamber of Commerce**
Box 9473
Panama City Beach 32407
904-234-8224

**Cedar Key Area Chamber of Commerce**
Box 610
Cedar Key 32625
904-543-5600

**Convention and Visitors Bureau of Jacksonville**
33 South Hogan Street
Jacksonville 32202
904-353-9736

**Daytona Beach Area Chamber of Commerce**
Box 2775
Daytona Beach 32015
904-255-0981

**Destin Chamber of Commerce**
Box 8
Destin 32541
904-837-6241

**Gainesville Chamber of Commerce**
300 East University Avenue
Box 1187
Gainesville 32602
904-372-0115

**Greater Fort Walton
Beach Chamber of Commerce**
Drawer 640
Fort Walton Beach 32549
904-244-8191

**Pensacola Chamber of Commerce**
117 West Garden Street
Box 550
Pensacola 32593
904-438-4081

**St. Augustine Chamber
of Commerce**
Drawer O
St. Augustine 32085
904-829-5681

**Tallahassee Area Chamber
of Commerce**
Box 1639
100 North Duval Street
Tallahassee 32302
904-224-8116

# CENTRAL FLORIDA

**Chamber of Commerce
of South Brevard**
1005 East Strawbridge Avenue
Melbourne 32901
305-724-5400

**Clearwater Chamber of Commerce**
128 North Osceola Avenue
Clearwater 33515
813-461-0011

**Cocoa Brevard Area Chamber
of Commerce**
400 Fortenberry Road
Merritt Island 32952
305-459-2200

**Greater Orlando Area Chamber
of Commerce**
Box 1234
Orlando 32802
305-427-1234

**Greater Sanford Chamber
of Commerce**
Drawer CC
Sanford 32772-0868
305-322-2212

**Kissimmee-Osceola County
Chamber of Commerce**
320 East Monument Avenue
Kissimmee 32741
305-847-3174

**Largo Chamber of Commerce**
Box 326
Largo 33540
813-584-2321

**Pinellas County Tourist
Development Council**
Newport Square, Suite 109A
2333 East Bay Drive
Clearwater 33546
813-530-6452

# SOUTHERN FLORIDA

**Arcadia Chamber of Commerce**
2 South DeSoto
Arcadia 33821
813-494-4033

**Boca Raton Chamber of Commerce**
1800 North Dixie Highway
Boca Raton 33432
305-395-4433

**Bradenton Chamber of Commerce**
222 Tenth Street West
Bradenton 33505
813-748-3411

**Cape Coral Chamber of Commerce**
2051 Cape Coral Parkway
Cape Coral 33904
813-542-3721

**Charlotte County Chamber of Commerce**
2702 Tamiami Trail
Port Charlotte 33952
813-627-2222

**Clewiston Chamber of Commerce**
Box 275
Clewiston 33440
813-983-7979

**Coral Gables Chamber of Commerce**
50 Aragon Avenue
Coral Gables 33134
305-446-1657

---

## *Travel Tip:* FOR THE HANDICAPPED

Getting around a new place can be trying for any traveler, but especially so for the person with a physical disability. The Society for the Advancement of Travel for the Handicapped (26 Court Street; Brooklyn, NY 11252; 718-858-5483) has a listing of more than 300 travel agencies that offer special trips and tours for individuals or groups, and Florida is a frequent destination. Send the society a self-addressed, stamped envelope for a complete list of travel agencies.

Those handicapped persons who prefer to make their own arrangements will be happy to know that the rental fleets of Hertz, Avis, and National all contain a limited number of hand-control cars. Amtrak has special seats for handicapped travelers, but advance reservations are recommended. Wheelchairs are available in major Amtrak stations, and seeing-eye and hearing-ear dogs may ride with passengers at no extra charge. The free booklet *Access Amtrak* explains special services for handicapped and older passengers; to get it, write the Amtrak Distribution Center; Box 7717; Itasca, IL 60142. Air passengers requiring wheelchairs can make appropriate arrangements through the airline at the time they make reservations.

**Fort Lauderdale Chamber
of Commerce**
208 Southeast Third Avenue
Fort Lauderdale 33301
305-462-6000

**Fort Myers Chamber of Commerce**
2254 Edwards Drive
Fort Myers 33901
813-334-1133

**Fort Pierce Chamber of Commerce**
2200 Virginia Avenue
Fort Pierce 33450
305-461-2700

**Greater Miami Chamber
of Commerce**
1601 Biscayne Boulevard
Miami 33132
305-350-7700

**Hialeah Chamber of Commerce**
59 West Fifth Street
Hialeah 33010
305-887-1515

**Hollywood Chamber of Commerce**
330 North Federal Highway
Hollywood 33021
305-920-3330

**Homestead Chamber of Commerce**
650 U.S. Highway 1
Homestead 33030
305-247-2332

**Key West Chamber of Commerce**
402 Wall Street
Mallory Square
Key West 33040
305-294-2587

**LaBelle Chamber of Commerce**
Box 456
LaBelle 33935
813-675-0125

**Lake Worth Chamber of Commerce**
1702 Lake Worth Road
Lake Worth 33460
305-582-4401

**Marathon Chamber of Commerce**
3330 Overseas Highway
Marathon 33050
305-743-5417

**Miami Beach Chamber
of Commerce**
1920 Meridian Avenue
Miami Beach 33139
305-672-1270

**Naples Chamber of Commerce**
1700 North Tamiami Drive
Naples 33940
813-262-6141

**Okeechobee Chamber of
Commerce**
55 South Parrott Avenue
Okeechobee 33472
813-763-6464

**Pahokee Chamber of Commerce**
115 East Main Street
Pahokee 33476
305-924-5579

**Palm Beach Chamber of Commerce**
45 Coconut Row
Palm Beach 33480
305-655-3282

**Pompano Beach Chamber
of Commerce**
2200 East Atlantic Boulevard
Pompano Beach 33062
305-941-2940

**Sarasota Chamber of Commerce**
1551 Second Street
Sarasota 33577
813-955-8187

**Stuart Chamber of Commerce**
400 South Federal Highway
Stuart 33497
305-287-1088

**West Palm Beach Chamber
of Commerce**
501 North Flagler Drive
West Palm Beach 33401
305-833-3711

# INDEX

Adventures Unlimited, 68
Air Traffic Control Center, 106
Alaqua Winery, 88
Alderman's Ford, 61
Alfred B. Maclay State Gardens, 121
almost free, 119-126
Altamonte Mall, 50
Anastasia Island, 10
Angus R. Goss Memorial Swimming Pool, 13
Anheuser-Busch Brewery, 88
A Place for Cooks, 48
Apopka, 29
Arcadia to Okeechobee, 117
Arch Creek Park and Museum, 65
Around Lake Okeechobee, 117
Art Deco District, 31
Art League of Manatee County, 40
Art Place at Cauley Square, 43
Atlantic Beach, 10

Bacardi Gallery, 43
Bahia Honda State Park, 126
Baldomero Lopez Swimming Pool, 13
Bal Harbour shops, 54
Baltimore Orioles spring training, 86
Banister Shoe Company, 138
Banker's Note, 128, 129, 134, 138
Barley Barber Swamp, 64-65
Barnacle State Historic Site, 126
Bass Museum, 42
Bass Shoe Factory Outlet, 129, 130, 132, 135, 137, 138, 141, 142
Bay Area Outlet Mall, 133
Bay Beach, 23
Bay Vista Photo Gallery, 42
beaches, 7-22
Belz Factory Outlet Mall, 135, 138
Big Pine Key, 22
Big Tree Park, 29
Biscayne National Park, 64
Blue Spring State Park, 124
Boatyard Village, 48
Bob Hicks Memorial Swimming Pool, 13
Bob White Airfield, 71-72
Bok Tower Gardens, 124
Boston Red Sox spring training, 81
Boyd Hill Nature Trail, 123
Branded Cargo, 138-139
Brevard County Libraries, 98-99
Bridlewood Farm, 59
Brokaw-McDougall House, 24
Bronson-Mulholland House, 25
Broward County library system, 100-101

Calico Corners, 130, 135, 139, 143
Calle Ocho, 55
Canaveral National Seashore, 16
Cape Canaveral, 16
Capital Menswear, 129

Capital Outlet Mall, 129
Captiva Island, 19
Carl Fisher Monument, 75
Carl T. Langford Park, 29
Carter's Children's Outlet, 130, 131
Cascaden Swimming Pool, 13
Castellow Hammock, 65
Castillo de San Marcos, 121
Casual Male, 135, 139
Cecil Field Naval Station, 106
Central Christian Church, 72
Central Florida Regional Hospital, 91
Central Florida Regional Library, 95
Centre Street Historic District, 24
Chalet Suzanne, 30
Charlotte Harbor, 117
Chekika State Recreation Area, 126
Chicago White Sox spring training, 84
Cincinnati Reds spring training, 80
Circle Gallery, 43
City Cemetery, 75
Clearwater Beach, 13
Clearwater City Hall, 107
Clearwater Horseshoe Club, 80
Clearwater Public Library System, 96-97
Cocoa Beach, 16, 17
Cocoa Village, 51
Coconut Grove, 55
coconut palms, 76
Cohen's Fashion Optical, 143
Colby Memorial Temple, 72
colleges and universities, 93-102
Collier-Seminole State Park, 125
Columbus Day Sailboat Regatta, 85
Conservancy, Inc., 64
Coronet Fabric Mills, 130
Countryside Mall, 48-49
Courtney Campbell Causeway, 13, 114
Creighton Male, 139
Crescent Beach, 10
Crown Hotel, 70
Cummer Gallery of Art, 35
Cutler Ridge Shopping Mall, 56
Cyrus Green Swimming Pool, 13

Dadeland, 54
Dania, 21
Dansk Factory Outlet, 133, 139
Danskin Factory Outlet, 137
Davidson of Dundee, 90
Daytona Beach, 10
Daytona Beach Jai Alai, 122
Daytona Beach Kennel Club, 122
Daytona Beach Outlet Mall, 131-132
Daytona Flea Market, 47
Daytona International Speedway, 122
DeBary Hall, 28
Delray Beach, 20
Denmark's Sporting Goods Store, 82

Deseret Ranch, 73
Detroit Tigers spring training, 81
Dickson Azalea Park, 30
Dinky Dock, 15
discount shopping, 127-145
Dogwood Trail, 116
Donald Duck Citrus World, 90
Downtown Fort Myers, 53
Downtown Orlando, 50-51
drives, 111-118
Drug Emporium, 135
Dunedin Historical Society Museum, 37

Easy Street, 117
Eden State Gardens, 26
Edison Mall, 53
Edward Medard Park, 80
Eglin Air Force Base, 104-105
E. G. Simmons Park, 12, 61
Elliott Teaching Gallery/Art Center of Eckerd College, 38
Emerald Coast, 8
Englewood, 19
Erna Nixon Park, 30
Eureka Springs, 61

Factory Outlet World, Kissimmee, 140
Falling Waters State Recreation Area, 68
Farmers Market, 75
Fashion Clothiers, 144
Fernandina/Amelia Beach, 9
Fernandina Beach Shrimp Festival, 69
Festival of States, 81
Fifth Avenue, 51
Fisherman's Village, 52-53
fishing, 86
Flagler College, 96
Flea World, 50
Florida A & M University, 95
Florida Audubon Society, 61
Florida Caverns State Park, 69
Florida Federation of Garden Clubs, 30
Florida Folk Festival, 69
Florida Freewheelers, 82
Florida Gulf Coast Art Center, 37
Florida Institute of Technology Botanical Gardens, 30
Florida Pottery, 129
Florida Power Corporation, 89
Florida Solar Energy Center, 73
Florida Southern College, 97
Florida State Fine Arts Gallery, 35
Florida State Museum, 36
Florida State University, 94
Florida Strawberry Festival, 7
Florida Trail, 60
Florida Twin Markets, 50
Forest Hills Swimming Pool, 13
Forma Gallery, 44
Fort Caroline National Memorial, 25

# 154 INDEX

Fort Christmas Museum, 40
Fort Clinch State Park, 69
Fort Cooper State Park, 123
Fort De Soto County Park, 12, 61, 81
Fort Lauderdale, 21
Fort Matanzas National Monument, 25
Fort Myers Beach, 19
Fort Myers to West Palm Beach, 117
Fort Walton Beach/Destin, 8
Foster Harman Gallery of American Art, 41
Fountain of Youth, 122
Four Winds Gallery, 41
Francis Wolfson Art Gallery, 43
freshwater fishing, 78
Fruit and Spice Park, 32
Frye Boot Outlet, 139
Funtime Fashions, 141

Gabrielle Imports, 144
Gainesville to Cross Creek, 113
Gainesville to Micanopy, McIntosh, 113
Galeria Camhi, 43
Galleria, 53-54
galleries, 33-44
Gallery at Grove Isle, 44
gardens, 23-32
Gasparilla Sound, 19
General Sanford Memorial Library Museum, 39
General Shoe Factory to You, 133
Genius Drive, 62
Gingerbread Square Gallery, 44
Ginjan, 49
Gloria Luria Gallery, 43
Golden Age Games, 82
Goodyear Blimp, 75
government sites, 103-110
Grassy Point/Live Oak Point, 19
Greynolds Park, 65
Gulf World, 120
Gulfarium, 120

Hale Indian River Groves, 91
Happy Foot, 132
Harbor City Rowing Club, 83
Hastings Records and Tapes, 135, 137
Haulover Beach, 21
Haulover Beach Fishing Pier, 126
Heritage Park, 28
Hialeah Park Race Track, 32
Hibel Museum of Art, 42
Highlands Hammock State Park, 125
Hillsborough County Courthouse, 108
Hillsborough County Historical Museum and Library, 38
Himmarshee Village, 31
historic sites, 23-32
Hollywood, 21
Holy Trinity Episcopal Church, 28
Homestead Air Force Base, 110
Hontoon Island State Park, 72
Houston Astros spring training, 82
Hunt and Peck, 139
Hurlbut Field, 105

Hutchinson Island, 20
Hyatt Regency Grand Cypress, 72

Ichetucknee Springs State Park, 11
I. Irving Feldman Galleries, 41
industrial tours, 87-92
Interbay Swimming Pool, 13
International Minerals and Chemical Corporation, Inc., 90
Islamorada Key, 22
Island Gallery, 44

Jacksonville area beaches, 10
Jacksonville Art Museum, 35
Jacksonville Beach Fishing Pier, 69
Jacksonville Beach to St. Augustine, 113
Jacksonville Museum of Arts and Sciences, 35
Jacksonville Public Library, 95
Jacksonville to Cedar Key, 113
Jacksonville to White Springs, 112
Jacksonville University, 95
Jacksonville Zoological Park, 121
Janes Scenic Drive in the Fakahatchee Strand, 63
Jaycee Beach, 15
Jersild Factory Outlet, 142
Jetty Park Campground, 16
J. N. "Ding" Darling National Wildlife Refuge, 64
Joan Hodgell Gallery, 40
Jupiter Island/Jupiter Inlet, 20
Just Labels, 133

Kansas City Royals spring training, 84
Kapok Tree Inn, 29
Kelly Park, 14
Kennedy Space Center, 10
Key Largo, 22
Key Largo Antiques and Art Gallery, 44
Key Largo to Key West, 118
Key West, 22, 56
Key West sunsets, 75
Kingsley Plantation, 25
Kissimmee Livestock Market, 62
Koreshan State Historic Site, 125

Lake Davis, 62
Lake Eola Park, 29
Lake Fairview Recreation Complex, 14
Lake Hollingsworth Drive, 115
Lakeland City Hall, 108
Lake Louisa State Park, 14
Lake Nature Park, 60
Lake Park, 80
Lake Surprise, 66
Langford City Park, 82
La Petite Gallery, 43
Larry and Penny Thompson Park, 65
Las Olas Boulevard, 53
Leading Labels, 140
Liberty Homes, Inc., 89
libraries, 93-102
Linens 'n Things, 130-131, 136, 138, 145
Lithia Springs Park, 124

Loch Haven Art Center, 39
Loehmann's, 133, 137, 138, 145
Longboat Key, 18
Long Point Park, 17
Loop Road, Everglades, 117
Lori Wilson Park, 17
Los Angeles Dodgers spring training, 85
Lowe Art Museum, 42
Lower Matecumbe Beach, 22
Lowry Park, 61

Macdill Air Force Base, 107-108
Madeira Beach, 13
Maitland Art Center, 39
Manatee Springs State Park, 11
Mandalay Surf and Sport, 49
Marathon Key, 22
Marco Island, 19
Marian Stevens, 44
Marina Park, 83
Marineland, 122
Marjorie Kinnan Rawlings State Historic Site, 121
Marshalls, 131, 134, 138, 141-142
Martin Luther King, Jr. Pool, 13
Mayfair, 55
Mayport Navy Station, 106
Mayport to Fernandina, 112
Mead Gardens, 30
Melbourne, 17, 115
Melbourne Square Mall, 51
Melbourne to St. Cloud, 115
Memorial Beach, 22
Merritt Island National Wildlife Refuge, 62
Metropolitan Museum and Art Center, 42
Miami Beach, 21
military sites, 103-110
Minnesota Twins spring training, 82
Miracle Mile, 56
missile display, 108-109
Mission of Nombre de Dios, 25
Montreal Expos spring training, 85
Monument of the States, 72
Morikami Museum, 32
Moss Park, 15
Mount Dora Antiquing, 50
Museum of Arts and Sciences, 35
Museum of Florida History, 35
Museum of Natural History, 38
museums, 33-44

Naples, 53
Naples Art Gallery, 41
Naples Beach, 19
NASA launches, 73
NASA Spaceport, USA, 73
National Key Deer Refuge, 65
National Wildlife Gallery, 41
Natural Bridge Historic Site, 24
Naval Coastal Systems Center, 106
Navarre to Destin, 113
Navy Orlando, 108
Neptune Beach, 10
Netsky Gallery, 44
New England Divers, Inc., 145

… INDEX 155

Newport Sportswear/Southland Shirts, 134, 136
New River, 75
New Smyrna Beach, 16, 115
New Smyrna Sugar Mill Ruins, 28
New York Yankees spring training, 85
North Shore Park, 13
Northwest Regional Library, 94
Norton Gallery and School of Art, 42

Ocala National Forest, 59
Ocala Stud Farm, 59
Odd-Lot Trading, 143
Oehlschlaeger Galleries, 41
Old Cutler Hammock Nature Center, 65
Old Cutler Road, 116-117
Old Town Hall, 110
Oldest House, 121
Olustee Beach Ocean Pond Recreation Area, 11
Omni International Mall, 54
Orange County Historical Museum, 39
Orange County library system, 98
Orange County Offices, 108
Orange Cup Regatta, 81
Orange Park Mall, 46
Orlando City Hall, 108
Orlando International Artsfest, 72
Orlo Vista Park Community Center, 15
Osceola Center for the Arts, 39
Osceola County Courthouse, 108
Osceola National Forest, 58
Outlets Limited, 131

Pabst Brewery, 90
Palm Beach County Building/West Palm Beach City Hall, 109
Palm Beach Mall, 53
Palm Beach Polo and Country Club, 85
Palm Beach Post and Times, 92
Panama City Beach, 9
Paradise Beach Park, 17
Park Avenue, 50
Paynes Prairie State Preserve, 59
Peanut Island Coast Guard Installation, 109-110
Peddler's Village, 51-52
Pelican Harbor Seabird Station, 65
Peltz Famous Brand Shoes, 136, 137
Pensacola Beach, 8
Pensacola Historical Museum, 34
Pensacola Museum of Art, 34
Pensacola Naval Air Station, 8
Pepperidge Farm Thrift, 134, 143
Perry Harvey Sr. Park, 71
Peter Kent, 145
Philadelphia Phillies spring training, 79
Pier Place, 81
Pinecrest, 75
Pine Island, 19
Pinellas County Antiquing, 49
Pinellas County Courthouse, 107
Pinellas County Historical Museum, 37
Pittsburgh Pirates spring training, 84
Plant Hall, 27

Plantation Key, 22
Playalinda, 16
Point O'Rocks, 18
Polk Public Museum, 39
Polly Flinders Factory Store, 129, 130, 131, 136,137, 142, 143, 145
Pompano Beach, 21
pools, 13
Port Charlotte Beach, 19
Port Charlotte Cultural Center, 100
Port Everglades, 110
Porter House, 32
Potter's Wax Museum, 122
President's Cup Regatta, 80
Publix Milk and Ice Cream Plant, 90
Push, Pull, and Paddle, 62

Quality Outlet Center, 139-140

Ravine State Gardens, 26
Redington Beach, 13
Regency Square Mall, 46
Rhodes Park, 17
Riverfront Handicap Pool, 13
Riverfront Park, 71
Rockin' Rhythm Quality Western Wear, 49
Roger's Christmas House, 70
Ron Jon Surf Shop, 51
Royal Palm Square, 53
Royellou Museum, 38
Roy Jenkins Swimming Pool, 13

Safety Village, 71
St. Armand's Circle, 52
St. Augustine Alligator Farm, 121-122
St. Augustine Antiguo, 47
St. Augustine to Daytona Beach, 113
St. Augustine walking tours, 69
St. Gabriel's Episcopal Church, 28
St. Joe Paper Company, 89
Saint Leo Abbey, 28
Saint Leo College, 98
St. Lucie County Historical Museum, 41
St. Mark's National Wildlife Refuge, 58
St. Nicholas Greek Orthodox Cathedral, 70
St. Petersburg City Hall, 108
St. Petersburg Library, 97
Sanibel Island, 19
Santa Fe Community College, 95
Sarasota Square Mall, 52
Science Center of Pinellas County, 38, 61
Science Museum of Palm Beach County, 126
Sea Captain's Memoirs Gallery, 44
Seaside Treasure Inc., 49
Sea Turtle Lecture, 62
Sebastian Inlet State Recreation Area, 17
senior aerobic exercise, 82
Shapes Activewear Outlet, 134, 136, 140
Shark Valley, 64
Shell Factory, 92
shuffleboard, 86
Siesta Beach, 18
sightseeing, 67-76

Simpson Park, 32
skin diving, 78-79
Slocum Water Gardens, 29
Smathers Beach, 22
snorkeling, 84-85
Socks 'n Such, 136, 140
South Beach, 22
South Tropical Trail, 115
Southern Cross Observatory, 42
Spacecoast Freewheeler Ten-Speed Bike Club, 83
Spessard Holland Park, 17
Spook Hill, 71
sports, 77-86
springs, 11
State Capitol, 106
Stranahan House, 126
Sugar Mill Gardens, 26
Sulphur Springs Swimming Pool, 13
Suncoast Botanical Garden, 29
Suncoast Seabird Sanctuary, 60-61
Sunshine Mall, 49
surf casting, 78
surfing contests, 82-83
Surfside, 21
Swimsuit Outlet, 137, 142
Syms, 143

Tallahassee Junior Museum, 35
Tampa Bay Buccaneers, 80
Tampa-Hillsborough County Public library system, 97
Tampa International Airport, 71
Tampa Municipal Swimming Pools, 13
Tampa Museum, 38
Tampa Outlet Mall, 136-137
Tampa Recreation Department tennis lessons, 80
Tavernier Key, 22
Texas Rangers spring training, 85
Thalheimer's Gallery, 41
The Art Museum, 42
The Art Resource, 43
The Bahama House, 32
The Beach Art Center, 38
The Bike Trail, 85-86
The Carefully Chosen, 43
The Depot Museum, 39
The Falls, 54
The Florida Publishing Company, 88
The Florida Theatre, 69
The Gulf Stream, 74
The Home Depot, 133, 135, 139, 145
The Keys, 22
The Lightner Museum, 47
The Marketplace, 51
The Miami Herald, 92
The Museum of Fine Arts, 38
The Old Mill, 131
The Old Well, 74
The Palm Beaches, 20
The Rain Barrel, 44
The Treasure Ship, 68
The Webb Wildlife Preserve, 64
The Zoo, 120

Tiki Gardens, 49-50
T.J. Maxx, 131, 134, 143
Tower Gallery of Art, 41
T-Shirt Junction, 50
Tupperware World Headquarters, 90-91
Turkey Lake City Park, 124
Turtle Mound Historical Site, 73
turtle watches, 62-63
Tyndall Air Force Base, 106

U.S. Coast Guard Base/Old Governor's Island, 110
U.S. Naval Air Station, 104
U.S. Naval Aviation Museum, 34
U.S. 27, 114
University Gallery, 36
University of Central Florida, 98
University of Florida, 95
University of Miami, 100
University of North Florida, 95
University of South Florida, 97

University of South Florida Planetarium, 71
Upper Tampa Bay Park, 61

Valencia Community College, 98
Van Heusen Outlet Store, 129
Venice Beach, 18
Village International, 139-140
Villazon and Company, 90
Volusia County Public Libraries, 96

Waldo Flea Market, 46
Walt Disney World, 10
Walt Disney World Village, 51
Watermelon Capital, 74
Water Ski Museum and Hall of Fame, 81
Webster Flea Market, 50
Wekiwa Springs State Park, 124
West Florida Regional Library, 94
Whitney Beach, 18
Wickham Park, 17

Wilderness Park, 80
wildlife, 57-66
Windermere, 115
window-shopping, 45-56
Windy Acres Polo Clinics, 82
Wines of St. Augustine, 90
Winston's, 130
Winter Park Public Library, 98
Winter Park Sinkhole, 73
Wirtz Gallery, 43
World's Chicken Pluckin' Championship, 81
World's Largest Christmas Tree, 74
Worth Avenue, 53
Wyndham Hotel, 62

Ximenez Fatio House, 25

Ybor City State Museum, 124
Ybor Square, 27
Yulee Sugar Mill Ruins, 28

# DAYS INN DIRECTORY

As part of the special September Days Club edition of *Florida for Free*, we've compiled a directory of all the Days Inns—great bargains at convenient locations—in the Sunshine State. We've included addresses and telephone numbers, but when calling long-distance be sure to use the toll-free number: 800-325-2525.

**Boca Raton–South/Deerfield Beach**
1250 W. Hillsboro Blvd.
Deerfield Beach, Florida 33441
(305-427-2200)

**Bradenton**
3506 1st St. W.
Bradenton, Florida 33505
(813-746-1141)

**Clearwater**
1690 US 19 N
Clearwater, Florida 33575
(813-799-2678)

**Cocoa–Kennedy Space Center**
5600 S.R. 524
Cocoa, Florida 32926
(305-636-2580)

**Daytona–Ormond Beach**
839 S. Atlantic Ave.
Ormond Beach, Florida 32074
(904-677-6600)

**Daytona-Interstate**
2800 Volusia Ave.
Daytona Beach, Florida 32015
(904-255-0541)

**Daytona-Oceanfront/Central**
1909 S. Atlantic Ave.
Daytona Beach, Florida 32018
(904-255-4492)

**Daytona-Oceanfront/South**
3209 S. Atlantic Ave. (A1A)
Daytona Beach, Florida 32018
(904-761-2050)

**Englewood**
2540 S. McCall Rd.
Englewood, Florida 33533
(813-474-5544)

**Fort Lauderdale–Oakland Park**
1595 W. Oakland Pk. Blvd.
Fort Lauderdale, Florida 33311
(305-484-9290)

**Fort Lauderdale–West Broward/Downtown**
1700 W. Broward Blvd.
Fort Lauderdale, Florida 33312
(305-463-2500)

**Fort Lauderdale–South/Airport**
2460 S.R. 84
Fort Lauderdale, Florida 33312
(305-792-4700)

**Lauderdale Surf Hotel**
440 Sea Breeze Ave.
Fort Lauderdale, Florida 33316
(305-462-5555)

**Fort Myers–North**
1099 US 41 N at Cleveland Ave.
Fort Myers, Florida 33903
(813-995-0535)

**Fort Myers–South/Airport**
11435 Cleveland Ave.
Fort Myers, Florida 33907
(813-936-1311)

**Fort Walton Beach**
135 Miracle Strip Pkwy.
Fort Walton Beach, Florida 32548
(904-244-6184)

**Gainesville**
6901 NW 8th Ave.
Gainesville, Florida 32601
(904-376-1601)

**Gainesville-South/Micanopy**
I-75 & Fla. 234, Rte. 2
Gainesville, Florida 33667
(904-466-3152)

**Jacksonville-North/Airport**
I-95 & Jax Int'l Airport Exit
Jacksonville, Florida 32229
(904-757-5000)

**Jacksonville-West**
5929 Ramona Blvd.
Jacksonville, Florida 32205
(904-786-6600)

**Jacksonville-South**
5649 Cagle Rd.
Jacksonville, Florida 32216
(904-733-3890)

**Key West**
3852 N. Roosevelt Blvd.
Key West, Florida 33040
(305-294-3742)

**Kissimmee**
2095 E. Spacecoast Pkwy.
Kissimmee, Florida 32743
(305-846-7136)

**Lake City**
I-75 & US 90, Rte. 13
Lake City, Florida 32055
(904-752-9350)

**Lakeland**
3223 US 98
Lakeland, Florida 33805
(813-688-6031)

**Melbourne**
4455 W. New Haven Ave.
Melbourne, Florida 32901
(305-724-5840)

**Miami–Civic Center/Downtown**
1050 NW 14th St.
Miami, Florida 33136
(305-324-0200)

**Miami-Airport**
3401 NW LeJeune Rd.
Miami, Florida 33142
(305-871-4221)

**Naples**
1925 Davis Blvd.
Naples, Florida 33942
(813-774-3117)

**Ocala**
4040 SW Broadway
Ocala, Florida 32675
(904-629-8850)

**Orlando North–Altamonte Lodge/Inn**
450 Douglas Ave.
Orlando, Florida 32714
(305-862-7111)

**Orlando North–Altamonte Inn**
235 S. Wymore Rd.
Orlando, Florida 32714-2599
(305-862-2800)

**Orlando–Sea World/
Convention Center**
9990 International Dr.
Orlando, Florida 32809
(305-352-8700)

**Orlando–Winter Park**
650 Lee Rd.
Orlando, Florida 32810
(305-628-2727)

**Orlando–Lake Buena Vista Resort**
12205 Apopka-Vineland Rd.
Lake Buena Vista, Florida 32830
(305-239-0444)

**Orlando–Days Park**
1600 W. 33rd St.
Orlando, Florida 32809
(305-423-7646)

**Orlando–I-4 at 33rd Street/Exit 32**
2500 W. 33rd St.
Orlando, Florida 32809
(305-841-3731)

**Orlando–Lakeside**
7335 Sandlake Rd.
Orlando, Florida 32819
(305-351-1900)

**Orlando–International Drive**
7200 International Dr.
Orlando, Florida 32809
(305-351-1200)

**Orlando–Airport Inn**
2323 McCoy Rd.
Orlando, Florida 32809
(305-859-6100)

**Orlando–Landstreet Inn and Lodge**
1221 W. Landstreet Rd.
Orlando, Florida 32809
(305-859-7700)

**Orlando–West of Magic
Kingdom/Epcot Center Entrance**
7980 Spacecoast Pkwy.
Kissimmee, Florida 32741
(305-396-1000)

**Orlando–East of Magic Kingdom
Entrance**
5840 Spacecoast Pkwy.
Kissimmee, Florida 32741
(305-396-7969)

**Orlando-Lodge/East of
Magic Kingdom**
5820 Spacecoast Pkwy.
Kissimmee, Florida 32741
(305-396-7900)

**Orlando–Lake Buena Vista**
12799 Apopka-Vineland Rd.
Lake Buena Vista, Florida 32830
(305-239-4441)

**Panama City**
4810 W. US 98
Panama City, Florida 32401
(904-769-4831)

**Pensacola**
6911 Pensacola Blvd.
Pensacola, Florida 32505
(904-477-9000)

**Pompano Beach**
1411 NW 31st Ave.
Pompano Beach, Florida 33060
(305-972-3700)

**St. Augustine-Interstate**
I-95 & Fla. 16, Rte. 2
St. Augustine, Florida 32084
(904-824-4341)

**St. Augustine—Downtown**
2800 Ponce de Leon Blvd.
St. Augustine, Florida 32084
(904-829-6581)

**St. Petersburg—Pinellas Park**
9359 US 19 N
St. Petersburg, Florida 33565
(813-577-3838)

**Sanford**
I-4 & S.R. 46
Sanford, Florida 32771
(305-323-6500)

**Sarasota-Airport**
4900 N. Tamiami Trail
Sarasota, Florida 33580
(813-355-9721)

**Tallahassee-North**
2800 N. Monroe St.
Tallahassee, Florida 32303
(904-385-0136)

**Tallahassee—Governor's Mall/South**
3100 Apalachee Pkwy.
Tallahassee, Florida 32301
(904-877-6121)

**Port Richey**
11736 US 19 & Fla. 52
Port Richey, Florida 33568
(813-863-1502)

**Tampa-North**
I-75 & Fla. 54 W
Zephyrhills, Florida 33599
(813-973-0155)

**Tampa—Fletcher Avenue**
701 E. Fletcher Ave.
Tampa, Florida 33612
(813-977-1550)

**Tampa—Busch Boulevard**
2901 E. Busch Blvd.
Tampa, Florida 33612
(813-933-6471)

**Tampa-East**
6010 Fla. 579 N
Seffner, Florida 33584
(813-621-4681)

**Tarpon Springs**
816 US 19 S
Tarpon Springs, Florida 33589
(813-934-0859)

**Titusville—Kennedy Space Center**
3480 Garden St.
Titusville, Florida 32796
(305-269-9310)

**Vero Beach**
8800 20th St.
Vero Beach, Florida 32960
(305-562-9991)

**West Palm Beach**
2300 W. 45th St.
West Palm Beach, Florida 33407
(305-689-0450)

**Wildwood**
I-75 & Fla. 44, Rte. 2
Wildwood, Florida 32785
(904-748-2000)